THE
GOD
YESHUA KNEW

SERENA BEAUCHAMP

THE GOD YESHUA KNEW—Copyright © 2008-2014 "Serena" Beauchamp and "Luc" Beauchamp. All rights reserved.

Updated versions of this book may be periodically released without notice. For information or updates regarding this book or additional books by the author, visit *SerenaBeauchamp.com*.

Painting of "Yeshua" at top of front cover: Christopher Scott Huffman
Cover Design: Gordan Blazevic, Croatia

ISBN: 978-1495346200 Amazon Paperback

SerenaBeauchamp.com

First Edition, February 2014
Version 1.0

Unless otherwise noted, most Scripture quotations are from the "NIV" Holy Bible New International Version®. Copyright © 1973, 1978, 1984, 2011 International Bible Society. Used by permission of Zondervan. All rights reserved. Other Scripture quotations marked as: "CEV" are from the Contemporary English Version Copyright © 1995 by American Bible Society. Used by permission. / "NLT" are taken from the Holy Bible, New Living Translation, copyright © 1996. Used by permission of Tyndale House Publishers, Inc., Wheaton, Illinois 60189. All rights reserved. / "AMP" are taken from the Amplified® Bible, Copyright © 1954, 1958, 1962, 1964, 1965, 1987 by The Lockman Foundation Used by permission. www.lockman.org / "NKJV" are taken from the New King James Version. Copyright © 1982 by Thomas Nelson, Inc. Used by permission. All rights reserved. / "KJV" and "YLT" are taken from the King James Version and Young's Literal Translation, both of which are Public Domain. / "TNIV" are taken from Today's New International Version. Copyright © 2001, 2005 by International Bible Society. Used by permission of International Bible Society. All rights reserved worldwide. "TNIV" and "Today's New International Version" are trademarks registered in the United States Patent and Trademark Office by International Bible Society. Use of either trademark requires the permission of International Bible Society.

Printed in the United States of America

*For those who have supported me on this journey; especially my beloved husband.
Thank you.*

CONTENTS

PREFACE — VII

INTRODUCTION — 1

PART I – MY JOURNEY BEGINS — 5

1 – Today's Heretic or Tomorrow's Reformer? — 7
2 – Locked Up and Hidden Away — 19
3 – Cherry-Picking in the Orchard of God's Word — 32
4 – Going Around in Circles — 39
5 – The Bible Comes of Age — 47
6 – Broken Dreams & Shattered Beliefs — 61
7 – Eternal Covenant of Truth — 68

PART II – THE HEART OF THE MATTER — 75

8 – Trying to Make God Happy — 77
9 – Paganism's Dark Inheritance — 84
10 – Yeshua the Jewish Rebel — 99
11 – Will the Real Christianity Please Stand Up? — 109
12 – I Don't Want Your Bloody Sacrifices! — 118
13 – Midnight in the Garden of Good & Evil — 124
14 – The Akeda Conundrum — 137
15 – Mithraism: A Convenient Template — 143

PART III – UNMASKING PAUL — 149

16 – The Father of Christianity — 151
17 – A Living Crucifix — 158
18 – A Conspiracy of Silence — 169
19 – The Path of a Mystic — 177
20 – Punished by God — 189
21 – A Thorn in the Flesh — 195
22 – A Tale of Two Benjamites — 202
23 – Abandoned and Alone — 209

PART IV – DECONSTRUCTING PAULIANITY	213
24 – The TRUE Gospel vs. the NuGospel	215
25 – The New Covenant Contradiction	223
26 – Eating Food Sacrificed to Idols	233
27 – Going Rogue	241
28 – Clash of the Titans	250
29 – Robbing Peter to Pay Paul	259
30 – Peter and the Wolf	267
31 – The Rest of the Story	274
32 – Sheeple No More	280
33 – Leaving Home	291

PART V – THE CALL TO GO FORTH!	297
34 – The Great Con	299
35 – God Is	313
36 – God Acts	319
37 – God Speaks	326
38 – God Sees Me!	338
39 – Becoming an Ancestor	342
40 – Taking Back Ground	348
41 – Consider the Cost	355
42 – Discovering the TRUE Gospel	364

AFTERWORD: NOTES FROM ISRAEL	373
MUSIC FOR THE SECOND REFORMATION	379
INDEX	397

PREFACE

In the course of my life I have written many religious songs and musical programs that have been said to contain *good doctrine* by my church's standards. My method has been complex, yet simple at the same time. Besides using my own deep and melancholy emotions to color the songs and try to help my audience connect with the deeper feelings, I have always backed up my words with the thoughts and authority of others who were highly respected. Some of the sources I have drawn from have been C.S. Lewis, Martin Luther, Ellen White, A.W. Tozier, William Barclay and of course, the Bible. My constant mantra, stemming from a long-standing lack of self-esteem has always been, "No one wants to hear what I have to say, so I need to be able to reference my writing with the words of someone much more important; the words of someone who is truly respected."

You can imagine my consternation at the thought of writing a book that actually speaks of my own feelings, my own struggles, and my own pain. Who would really want to read that?

As I was considering this thought one day, struggling with the notion of how to express myself to a world that most likely does not care what this simple girl thinks, I felt the beloved Voice of the Eternal One speaking words that only my soul could hear.

> *My child, I do not just want you to be quoting the words of others.*
> *I want you to find* YOUR *voice.*
> YOUR *words.*
> YOUR *experience.*
> *Rather than only quoting others because you don't feel worthy of having words of your own,* YOU *will become the one that others will be quoting.*
> *You need to find* YOUR *voice!*

Well, I am doing my best to obey. If God sees me and values me, then perhaps I'm worthy of standing up and being heard.

This book is not only about my journey to find the God Yeshua knew; it is also a journey about my quest, my struggle, and my search to find my own soul's voice.

INTRODUCTION

I am at heart a cowardly lion. For the last few years I have wanted so badly to share some of the really cool things I have learned about our loving God with others. But instead of shouting my exciting discoveries from the proverbial rooftops, I have instead attempted to hide in the proverbial closet! Not wanting to be the person who causes controversy, I have gone out of my way to hide or at least stifle discussion about my beliefs. While my friends and family members have freely debated and espoused their beliefs in my presence, I have remained silent because I don't want to make my loved ones feel uncomfortable.

I guess my propensity for peacemaking and not wanting to argue with others comes from being the typical middle child. Growing up, I always wanted people to just get along. When it came time to choose *fight or flight*, for me it was *flight* all the way. I would much rather run than exchange blows, physical or verbal! That is why sharing the new tenets of my faith has been so very hard for me—I don't want people I love to get angry with me, and I am also deeply afraid of rejection.

My very assertive husband tells me, "Why does it even matter who rejects you or not? You care way too much about what people think!" And it's true. I've always been a people-pleaser. I have a long history of being the *good girl*, the anti-troublemaker, and the compliant daughter. Growing up with a dad who was very involved in "The Work" as a Seventh-day Adventist educator, I was always mindful of the fact that others would be watching my actions and judging my parents if I stepped out of line. Being a conciliatory sort, the thought of reflecting badly on these two godly people who sacrificed so much for me was more than I could ever bear. To illustrate how much I wanted to only please my parents, let me tell you this: I do not remember ever being spanked because, "That really makes Mommy and Daddy sad" hurt far worse than the end of a belt ever could.

Living up to the high standards that have always been expected of me is the primary reason why this journey has been so difficult. Moving from one religious tradition to another is not a decision that anyone, including myself, makes lightly. In fact, it is probably the hardest decision I will ever make, because it has struck at the very core of my emotional, psychological, and religious fiber. It means no longer fitting in with my entire social culture, no longer having shared belief to hold me close to friends and family, and always feeling like people no longer want to be around me because they can only perceive me as having *backslidden*.[1]

Furthermore, many of those close to me do not want to hear what spiritual questions brought me to this point. I suspect this is because they are very likely afraid deep in their hearts that if they even entertain these same questions, they

---

[1] The term *backsliding* is generally used in religious circles to refer to former believers who have reverted back to a sinful lifestyle—or *turned away from the truth*.

might find themselves inadvertently following the same so-called heretical path.

While a few friends have been understanding and supportive of my journey of faith, I have been roundly surprised and dismayed by the tone and attitudes of others. One friend said that I have *poor spiritual judgment*; another insisted that I was an *enemy of God* and exclaimed that she'd never want to read this book detailing my spiritual pursuit. Others have quietly backed out of my life, never to be heard from again or only to greet me politely on those rare occasions when we happen to bump into each other.

My dear husband has borne the brunt of the blame for my perceived defection from the church of my childhood in the minds of many who cannot imagine that I, of my own volition, have made the choices and undertaken the studies that have brought me to the understanding that I now have. "If she had only not married someone outside of our religion, she'd still be safely in the fold!" is the general thought.

What these individuals do not realize is that every step I have taken, I have made on my own! Luc and I have searched for answers together but we have taken nothing for granted; even the *truthfulness* of our own spouse's opinion! I have challenged Luc about his beliefs on multiple occasions, and he has done the same with mine. Together we have searched, prayed, cried, and agonized. Together we have hashed out answers and come to conclusions arrived at only after hours, days, weeks, months, and even years of logical thought, fervent prayer, and intensive study.

Some people who used to be close to me have tried to imply that because I now have factual fundamental disagreements with mainstream Christianity in general, and my denomination in particular, I am somehow no longer walking with God. These individuals are saying that because I have turned away from God in their opinion that I am now *lost*. They feel extremely sad and even *angry* over the fact that I "once knew the truth but now have wandered away."

The reality is quite to the contrary. I have not abandoned God whatsoever! It has been the hand of God that has led me every step of the way to where I am in my knowledge and understandings today. Perhaps from a purely denominational perspective, people may want to disagree that it has been God who has been leading me. However, the fact is that I have never once turned away from my Heavenly Father!

I know that in many people's eyes, I have gone from *Good Girl* to *Badventist* to *Heretic* to *Apostate*. If you are one of my beloved friends or family members who have felt this way about me, I know that you mean well and that your concern for me is genuine. I, too, have been where you are! I have also watched beloved friends turn away from *the church* completely. I, too, have agonized at the thought that I may never see these friends in Heaven because they no longer *believe* the *right* things. I, too, have sobbed over their presumed fate, so I understand the grief that you might experience deep in your heart for what you feel is the loss of my salvation.

But honestly, have you ever really stopped to ask me where I am in my walk with God today? Will you believe me when I tell you that my connection with my Heavenly Father is stronger than ever because of what I have learned about His beautiful and forgiving character?

Please let me tell you this story in the hopes that just maybe, you too will be willing to get to know the God Yeshua knew, and the God I am still discovering.

PART I
MY JOURNEY BEGINS

CHAPTER 1

Today's Heretic or Tomorrow's Reformer?

No one starts out intending to be a so-called heretic. I did not begin my spiritual quest planning to leave my cherished religion that was the faith of my fathers, my grandfathers, my great- grandfathers, my great- great- grandfathers, and my great- great- great- grandfathers. I really just wanted to find a reasonable answer and valid explanation for a Biblical inconsistency I had discovered.

While searching for this answer Luc and I embarked upon a deep study of the Scriptures, the Bible, and the history of our Christian faith. We did not limit ourselves to the Bible and SDA publications such as the *Conflict of the Ages Series*, the *Testimonies*, and the *SDA Bible Commentary*.[2] Instead, we

---

[2] Adventist theologian Clifford Goldstein recommends, "Keep seeking with a fervent and honest heart. As long as you stick to the Bible (and Ellen White's

undertook an extensive investigational scholastic-like work where we tried to excavate and examine all available information about early to modern Christianity. We attempted to leave no stone unturned.

LET'S START AT THE VERY BEGINNING...

Growing up Adventist, I had always been taught that being able to defend one's beliefs was of paramount importance. Introducing doubt into the equation was never even a consideration—I knew my church, the remnant church spoken of in Revelation,[3] had the *complete truth*; and if someone believed that the Bible was God's Word I should be able to convince them of the validity of my beliefs. That said, it was also understood that some things were dangerous to one's faith—and marrying a non-Adventist was at the top of the list of no-no's.

I kept this thought at the forefront of my mind when I started dating Luc. Luc and I met on the Internet some time before finding one's significant other online was a common or acceptable practice. Although this was an unconventional way to find someone to date, Luc and I really hit it off. However, we both had some serious reservations about the long-term ramifications of a successful real-life relationship. On my end, and this was probably the most important thing for me, Luc wasn't an Adventist but a self-proclaimed *Bapticostal*. My denomination was a fundamental part of who I was, so I knew this could cause a real problem if I couldn't

---

books and articles) you will not go wrong."
http://www.adventistreview.org/2003-1530/story4.html 08/01/2010
[3] Revelation 12:17

convince him to become an Adventist. However, he assured me that he believed what the Bible said and that he just wanted to find and embrace the truth.

Ironically, one of Luc's main reservations stemmed from the fact that the girl he was falling in love with was a devout Adventist. He had grown up despising an Adventist family down the street, and couldn't imagine falling for and possibly marrying an Adventist! Yet even though we were on opposite sides of the continent, we felt a powerful connection at a heart level. We began to call and write and get to know each other as best we could across the miles, to see if there was something there that made this particular long-distance relationship worth pursuing.

Since faith in God was of the utmost importance to both of us, we discussed Biblical doctrines a great deal during the getting-to-know-you process. Gradually Luc became to see things the way I did regarding the state of the dead, the duration of hell, and the Secret Rapture versus a visible Second Coming. As far as the Sabbath was concerned, when he came to visit me he was perfectly willing to attend my hometown Adventist church on Sabbath with me.

Feeling satisfied that this *do not yoke yourselves with unbelievers* hurdle had been overcome, my beloved and I happily eloped in December of 1999 and started our new life together. I was very active in the music program at my home church, and played the piano and sang for praise service every Sabbath. Luc came to church with me every week and really started to embrace my friends, my church, and even the Adventist beliefs. He did have some lingering questions about the Sabbath, so I encouraged him to study into it and write a book about his findings.

Luc took my advice to heart. He read a lot of books about the Sabbath, explored Dr. Samuel Bacchiocchi's very scholastic research, and eventually ended up with a 150-page tome entitled "When Christians Keep Sabbath". The manuscript affirmed that the Sabbath was indeed valid and a real blessing. It also concluded, based on Paul's advice to believers found in Galatians and Romans, that in the end it really didn't matter if you observed the Sabbath or not.

The book's ending left me horrified. "Honey, you have all this great research! How could you come to such an illogical conclusion and miss the *entire point?*"

Clearly, my beloved husband needed my assistance in order to come to the correct conclusions. So, we both started reading everything we could put our hands on to learn all there is to know about the history of the Sabbath.

Lucifer or Satan?

It was while we were in this spirit of intensive study that we ran into a troubling Biblical inconsistency. We discovered that the scholars of the *International Bible Society* (IBS) had removed the name *Lucifer* from the *New International Version* (NIV) translation of the Bible. I couldn't understand why they would do that—everyone knew that *Lucifer* is another name for Satan! The highly respected *King James Version*, the *real* Bible, specifically referred to *Lucifer* directly in Isaiah 14:12, so this doctrine was entirely Biblical. That, more than anything, made the *Lucifer was the name of Satan before the fall* doctrine an inerrant aspect of my faith. Ellen White's frequent usage of the name confirmed it as *truth* for me.[4] Why would the IBS take this rather drastic step?

Sister White said in the introduction of *The Great Controversy*,[5]

> As the Spirit of God has opened to my mind the great truths of his Word, and the scenes of the past and the future, I have been bidden to make known to others that which has thus been revealed—to trace the history of the controversy in past ages, and especially to so present it as to shed a light on the fast-approaching struggle of the future.[6]

In this introduction she tells her readers that she has the full story of what went on straight from the mouth of the Lord Himself. With this as her declaration of inspiration, she proceeds to refer to *Lucifer* by name no less than 15 times in chapter 29, *The Origin of Evil*. She uses this name multiple times in her other writings as well. This is why those like me who grew up Adventist knew beyond a shadow of a doubt that this being was literally named *Lucifer*—the Bible said it and Sister White's *Pen of Inspiration*[7] verified it.

---

[4] Adventism considers Ellen White to be a modern-day prophet of God. She has written a great many letters, books and articles.

[5] 1907 edition

[6] page xi

[7] In Adventist circles Ellen White is commonly referred to as "the Pen of Inspiration" (or just "Inspiration") and "the Spirit of Prophecy" or "SOP". She is also referenced in other ways, such as when Adventist believers say "we have been told that..." or "Inspiration tells us..." or "the Red Books tell us..." It is a part of Adventist lingo that initially confuses new or non-Adventist believers.

Realizing that something didn't add up, I decided to research the *Lucifer* issue myself. In this Information Age where most answers are just a click away, it did not take long to find out that the actual word *Lucifer* was not found anywhere in the Hebrew Scriptures. In fact, *Lucifer* is a distinctly Latin word that was introduced into the Bible when Jerome of Antioch translated the Hebrew Scriptures into Latin in 405 A.D. The Hebrew word that was translated as *Lucifer* is *halel*, which more or less means *light*. *Halel* is the root from which we derive the English word *halo*. Furthermore, *halel* is not even a proper noun; it is an adjective used to *sarcastically* describe someone like a human king who is highly visible like the morning star, or has the appearance of *light*.

After Jerome's translation of the book of Isaiah into Latin, some within the leadership of the Roman Catholic Church began to mistakenly assume that the person being described within Isaiah 14:12 was Satan. They ascribed this passage as being a discussion of Satan and it was they who assigned the devil his new Latin moniker, *Lucifer*.

It is interesting to note that during the Protestant Reformation, Martin Luther did not import the word *Lucifer* into his *German* translation of the Bible. However, this *Latin* word was again deliberately and quite mistakenly carried over into the *English* translation of the King James Version of the Bible because these period Christians simply expected it to be there.[8]

---

[8] I find it curious that the Catholic Fathers maintain that "Lucifer is not the proper name of the devil, but denotes only the state from which he has fallen." http://www.newadvent.org/cathen/09410a.htm 7/5/10
In this matter, Protestantism has taken the story of *Satan equals Lucifer* much further than Catholicism itself does!

In the early part of the twentieth century other mainstream Bible versions such as the ESV and the ASV had already removed the world *Lucifer* from their English translations of the Bible. Then in 1978, the *International Bible Society* published their NIV Bible translation that also rightly corrected this error of tradition and mistranslation. Since they have chosen to right this entrenched wrong, the IBS has been strongly criticized for "trying to remove the devil from the Bible".

Because of this word translation issue, a simple adjective in the Hebrew has turned into an entire doctrine. In the thick of Adventism, many people do not know that *Lucifer* is not really another name for the devil. Yet it is this fictitious story that is being taught in our schools and churches as gospel truth.

Deciding to seek answers from approved Adventist sources first, Luc wrote to ask the editor of a major Adventist periodical about this issue. The editor verified that he knew the real truth about the name *Lucifer*, yet berated and chastised Luc for simply bringing up the point. Declaring that that we were making a mountain out of a molehill, he explained that millions of books were now already in print by our esteemed Christian leaders, revered evangelists and beloved authors. They all (mistakenly) had referred to Satan as *Lucifer* and as such, their books could not now be recalled, let alone corrected! It was just too late to go about correcting the error, especially with the elder generations who had been raised believing *Lucifer* was the actual name for the devil.

This gentleman was then and remains now an influential representative of today's top Adventist leadership. He was purposefully engaged in upholding and perpetuating this erroneous lie; yet *we* were the ones being belittled and vilified for bringing the truth to the surface and questioning it!

Does it matter if you continue to perpetuate a falsehood if you know that what you are promoting is not the truth? Is it okay to insist that Satan's *real* name is one that the Hebrew Scriptures never address him as *and* to quote as your authority to do so those very same Scriptures? This is what is commonly known in scholarly circles as *circular reasoning*.

Adventists have been advised to "allow the Bible to interpret itself, line upon line, precept upon precept."[9] We are told to *not* look at the texts with a critical eye; trying to analyze who really wrote them, what context their words were surrounded by, and whom they were intended for. Conversely, we are also told that God is picking out tiny details here and there to signify that there is a *future antitypical meaning* to the prophecy that will be fulfilled later on or, in this case, which somehow happened long before the original event being prophesied actually took place. Can we really have it both ways?

THE HEBRAIC PERSPECTIVE

It seems that we often try to make the simple Hebrew Scriptures much more difficult than they really are. If one simply reads Isaiah 14 with a rational and logical frame of mind and allows it to interpret itself, it is plain to see that it cannot be speaking about the devil or *Lucifer*. Rather, this passage is a pointed prophecy against the literal king of Babylon. The

---

[9] Ted Wilson, General Conference of SDA president, Sermon at GC of SDA, 07/04/2010

prophecy is colorful and poetic but it contains no *type of the devil*, and no character called *Lucifer*.

> All your pomp has been brought down to the grave, along with the noise of your harps; maggots are spread out beneath you and worms cover you ... Those who see you stare at you, they ponder your fate: "Is this the man who shook the earth and made kingdoms tremble, the man who made the world a desert, who overthrew its cities and would not let his captives go home?[10]

Adopting a more Hebraic mindset, it becomes obvious that this is not a description of an archangel, but of a mortal man—most likely a highly exalted head of state—lying in a grave decaying in death.

Abraham Ibn Ezra was a Jewish rabbi who lived from 1092 to 1167. His commentary on Isaiah suggests:

> There is an old tradition that when Nebuchadnezzar had died, and was buried, he was dragged out of his grave again, because the people of his kingdom were in doubt whether he really was dead, and feared he might again return to them as he had done before. This is perhaps really the fact; there is at least no doubt, that this verse refers to Nebuchadnezzar, who was the first of the Babylonian kings that reigned over Israel.[11]

---

[10] Isaiah 14:11, 16-17
[11] Translation of the Commentary on Isaiah, pp. 71-72; Item 19.

Finding Out the Truth

So there it was. The Roman Catholic Church had manufactured the whole *Lucifer* story and now my own beloved Adventist Church was continuing to perpetuate the lie.

How distressing it was to find out that my own church had lied to me! My pastors had learned about this issue in seminary, yet I do not remember ever hearing a single one address this issue. None of my Bible teachers addressed it in any of the religion classes I attended and excelled in, and I went through some 17 years of Adventist schooling!

As someone who had grown up Adventist, I had been taught over and over that the Bible has no errors whatsoever and that all of its books are in perfect agreement. "If the Bible has any error," I was told, "then the whole thing should be thrown out! Either the Bible stands together or it falls together!" Yet, this matter illustrated that the Bible had an error, and a big one! Isaiah 14:12 had been the *only* text where the name *Lucifer* appeared in the entire Bible! Its correction and removal meant that Christianity suddenly had *no* Biblical support for using this name for the devil. For a Bible-believing Christian like myself, that is a pretty big deal!

Unfortunately, Adventists seemed to be some of the least willing to change their thinking regarding this issue over the specific *name of Lucifer* doctrine because "Sister White said that 'Lucifer' was the devil's name in heaven, so that must make it truth!" Not only does the *Lucifer* lie sully the inerrancy of the Bible, but it threatens Sister White's validity as an inerrant mouthpiece for God as well.

Other Evangelical Christians will automatically dismiss the error as much ado about nothing, adopting the viewpoint that "This is just a name translation (they mean 'transliteration') issue. Lots of names have been translated (transliterated) within the Bible."

Unfortunately, this is not just a "name transliteration issue". If it were, then the scholars of modern 20th century translation wouldn't have bothered correcting and removing it! A transliteration is still a proper name. *Lucifer* is not a proper name, it is an adjective; and it is no longer in the modern translation of the Bible![12]

I asked an Adventist pastor friend of mine about this problem and was met with a rather terse response. Other devout Adventist friends downplayed the importance of this issue since it was not *salvific*. They continued to call Satan *Lucifer* regardless of the facts that I shared.

Clearly, this is not a salvific issue; but it *is* a matter of honesty and integrity. My church leadership had taught me something that was patently false, and most of them knew they were teaching a lie. This singular doctrine became quite a faith-shaking matter that left me wondering, "What other things have I been taught that are simply not true?"

Even more disturbing was the realization that I could no longer claim to have all the answers! Previous to this realization I had been certain that there were no doctrinal gray areas; my denomination had it all right. Luc had grown up with the same sense of "we are right and everyone else is wrong" in his churches as well. Yet the fact remained that something as pivotal as the name used for Satan within the Bible itself was a lie! Why didn't our pastors and teachers tell us this?

Shocked out of our rather self-righteous complacency, Luc and I began to study, pray, and look to God for His truth

---

[12] Those Bible versions of the King James tradition, such as the NKJV, continue to errantly insert the name *Lucifer* into their texts.

about this faith-shaking error. We began to realize that Christendom was putting far too much trust in the people and traditions handed down from its previous generations—and that our rather blind faith included the naïve assumption that our Christian ancestors had inserted the absolute correct content into the Bible itself.

Considering the chilly reception I had received when attempting to bring up this troubling point with my pastor friend, it didn't take me long to realize that there are some intellectual questions regarding the Bible that the denominational leadership does not want to hear. Unfortunately, even though I no longer felt welcome to ask them, my questions remained.

At the beginning of what would become a lengthy and unexpected spiritual expedition, I never even considered whether asking these questions would make me today's heretic or tomorrow's reformer. In the end, only history and God Almighty would be able to tell.

CHAPTER 2

Locked Up and Hidden Away

After I started to look more deeply into the culture of Christianity and the history of my beliefs, I found myself picking up a book discussing all the different names that describe God in the Bible. It was fascinating to learn that God's name is not actually *the Lord*, but instead is another word that we never even use.

Whenever you see the phrase *the Lord* spelled out within the Bible in small capital letters, the underlying word you find written in most of the Hebrew Scriptures is יהוה. This grouping of four Hebrew letters is often referred to as the *Tetragrammaton*, and is generally thought to be referring to God's *actual* proper name.

There is a lot of controversy about how the *Tetragrammaton* is pronounced, due to questionable vowel points that have been inserted between the consonants. When I first started researching this issue, *Yahweh* was the pronunciation that seemed to have the most amount of support in Messianic circles.

So Many Opinions, Which One is the Truth?

After spending a good six or seven years calling God *Yahweh* and teaching my children to do the same, a new Facebook friend strongly expressed that he believed *Yahweh* isn't the correct way to say or spell God's Name, it was *YaHuWaH*. A lively discussion (dare I say argument?) ensued, and it became apparent that more information was needed.

After researching the matter further, I found that there are a lot of conflicting opinions regarding how to pronounce and spell God's Name. Additional pronunciation variations include Christianity's revered standard, *Jehovah*; as well as *Yahowah* and *Yehovah*. Furthermore, a lot of the Messianic Christian believers espousing these specific pronunciations are militant about insisting that only their preferred variation is correct and anything else is a personal insult to God. Some folks will lecture that if you innocently use the word *God* or even the incorrect pronunciation or spelling of the *Tetragrammaton*, you are not actually worshiping our Creator at all but some Babylonian or Egyptian deity!

In addition to the fact that being told you are worshiping Satan is a serious conversation and relationship killer, this rigid viewpoint is a real turnoff to those who have been worshiping their Creator the best they know how. This unloving stance really tends to discourage seekers from learning about God's TRUE Name at all, because they are so repulsed by the unfriendly and unloving vitriol expressed by the *Name of God* believers.

Opinions on this matter were so abundant and bombastic that I began to feel confused. In my heart, I inherently knew that I needed to seek out and learn about this matter from a scholar with an authentic Jewish background, as opposed to someone with an active Messianic agenda.

After seeking God's leading on the matter, I was referred to a Jewish rabbi and scholar who explained that the name I had been using, *Yahweh*, was not the TRUE Name of God that has been known to Jews for millennia. Sadly, Judaism has not felt compelled to share their most accurate information with Christians, so Christianity as a whole has remained blissfully unaware that they don't even *know* God's TRUE Name. Furthermore, the early Masoretic scribes *hid* the truth of God's actual proper Name by inventing the YHWH Tetragrammaton, which really ends up being more of a descriptive title.

Dr. Shmuel Asher, a *Karaite* scholar and rabbi who specializes in Ancient Hebrew Studies, explains,

> Not only did our ancestors hide the name by the invention of their *YHWH—Tetragrammaton*, (יהוה) which is generally translated as *Jehovah*. Over much time they have sold this by-product to all religions, even in the Jewish community, that this was in fact the name which we are commanded to use instead, while very carefully side-stepping the proper Name that was actually given to Moshe (Moses) on Mt. Horeb. IF that wasn't clear, I will clarify; *all professional orthodox and many non-orthodox clergy know the* TRUE *Name!* It's you who do not! We are taught this TRUE

name, and even sing songs[13] using this name that supposedly does not exist. However, the reasons given to us for hiding it from all Gentiles are as follows: 1) So the pagans can't learn it and utilize its formidable power. 2) So that the common people do not defile it and treat it as common or base. However, when asked *where* this commandment is to hide the proper name of GOD from his people, *all* people, we get no good answer. That is because a truthful Torah answer does *not* exist.[14]

The TRUE Name of God is found several places in the Hebrew Scriptures. In Exodus 3:14 it is denoted in full as "AHEYEH *ashar* AHEYEH". This is the complete phrase that has been translated into English, as "I AM THAT I AM". We find AHEYEH (אהיה) used as a proper name in two other places in Exodus 3 as well. In addition, it is found in Genesis and is also used as a first person proper name in Exodus 4. It is worth mentioning that Moses was given AHEYEH *ashar* AHEYEH description as more as a clarification, since Moses had already been introduced to God's Name "AHEYEH".

---

[13] Here is a YouTube link to an example of a song that is very familiar to most Jews containing God's TRUE Name. This version of the song was recorded in the 1970s and the lyrics were actually *written* in the 17th Century by the poet Shalom Shabbazi! This certainly helped me understand that Judaism has long known God's true and proper Name.
http://www.youtube.com/watch?v=FB9_nVfNSsU

[14] Dr. Asher's extensive, very educational study regarding God's true Name from a Karaite Jewish perspective is found here.
http://ancienthebrewlearningcenter.blogspot.com/p/true-name.html quoted 03/25/2012. Additional information regarding early Jewish scribal changes to the Scriptures can be found in his book, "The Land of MEAT and Honey", available at www.amazon.com.

Dr. Asher continues,

> Here are the details that separate the proper name from the *YHWH expression*, which was made up and instituted long after Moshe died:
>
> The { א }—Alef prefix makes a verb refer to one's self–(personally).
> The { י }—Yod prefix relates the verb to someone else–{impersonal}–{yhwh = He WILL be} vs. {AHYH = I exist forever}.
> Thus אהיה or AHYH is the proper name![15]

Dr. Asher explains that the three-word phrase AHEYEH *ashar* AHEYEH is not really a phrase, as we would understand it in English. Rather, it was God's way of telling Moses that He was from before, exists now, and will exist into forever. This is how things were understood in the ancient Hebrew language and culture. Kind of like "I was Serena before and am Serena now and will be Serena in the future." Dr. Asher then raises a troublesome point.

> Now here is where the big issues begin for most people who are not brought up within the Jewish community or culture, knowing the many hidden truths like this one. Exodus 3:15 has been manipulated, and the *YHWH* = *Jehovah* has been added in order to facilitate and perpetuate hiding the TRUE name. We [Jews] know that the YHWH—Tetragrammaton was a mechanism devised to be the tool used to actively aid in

---

[15] http://ancienthebrewlearningcenter.blogspot.com

hiding His TRUE Name. Even building on top of this by making it punishable law to say the name; this practice comes to us directly from the practices of pagan Babylon. This YHWH title is closely associated with all manner of Kabalistic rituals through Gematria, as well as ancient and modern Masonic religious rites, the Catholic Church, and other satanic occult rituals. Unknown to most people, this YHWH title is found and used by all of the above.[16]

Let me emphasize that this is not just a name transliteration issue, but is rather a deliberate mistranslation of a proper name—God's own Name—by intentionally replacing God's actual Name with a title; which becomes, in effect, an alternate name. Think about it. In Exodus 3:14, you hear God saying, "My name is אֶהְיֶה אֲשֶׁר אֶהְיֶה." But the way we are told it, a breath later in the next verse God has supposedly changed His mind and is telling Moses, "Hey Moses, even though I just told you my name is אֶהְיֶה אֲשֶׁר אֶהְיֶה", tell the people that יהוה has sent you!" This is roughly the equivalent of me saying, "My name is Serena. Tell your friends that Sharon sent you."

Christians never stop to think that this does not make any logical sense, because we do not know Hebrew and are not looking at this from the Hebraic perspective. The bottom line is, whenever you see "the LORD" spelled out within the Bible in small capital letters, the actual underlying Hebrew word was originally אהיה which when correctly translated is very likely pronounced *ah-ee-YEH*.[17] This was later removed,

---

[16] http://ancienthebrewlearningcenter.blogspot.com
[17] The first two syllables of AHEYEH kind of run together like you are saying "aye aye, captain". To me it is easier to phonetically think of it as "aye-YEH".

and the YHWH (*Yahweh*) third person title, known as the Tetragrammaton, was installed in its place.

This issue illustrates that duplicity is not only found on the Christian side of the equation, but on the Jewish side as well. The layers of deliberate deception just keep getting deeper and deeper!

Most Christians are generally brought up believing that all Scripture is 100% inerrant and inspired. Because of this foundational belief, we often have a hard time accepting that many of the Scripture passages found in the Holy Bible are, for lack of a better word, doctored. Dr. Asher states,

> Many people have had huge issues when succumbing to the realization that the ancient scribes made so many deletions and additions to their Masoretic copies. Of course, these Masorite copies are the source texts most all Greek and Latin language Bible versions are derived from, and were subsequently translated into the later European languages. The fact remains, here we are, it is not going away, and it really should be our collective duty to clear it up; to get back to as close as possible to our original source of truth and power.[18]

A Divine Directive

While it is troubling to consider that the ancient scribes took it upon themselves to hide the name of God, it is even more shocking to understand that there is a deeper reason for this phenomenon that points back to the Eternal One Himself. At

---

[18] http://ancienthebrewlearningcenter.blogspot.com

some point well before the Christian era, *God Himself* removed His name from Israel. The reason for this removal was that the priesthood of Israel had ceased listening to the Almighty, and had wandered away from Him. They began adopting and intensifying the tenets of pagan practice; including them as part of their worship of the God of Abraham. It was for this reason that God said,

> "I judged (Israel) according to their conduct and their actions. And wherever they went among the nations they profaned my holy name, for it was said of them, 'These are AHYH's people, and yet they had to leave [AHYH's] land.' I had concern for [I cared what other nations believed about] my holy name, which the house of Israel profaned among the nations where they had gone."
>
> "I swear by my great name," says AHYH, "that no one from Judah living anywhere in Egypt [also a metaphor for someone living in sin outside of God's Law] will ever again invoke my name or swear, 'As surely as the Lord AHYH lives.'"[19]

By instituting the pagan practices and rituals of a foreign god into their worship of AHEYEH, Israel had for all intents and purposes chosen to follow *another god* instead of her TRUE God. So, as the prophets said, *God removed His* TRUE *Name* from her midst. The great irony is that these scribes who actively hid God's TRUE Name from the people, as they continue to do today, thought that this was all their own idea!

---

[19] Ezekiel 36:16-21 NIV / CEV /NASB; Jeremiah 44:25-26, [amplifications supplied]. See also Amos 6:8-11; Hosea 2

This discovery was unnerving to say the least, but the evidence showing that God's name is *still* being removed from His followers was undeniable. Have we in Christianity unwittingly adopted the very same ungodly pagan thoughts, practices and ideas about God that were present in ancient Israel? Have Israel's own sins—*the sin of the fathers*—now followed the children even into Christianity's beliefs and views of our heavenly Father? Protestantism grew out of Roman Catholicism, which grew out of Judaism, which had already been highly modified to suit its own distinct agenda. What is it within these religions that God still finds so objectionable that He would continue hiding his very name from Christianity in the modern era?

The Use of God's True Name in Christianity

There is another layer of deception that needs to be peeled back in order to get to the heart of this *Name of God* issue. In addition to the fact that the Masoretic scribes have actively hidden the Name of God, Christianity itself also has an unspoken aversion toward using God's name and prefers to use instead the title, *the* LORD. The Tetragrammaton, although it is a scribal invention and not God's TRUE Name, is used over 6,000 times throughout the Hebrew Scriptures; yet never once does anyone within Christianity ever read even an approximation or guesstimate of God's Name in the pages of *any* major modern Bible translation. Instead, God is continually referred to by the title *the* LORD alone.

So deep has this Christian aversion to God's TRUE Name become that the translators and editors of the Revised Standard Version (RSV) translation of the Bible actually took it upon themselves to demand that God's actual Name was entirely inappropriate for any Christian to read from the Scriptures! Take note of the RSV's opening notes regarding the Name of God:

> While it is almost if not quite certain that the Name was originally pronounced 'Yahweh,'... the use of any proper name for the one and only God, as though there were other gods from whom He had to be distinguished, was discontinued in Judaism before the Christian era and is entirely inappropriate for the universal faith of the Christian Church.[20]

Who made these Bible editors the sole arbiters of what is and is not entirely inappropriate for the universal (i.e. *catholic*) faith of the Christian Church? After all, God specifically defended God's own name and oneness by saying unto Moses,

> "AHEYEH *ashar* AHEYEH" [I AM THAT I AM] and he said, "So will you tell the children of Jacob; { AHEYEH } has sent me to you."[21]

But then God adds this directive that Christianity tends to disregard or ignore completely:

> God also said to Moses, "Say to the Israelites, 'AHEYEH [I AM], the God of your fathers—the God of Abraham,

---

[20] From the opening notes at the beginning of the editors of The Holy Bible, Revised Standard Version, Nashville: Cokesbury, 1952. This is the Bible that I used all the time growing up, as it was given to me when I was a child.
[21] Exodus 3:14 As translated at http://www.ancienthebrewlearningcenter.blogspot.com/p/true-name.html

the God of Isaac and the God of Jacob—has sent me to you.' *This is my name forever, the name by which I am to be remembered from generation to generation.*[22]

God actually commands us to remember and call Him by His TRUE Name! Ironically, we sing song after song extolling ourselves to *praise the name of the Lord*. Yet we never actually praise God by Name! We claim the promise that,

> The name of the LORD is a strong tower, the righteous run to it and are safe.[23]

Yet we never come near the strong tower of God's own TRUE Name, but continue to distance ourselves from the Almighty by holding dear to God's title alone. The true translation of this passage from Solomon's Proverbs should rightly be,

> The name of AHEYEH is a strong tower, the righteous run to it and are safe.[24]

Although many Jews don't have much to say about Yeshua, there are some Jewish scholars who believe that Yeshua

---

[22] Exodus 3:15

[23] Proverbs 18:10 NKJV

[24] Having been around a fair number of Messianic and "Torah-observant" believers who have strong opinions on how God's Name should be pronounced, I considered using the standard Tetragrammaton to denote God's true Name in this book, since that is the variation with which most people are accustomed. However, because I cannot in good conscience continue to perpetuate the lie begun by the early Masorite scholars and continued by Catholicism, I will be using the true Tetragrammaton—AHYH—in this book, even in Scripture quotes; rather than the scribal invention of YHWH or YHVH as is written in the bulk of the Hebrew Scriptures.

himself knew the TRUE Name of God and used it regularly. Again, Dr. Asher states,

> Jesus, whose actual proper name may be better represented as *Yehshiyeh*, was not persecuted right from the start by the Pharisees for saying mean things. They looked to kill him ... mainly for outwardly speaking and teaching the Name in public; which in turn exposed the long Talmudic traditions of hiding the TRUE Name of The Most High from the unwashed population; as well as making certain to tell everyone who exactly lied to them. This was a much larger issue than even most scholars today understand.[25]

From a personal perspective, I noticed early on that most of my friends and family showed no desire to even speak God's Name. Furthermore, they looked at me like I was an oddly shaped slice of religious fruitcake when I used it myself! They just did not seem to care that they were addressing God by an impersonal title, because their tradition of addressing God only as *the* LORD was more important. How I wish they could hear Yeshua say, as he did to the Pharisees,

> You have a fine way of setting aside the commands of God in order to observe your own traditions![26]

I did take comfort from the fact that people in the modern era are starting to find and use God's TRUE Name again. Is it because, perhaps, they are finally starting to root out the paganism in their belief system?

---

[25] http://ancienthebrewlearningcenter.blogspot.com
[26] Mark 7:9

Calling upon the Name of Aheyeh

God's Name sounded quite foreign to my non-Hebraic ears, but I wanted—no *needed*—to know more! And so I tentatively started calling upon God using His TRUE Name, the best I knew how. I gingerly and a bit self-consciously introduced it to others, as well. Somehow, I knew that God appreciated hearing me call on Him by Name. The introductions had been made, and we were now on a first name basis. It felt like such a gift. Me. ME! Speaking to the God of the Universe like a friend!

As I started praising my Father by Name, the little flame of understanding in my heart started to grow. Slowly but surely, I was starting to become acquainted with the God Yeshua knew.

CHAPTER 3

❖

CHERRY-PICKING IN THE ORCHARD OF GOD'S WORD

*No man ever believes that the Bible means what it says:
He is always convinced that it says what he means.*
—George Bernard Shaw

Every time a serious conversation on Biblical doctrines and topics takes place, you start hearing things like the following. *"I sure don't understand how you got that from that text,"* or *"Why are you reading Leviticus when you should be quoting Paul? He's much more relevant for our time!"* or *"If you think that Scripture A is true, wait until you hear what Scripture B says!"* Then, someone starts throwing out accusations that the other person is *picking and choosing* which Scriptures are *relevant* and the whole conversation rapidly goes to hell in a hand basket.

The true irony really only appears when a non-believer shows up with questions about Biblical inerrancy. Both

Christians, who have just been fighting bitterly over whose interpretation of Scripture is correct, will quickly stand back-to-back and tell the non-believer that the entire Bible is inspired and there are no contradictions to be seen in it at all.

It is usually at this point that the non-believer is informed that what appears to be a contradiction is not really a contradiction at all, but that you must first be *filled with the Holy Spirit of God* in order to really understand the *deep spiritual meaning* between the [contradictory] texts. As if that is going to somehow convince him when he can see for himself that there is a glaring contradiction! If the non-believer dares to continue to disagree, he is generally given some variation of the following ultimatum: "You're going to hell if you don't just stifle your questions and believe what God has put into the Bible!"

In spite of the thousands of denominations that have arisen in Christendom because of some obvious ambiguity over which texts are more or less correct than others, it is just not okay for you as a Christian (unless you are an Episcopalian) to admit that you do not like certain passages, or think that they are not true or binding for our time. If you in fact do admit this, you are generally made to feel like a heretic with *weak faith* for doing so. The one exception is if you are discarding an *acceptable* passage because your denomination has told you it is all right to do so (e.g., tossing out God's TRUE Law as binding if you define yourself as a *New Covenant* believer).

While studying and researching the Scriptures, the context they were written in, and eventually the history of the Bible canon itself, I finally came to the inescapable conclusion that far from treating every verse in the Bible the same, I personally do make distinctions as to which Scriptures I allow to have authority over me and those which I discard as irrelevant and unnecessary. I also disregard those passages that I feel make no logical sense! And you know what? Every other Christian—and Jew, for that matter—does the exact same thing. I have just decided that it is okay to admit it.

An interesting email came in from the Internet the other day that illustrated this issue in a very thought-provoking manner. It was an open letter written by a concerned individual in response to Dr. Laura Schlesinger, a conservative radio host who was at the time of this letter's writing a very devout Orthodox Jew.[27] In her radio show, Dr. Laura said that homosexuality is an abomination according to Leviticus 18:22, and cannot be condoned under any circumstance. The writer of the letter had a few questions and concerns regarding this issue:

Dear Dr. Laura:

Thank you for doing so much to educate people regarding God's Law. I have learned a great deal from your show, and try to share that knowledge with as many people as I can. When someone tries to defend the homosexual lifestyle, for example, I simply remind

---

[27] In 1996, Dr. Schlessinger and her son Deryk converted to Conservative Judaism, then switched to Orthodox Judaism in 1998. She has said that her husband Lew, who was raised an Episcopalian, also converted, but he later admitted he had not completed the conversion. In 2003, Schlessinger announced on the air that she was no longer an Orthodox Jew, that she felt frustrated by the effort she had put into the religion, and complained that she felt little or no connection with God.
http://www.nndb.com/people/427/000022361/

them that Leviticus 18:22 clearly states it to be an abomination ... End of debate.

I do need some advice from you, however, regarding some other elements of God's Laws and how to follow them.

1. Leviticus 25:44 states that I may possess slaves, both male and female, provided they are purchased from neighboring nations. A friend of mine claims that this applies to Mexicans, but not Canadians. Can you clarify? Why can't I own Canadians?

2. I would like to sell my daughter into slavery, as sanctioned in Exodus 21:7. In this day and age, what do you think would be a fair price for her?

3. I know that I am allowed no contact with a woman while she is in her period of menstrual uncleanliness - Lev. 15: 19-24. The problem is how do I tell? I have tried asking, but most women take offense.

4. When I burn a bull on the altar as a sacrifice, I know it creates a pleasing odor for the Lord - Lev. 1:9. The problem is my neighbors. They claim the odor is not pleasing to them. Should I smite them?

5. I have a neighbor who insists on working on the Sabbath. Exodus 35:2 clearly states he should be put to death. Am I morally obligated to kill him myself, or should I ask the police to do it?

6. A friend of mine feels that even though eating shellfish is an abomination, Lev. 11:10, it is a lesser abomination than homosexuality. I don't agree. Can you settle this? Are there 'degrees' of abomination?

7. Lev. 21:20 states that I may not approach the altar of God if I have a defect in my sight. I have to admit that I wear reading glasses. Does my vision have to be 20/20, or is there some wiggle-room here?

8. Most of my male friends get their hair trimmed, including the hair around their temples, even though this is expressly forbidden by Lev. 19:27. How should they die?

9. I know from Lev. 11:6-8 that touching the skin of a dead pig makes me unclean, but may I still play football if I wear gloves?

10. My uncle has a farm. He violates Lev. 19:19 by planting two different crops in the same field, as does his wife by wearing garments made of two different kinds of thread (cotton/polyester blend). He also tends to curse and blaspheme a lot. Is it really necessary that we go to all the trouble of getting the whole town together to stone them? Lev. 24:10-16. Couldn't we just burn them to death at a private family affair, like we do with people who sleep with their in-laws? (Lev. 20:14)

I know you have studied these things extensively and thus enjoy considerable expertise in such matters, so I'm confident you can help.

Thank you again for reminding us that God's word is eternal and unchanging.

Your devoted disciple and adoring fan.[28]

Facetious? Yes. But true? Also yes!

It is easy to relate to this email because we all tend to pick and choose which parts of Scripture we believe are valid and binding for our times. That is why it becomes a bit ludicrous—and blatantly hypocritical—when we deny others the privilege of doing that which we ourselves do on a regular basis.

Ironically, many Christians will insist they are not *cherry-picking* Scripture, when in fact they are doing that very thing! One Christian friend's rationale for holding some laws to be valid and not others illustrates this point:

> It's not *cherry-picking* but rather *gleaning* from these ancient laws the principles necessary for governing our lives. Obviously the laws were written for a tribal community and some of the laws aren't applicable to our modern society but when it comes to our bodies and how to take care of them, what to eat, sexuality ... yes, they are still valid!

---

[28] The actual authorship of this letter has been disputed, although the name Kent Ashcraft keeps coming up. The letter was written in early 2000.

With this response, my friend has done what Christianity has taught her to do when faced with its own hypocrisy; that is, to redefine or recast its own actions in an effort to make it appear that its own hypocrisy is somehow okay because of the excuses it has provided. In this case, my friend indeed discards a certain number of the laws as fitting only for a *tribal* people but holds the ones that are important to her today—such as the law regarding homosexuality—to be valid. If this is not *cherry-picking* Scriptures, I do not know what is!

Another Christian friend's response to the above "Dr. Laura" letter was to obfuscate,

> The point is there is a standard. There is right and wrong. People can believe what they want, based on their feelings, their emotions, whatever. I choose to believe in the Word of God. It's the only thing that hasn't failed me, though I have failed it. That is the standard, telling me truth from error. Were anyone to come to me, and try to convince me otherwise, I would likely be pretty wary of them.

The question that neither friend dares to ask is this: Who is to determine what is authoritative and inspired for you and what is not? How do you know which Scriptures have really been spoken from the mouth of God?

CHAPTER 4

❖

GOING AROUND IN CIRCLES

Dr. Larry Richards, an Adventist professor at Andrews Theological University, has presented an interesting paper with a very logical thought process regarding the Bible canon and which writings are inspired. He writes:

> I have, to be sure, argued that the traditional arguments made in defense of the authoritative nature of Scripture (and therefore in an indirect sense, of the truth contained in Scripture) are often not very sound, and are meaningful at best only for those who already believe... We shall look at three questions which represent the concerns most often raised. The line of thought that runs through these inquiries suggests that I have taken something away, something that previously offered certainty. Some persons, no doubt, have held a position much like the one I'm go-

ing to now cite from, Edward J. Young (Introduction to the Old Testament, 1949) who wrote these words:

'Canonical books... are those books which are regarded as divinely inspired. The criterion of a book's canonicity, therefore, is its inspiration. If a book has been inspired of God, it is canonical, whether accepted by men as such or not. It is God and not man who determines whether a book is to belong to the canon. Therefore if a certain writing has indeed been the product of divine inspiration, it belongs to the canon from the moment of its composition'.

First of all, the statement sounds good, does it not? (We have pointed out, however, that inspiration was not a criterion for canonicity in the early church). Notice the third sentence. How often I have heard this comment: "If a book has been inspired of God, it is canonical, whether accepted by men as such or not." But I must ask, who answers the question about whether a book has been inspired of God? I agree, if God inspired the book, it is God's word. But someone must decide (either an individual or community), whether or not God inspired the book! Who?

Young goes on to make another commonly heard statement: *'It is God and not man who determines... canon.'* Once again, I'll say yes, God determines. But the, it follows that I must also ask: "How do we determine what God has determined?" How do we know God's thinking on this? Who tells us? Does God? If God, how does He tell us?

Dr. Young's final point in the above paragraph reflects a very unscholarly judgment. Magic is not the order of the day. In the following quotations from the same book, we may again read the typically held position—a product of Reformation heritage. Note the obvious circular nature of the comments:

'The Christian recognizes the Scriptures as inspired, because they are such, and bear in themselves the evidences of their divinity. Basic, therefore, to any consideration of how man comes to recognize the Bible as God's word is the fact that it is indeed divine'.

Young is simply saying that Scripture is true because it is. The person who comes to the Bible knows it's God's Word because it is divine. This line of reasoning is shallow even for a believer.[29]

Dr. Richards is bravely saying what most Christian leaders do not dare to say, for fear of causing their parishioners to have a *crisis of faith*. So the status quo remains that with little exception, Dr. Young's viewpoint is the sum total of the analysis given to Christians by their various church leaders regarding why the Bible in its entirety is inspired. *The Bible is inspired because it says it is inspired.* It is completely *circular reasoning*, rather like a self-professed prophet who writes or declares that he or she is a prophet and therefore, he or she must be one because his or her inspired work says so!

One of the most frustrating examples of this phenomenon is the so-called prophet who will solemnly predict to his or her followers, "There will be people who come along and

---

[29] RICHARDS, W. Larry, *Ellen G. White's Writings: An Extension of Canon?* Copyright © 2002 W. Larry Richards. Unpublished Work. Andrews University. http://www.andrews.edu/~larryr/Articles/Richards.Canon.pdf

disagree with me." Will this prophecy come true? Well, DUH! It is highly likely that it will! "See," the devoted followers then proclaim. "This verifies that so-and-so was indeed a true prophet! He/she *prophesied* that this would happen!"

The Bible is inspired because it says it is inspired is one major issue that Roman Catholics take with the Protestant doctrine of *Sola Scriptura,* or *Scripture Alone.* Protestants are taking this *Roman Catholic* creation—the Bible—and using it to tell Catholics how they themselves are wrong! In a stroke of irony, both Catholics and Protestants are taking Judaism's created Scriptures and telling Judaism that they are wrong in their interpretation of their own Scriptures, as well!

Catholicism does not say the Bible is divine because of what it says, but because their church leadership has declared it to be divinely inspired. In the Roman Catholic mindset, it is *the Church,* and not the Scriptures that are merely a product of the Church, that ultimately has the authority to define what is divine and what is not.

In like manner, many so-called *Torah-observant* believers who are former Christians or current Messianic Jews feel that they are superior to or more obedient to God than traditional Jews. These *Messianic* believers elevate Torah to the point of believing that every single word in it is from the mouth of God; yet they disregard the fact that Judaism itself brought them their Torah, and may have some relevant insights about not only its interpretation and current application, but its compilation as well!

Dr. Richards goes on to say,

> To argue for "inherent worth" alone is to argue strictly on the subjective judgment of a reader. That is, Luther reads 2 Maccabees and testifies: the text does not au-

thenticate itself. How did he determine this? Obviously his own religious experience, his education, his presuppositions, his understanding of canon history, etc.—none of these can be separated from the judgment he makes. Eck, on the other hand, brings a different background to the same document and concludes the opposite of Luther. For Eck the text of 2 Maccabees belongs to the canon.

Any Christian in any age, however, who argues that a document is authoritative for them because of what that book has done in his/her life, may, and only then, testify that it has inherent worth. That is the relationship between the Reformation criterion and the one I'm proposing. Results come first; the response leads to a statement about self-authentication. The statement alone, that is without some means of testing it, opens the door for a multitude of different canons. Luther himself would have eliminated some books (such as James) from a canon list which was not in dispute by Catholic or Protestants!

The second question is, if Scripture is authoritative only after it is declared such (by a person or a community), are we able to say it is still authoritative even if everyone should deny the authority?

If every person should deny a document's authority, it obviously would not have authority. A document only has control over, or offers guidance to, one who agrees to such. "That is what authority means. "Authority" by definition requires at least one person to acknowledge the authority, or it does not exist.[30]

---

[30] RICHARDS

A real-world example of this fact is that the average Adventist will generally call Ellen White's writings *authoritative and inspired*, while a former Adventist or a Baptist will scornfully call her a false prophet and classify her writings as just another woman's opinion.

> None of this line of reasoning is intended to argue that a truth becomes truth only by our feeble acknowledgments. Truth is indeed truth prior to our understanding; we do not make something true because we say it's true; on the other hand, truth is only truth for any person or body of persons after they "know" it. My recognition does not make it truth; it only becomes truth for me, though, once I believe! You mean, someone asks, it's only true/authoritative after I (or someone) says it is? No, it may be true/authoritative for someone else apart from my stated belief. But in terms of a person's real world, that truth/authority makes no impact until it exercises authority over the person. And it can only exercise authority after the person consents.
>
> Third, in the end, how can anyone be certain about what is authoritative and whether or not there is such a thing as absolute truth? Where or how are such crucial questions answered?[31]

Dr. Richards' point is profound in its simplicity. As Christians, we routinely find different parts of Scripture that we do or do not give authority over us. One person will give Leviticus 18:22 authority over their life because they are

---

[31] RICHARDS

strongly against homosexuality; yet they consider Leviticus 19:19, just one chapter over (*do not wear clothing with two different kinds of fiber in it*) to be a completely irrelevant law. Another Christian will hold as Gospel Truth the apostle Paul's counsel that *women are not to teach in church,* while another will dismiss this directive as the product of a bygone age.

Dr. Richards ultimately concludes that we should test inspirational documents and see what kind of fruits they bear in our own lives. Yeshua said much the same when he said,

> Every good tree bears good fruit, but a bad tree bears bad fruit. A good tree cannot bear bad fruit, and a bad tree cannot bear good fruit. Every tree that does not bear good fruit is cut down and thrown into the fire. Thus, by their fruit you will recognize them.[32]

Here we have a very interesting point. What fruits have the different portions of Scripture borne through time? How have they impacted the lives of those they have touched?

To make this *fruits* concept even more personally relevant, each one of us should be brave enough to ask the following questions:

What kind of life do I lead?

How many people do I bless through my very existence?

---

[32] Matthew 7:17-20

Does my personally selected authoritative Scripture make me more or less loving and tolerant to those around me?

Does my religion make me kinder and more humble, or does it leave me feeling angry and *self-righteously* superior?

Am I such a loving and compassionate person that others who do not hold *any* Scripture passages to be authoritative would actually want to further investigate what I believe? Would they want to know the God that I claim is leading me?

What kind of fruits have the Scriptures that I hold dear produced in my own life?

Even though I had learned to quote pages and pages of Bible texts when I was a child, it was now time to learn more about the history of the Bible itself. Perhaps if I discovered more about the circumstances surrounding the Bible's formation, the contradictions I was also discovering within the Scriptures would become less troublesome. Little did I realize the depth of history I was about to uncover.

CHAPTER 5

❖

THE BIBLE COMES OF AGE

After discovering that God's TRUE Name had been hidden and a new name for Satan had been added into the Scriptures, it became painfully apparent that there were some issues going on with the Bible that were going to be difficult to deal with. However, I felt irreverent and borderline heretical to even entertain any questions about it because of my utmost respect for *God's Word*.

I realized that my Holy Bible did not *literally* arrive by FedEx® from Heaven, bound in a sturdy leather cover with a tasteful *KJV* stamped in gold on the front. However, it might as well have, because the strong feelings of reverence that I felt when carefully opening those gilt-edged pages made it *feel* like the contents had been handed down from the clouds.

To someone who has been raised as a Christian, the Bible itself represents a deep but holy mystery that instills an almost mystical perception of the Scriptures it contains. Some Christians will refuse to write in their Bible for fear that God might be angry at them for defacing the Word of God. Others are taught, as I was, that it is disrespectful to set any physical object on top of the Bible, because to do so would be like dishonoring God Himself.

While my church and Bible teachers indeed taught me all kinds of very good lessons from the Bible, I actually learned very little about the Bible itself. In many ways, I believe this dearth of knowledge among Christian laypeople about the Bible's origins is, in fact, by design. When you truly begin learning about how the Bible came to be the book we have today, a certain layer of mythical reverence is suddenly stripped away. Because of your increasing knowledge about this library of Scripture, that child-like mystery you once had about God's Word vanishes forever. You can never unlearn that which you discover when you *eat of the Tree of Knowledge*.

Despite feelings of personal discomfort, I began to realize that it was time to better learn not only the history of my Church and faith, but also the history of my own most sacred spiritual treasure; the Bible.

The Bible's Historical Roots

It is common knowledge within the scholastic Christian community that throughout the first through fifth centuries, a myriad of Christian sects were writing and distributing all kinds of books and epistles detailing what they thought and how they believed.[33] This was a way of recording history, as they knew it from what they had been told. Some of these

---

[33] EHRMAN, Bart, Lost Christianities: The Battles for Scripture and the Faiths We Never Knew, 2005, Introduction, pp. 1-9

writings were not in keeping with what Yeshua HaMaschiach had taught; but many of them indeed were.

However, such methods of historical preservation combined with a lack of communication led to easy historical revisionism. As such, Gnosticism from Greece was brought into the Church along with other popular pagan beliefs from Rome, such as Mithraism and Solis (sun) worship. The people of these centuries had no real way of knowing who was actually telling the truth and who was simply repeating pagan tradition under the banner of *Christianity*.

By the turn of the late second century, the Roman Catholic leaders were not the only ones developing various lists of books that they considered inspired and authoritative. Leaders of other developing churches were also formulating their own lists of books they considered to be *canon*, or standard.[34] To early Catholicism's way of thinking, the development and solidification of a standardized list of *accepted* or *orthodox* books that could be read in church would go a long way in keeping those pesky *heretics* and their dogma out of the still developing Church.

Many Christians believe that the Emperor Constantine determined which books would make it into the Bible canon. However, the Council of Laodicea in circa 364 AD was the first official Roman Catholic Church Council to make a formal ecumenical (meaning all-encompassing and church-wide) attempt at solidifying their own orthodox listing of canonical books—some 30 years after Constantine's death. One of the steps the Council of Laodicea took in dealing with Christians it considered heretics was to decide what was and was not considered acceptable to read in church.[35] The Laodicean

---

[34] "Canon", from the Greek term *kanon*, meaning *a standard of measure*.
[35] Canon 59 & 60

Council thus set the Church on a path toward ecumenical recognition of what would and would not be considered *orthodox* as canonical Scripture.

At the same time the Laodicean Council was establishing its official list of canonical books, it was also declaring broad changes to the Law of God. It even stated that Christians were *no longer permitted* to rest on the Sabbath, or keep the Passover with the Jews.[36]

By issuing these standards of *catholic* (universal) behavior for Roman Christians, it became obvious that Rome's ostensibly *catholic* version of Christianity was not completely universal in its acceptance among all period Christians of the day. Rome was obviously having at least some difficulty dealing with *non-Roman* Christians, as these *non-orthodox* (heretical) Christians were indeed still keeping Sabbath and celebrating the Passover well into the fourth century and beyond![37]

---

[36] Canon 29 reads, "Christians must not judaize by resting on the Sabbath, but must work on that day, rather honoring the Lord's Day; and, if they can, resting then as Christians. But if any shall be found to be judaizers, let them be anathema from Christ." Canon 37 reads, "It is not lawful to receive portions sent from the feasts of Jews or heretics, nor to feast together with them." Canon 38 reads, "It is not lawful to receive unleavened bread from the Jews, nor to be partakers of their impiety."

[37] Christians were keeping a Torah-observant Sabbath well into the fifth century with various sects (i.e.. denominations) continuing to do so well into the modern era. My own ancestors actually predate the SDA Church and were founding members of the first Seventh-day Baptist Church in the colonies in the mid 1600s.

The Developing Bible Canon

After the rabbis remaining at Jamnia had settled what would become the Hebrew canon (the *Tanakh*, which is what Christians generally refer to as the *Old Testament*) circa 100 AD, the church fathers in Rome added books from the Greek Septuagint into the established Jewish canon. It is important to note that the Septuagint itself was not a decidedly static collection of books either, but was rather a loosely accepted collection of ancient Jewish writings that mainly included the Torah, the Prophets, and the Writings, along with other historical Jewish books and writings.[38] These Writings included the so-called Intertestamental or *Apocryphal* books, which the Church in Rome declared to be *inspired* canon.[39]

To Rome's official listing of Jewish books, the early church fathers also then added other *current period* books from men they thought prominent from less than 100 years prior (i.e. the first century). Imagine if our church leaders of today decided to add a book from Mary Baker Eddy, Ellen White, or Joseph Smith to the Bible! This is exactly how many of these *non-Roman* Catholic Christians felt about Rome's ostensibly inspired Bible canon! The books Rome added to their canonical list included just four Gospels and the Marcion canon, which included most of Paul's letters.

---

[38] An interesting fact about the *Writings* is that the Essenes, an early denomination of Judaism, did not appear to accept the book of Esther as canonical since this book is not found in any of those discovered among the Dead Sea Scrolls. The book was indeed available as a period Jewish book, yet the Essenes evidently chose not to use it. Curiously, this book never mentions God in it, not even once!

[39] Note that the Jewish canon does not include these Intertestamental (Apocrypha) writings as inspired, but rather considers them simply historical.

Irenaeus of Lyons (2nd century AD - c. 202 AD), a disciple of Polycarp, was Bishop of Lugdunum in Gaul, Roman Empire (now Lyons, France). He was an early church father and apologist, and his writings were formative in the early development of Christian theology. Regarding the number of gospels to be selected, Irenaeus declared:

> It is not possible that the Gospels can be either more or fewer in number than they are, since there are four directions of the world in which we are, and four principle winds ... The four living creatures [of Rev. 4:9] symbolize the four Gospels ... and there were four principle covenants made with humanity, through Noah, Abraham, Moses, and Christ.[40]

By today's scholastic standards, Irenaeus would be laughed out of the Church as a superstitious idiot if he presented this same kind of *empirical evidence, numerology* and *vapid reasoning* to specifically include *four* Gospels. Yet how many gospels do you find included in your Bible today? Four!

Irenaeus' canonical list of *inerrantly inspired* books also included an early Christian writing called the *Shepherd of Hermas*[41]—a book that was later *dropped* from the canon by

---

[40] METZGER, Bruce, *The Canon of the New Testament*, Oxford University Press, 1997, pp. 154-155

[41] *The Shepherd of Hermas* (sometimes just called *The Shepherd*) is a Christian work of the second century, considered a valuable book by many Christians, and occasionally considered canonical scripture by some of the early Church fathers. *The Shepherd* had great authority in the second and third centuries. It was cited as Scripture by Irenaeus and Tertullian and was bound with the New Testament in the Codex Sinaiticus, and it was listed between the Acts of the Apostles and the Acts of Paul in the stichometrical list of the Codex Cla-

the also *inerrant and inspired* decision of later bishops of the Church.

In addition to dropping or adding additional books, the early Christian sectarians set about making alterations to the Scriptures. But just adding a word here or changing a word there was not enough for the early Roman sect of Christianity—whole events, even entire chapters were being added to the Bible![42] Conversely, many verses were being dropped from manuscripts simply because these period scribes and elders did not like what they said.

One example illustrating this occurrence is that the Gospel of Matthew was originally written in either/both Hebrew or Aramaic, not Greek. Unfortunately, the only surviving manuscripts are much later Greek variants of the original Hebrew and /or Aramaic manuscripts. The first two chapters of Matthew are missing from the earliest, more reliable ancient manuscripts. These chapters were later additions to the original book of Matthew, which seemed to serve no other purpose than to decidedly assert the Hebraic lineage of Joseph and the *virgin birth* of Yeshua.

At issue with the *virgin birth* story in the Greek versions of Matthew is that 1) the *virgin birth* account is an adaptation of Mithraic mythology and 2) the references to Isaiah 7 as a prophecy of Yeshua being born of a *virgin* are the work of terrible scholarship and a very poor misinterpretation and mistranslation of the original Hebrew of Isaiah 7:14. In Isaiah 7:14, Bible scholars indeed note that the translation of the Hebrew does not indicate a *virgin*, but rather merely a *young*

---

romontanus. Some early Christians, however, considered the work apocryphal. (Wikipedia.com)

[42] EHRMAN, Bart, *Misquoting Jesus: The Story Behind Who Changed the Bible and Why*, 2007, Section 2, Copyists of the Early Christian Writings, pp. 45-70

woman. Take note also that within the prophecy of Isaiah 7, the young woman is in fact Isaiah's own wife who is already pregnant! The editors of the CEV note:

> Isaiah 7:14 virgin: Or "young woman." In this context the difficult Hebrew word *did not imply a virgin birth.* However, in the Greek translation [of Isaiah] made about 200 (B.C.) and used by the early Christians, the word *parthenos* had a double meaning. While the translator took it to mean "young woman," [the editor of the Greek version of] Matthew understood [totally or deliberately misunderstood?] [parthenos] to mean "virgin" and quoted the passage (Matthew 1.23) because it was the appropriate description of Mary, the mother of Jesus.[43]

While the editors of the CEV seem to deliberately whitewash this deeply troubling issue of mistranslation, the fact of the matter remains that 1) the full and true context of this text in Isaiah is not speaking about a *virgin; parthenos* only means *young woman,* and 2) whoever wrote these first two chapters of Matthew (it was not Matthew!) ignorantly and/or deliberately mistranslated Isaiah 7:14 as the means of attempting to support their need for a *virgin birth* story from within the Hebrew Scriptures. This section of Matthew is without question a later Roman Catholic addition to the original Matthean text. Other more accurate versions of the Bible, such as the UPDV, have completely removed the virgin birth story from the book of Matthew because it is clearly a later Roman Catholic addition to the book.[44]

---

[43] [Bracketed] commentary supplied
[44] Updated.org/matthew.shtml

Few Biblical scholars will disagree with these facts. Furthermore, Matthew was not the only book to have been edited by Roman Catholic apologists. Another deeply troubling issue is in regards to the latter verses of the Gospel of Mark. The NIV notes,

> The most reliable early manuscripts and other ancient witnesses do not have Mark 16:9-20.

This comment by the NIV translators should be alarming to any Christian. "What do you mean the most reliable manuscripts don't have these verses? So these verses come from *unreliable* manuscripts? Then why are then in my Bible?" That is *exactly* what the NIV editors are stating, then subsequently downplaying. They only left those verses in the book of Mark because devout believers are expecting them to be there, not because they actually belong there. Take note that the NIV editors also rightly removed the word *new* from Yeshua's supposed phrase *new covenant* within the books of Mathew and Mark, because the most reliable manuscripts do not have the term *new* within them.[45]

ELEVATING AND DEPRECATING THE SCRIPTURES

Over a period of several hundred years, the subsequent various Roman Catholic Church councils added, edited and dropped books from the canon based on the decisions—official votes—of the period leadership in power.

Take note of the odd quandary that dropping a book presents to the mainstream modern Protestant doctrine of

---

[45] Matthew 26:28, Mark 14:24, "Some manuscripts *the new*".

Biblical inspiration and inerrancy: dropping any book from the canon that has been added by a previously and ostensibly *inspired and infallible* church council means that either: a) God was being expedient with the canon or changed His mind, b) the church had previously willfully ignored the will of God, c) the decisions made by previous councils were in error, or d) the various councils had simply done whatever they wanted with the canon to serve the opinions of the current leadership.

No matter which way you slice it, the factual history of the development of the Bible canon does not lend very good support for the Protestant doctrine of *Sola Scriptura*, or *Scripture Alone*, as being a sound foundation upon which to build an understanding of the *Word* and the *Character* of God.

Can you imagine this same scenario happening today? Imagine if as an Adventist Christian, you heard that the vast Baptist denomination was officially planning to *drop* a random book from the Bible because that book unequivocally supported the keeping of the Sabbath Commandment; and the Baptists wanted no part of the Sabbath because they wanted to go to church on Sunday? Would you as a Sabbath-keeping Christian really consider these Baptists to be *inspired* because their General Conference held a vote to abolish and banish from the Bible any early Christian support of the Forth Commandment? Yet this is exactly what the Roman Catholic Church did when it effectively nullified the *Gospel of the Hebrews*[46] with a simple vote of its powerful membership in Rome. Irenaeus' *orthodox* list of books specifically excluded

---

[46] The *Gospel of the Hebrews*, also called the *Gospel of the Ebionites*, is a non-extant (now extinct; the Catholic Church destroyed any copies it found) book similar in content to the Gospel of Mathew. We know if its existence through the writings of the Church Fathers who wrote of it and even quoted from it.

the *Gospel of the Hebrews*, most likely be[came t]he seventh-day Sabbath observance (among a [... so] very Hebraic/Jewish understandings); [...] Christians were observing well beyond th[e ...] centuries!

THE BIBLE IN TROUBLE

Near the end of the fourth century, the Bible as a canon of Scripture, as decreed by the Roman Catholic Church, had been fully established. By this time, thousands of Latin copies of the Bible had been hand-written and translated by various scribes, with some copies being better and more accurate than others. This problem of many divergent copies prompted Pope Damasus I in 382 to commission Jerome of Antioch to create a standardized Latin version that could be read to the common people; hence the name *Latin Vulgate*, a Bible for the *vulgar* (i.e. common) masses.

Oddly, however, the Vulgate translation was not really for the *common* people. While Latin might have been the official and legal language of Rome, it was not the common tongue throughout the majority balance of the Roman Empire. If you were a commoner with very little education living in the outer regions of the Empire, the chances of you speaking and understanding Rome's Latin would have been slim to none. Henceforth, the *language of the Bible* would be utterly lost to you.

A Latin-only version including the whole *Lucifer* (mis)translation issue was not the only problem Christians faced with the developing Bible canon. Jerome was in deep disagreement with Pope Damasus over the canonical list of books itself! Jerome did not want to include the books that to be known as the *Apocrypha* in his translation, but did because he was ordered to do so by his employers.

The controversy surrounding the inclusion of the *Apocrypha* raged for centuries. So great was the disagreement about the *inspiration* of the Apocrypha that in the sixteenth century, Martin Luther and other Reformers made an informed (newly inspired?) decision to *exclude* (drop, de-canonize, remove) these books from the Bible canon that the Roman Catholic Church had well established via its *inerrant inspiration* a thousand years earlier. In effect, the Reformers were saying, "We do not accept the authority of these books *nor* do we accept the authority of the Church that insists they are inspired!"

Whether we wish to admit it or not, the issue of the inspiration of the Apocryphal books presents a huge doctrinal enigma to the Christian Church. It also highlights a deep contradiction for the doctrine of Biblical inerrancy, inspiration and infallibility. That contradiction is simply this: on the one hand we indeed claim God's inerrant and infallible inspiration in assembling the books of the Bible; yet, on the other hand we also claim that the Apocryphal books that were *originally* inspired for inclusion are now *not inspired*.

As Christians, we cannot have it both ways without becoming hypocrites of the highest order!

Christian scholars as a whole are all too ready to agree with these facts in the development of the Bible canon. But when one subsequently concludes that Biblical inerrancy is impossible because of these *political contests* between the various factions of early Christian leaders, one hears all manner of illogical denials. For example, the late Dr. Samuele

Bacchiocchi once told Luc in an email that "...the Bible is not the product of the Catholic Church!"[47]

Or how about this statement from the highly esteemed Dr. Bruce Metzger,

> You have to understand that the canon was not the result of a series of contests involving church politics. The canon is rather the separation that came about because of the intuitive insight of Christian believers.[48]

Are we all looking at the same facts? It would appear that these esteemed scholars are not looking very critically at the facts of history! As we have seen, there were indeed deep political contests between factions of Christians; each writing, compiling, editing and arranging their own canons of *Scripture*!

The development of the current Bible canon is not some unfathomable mystery of God. Its development is well documented throughout the annals of Christianity.

True and total inerrancy, inspiration and infallibility would logically preclude any changes (and indeed any editorializations) within the canon whatsoever. This quandary can easily be answered by simply recognizing that historically there have been many canons of Scriptures fostered by many factions and denominations of the early Christian Church.

---

[47] Dr. Samuele Bacchiocchi, in an email to my husband, Beau, during a discussion about the Apocrypha.
[48] Dr. Bruce Metzger, quoted from an interview by Lee Strobel in The Case for Christ: A Journalist's Personal Investigation of the Evidence for Jesus, 1998, Chapter 3

We must recognize that the Catholic Fathers and Protestant Reformers who changed and reorganized the current canon, did so on their own authority with the best knowledge they had available.

This is not to say that God did not participate in the inspiration, writing and assembly of the canon; in fact, evidence points to the contrary! In our fullest understanding of the assembly of the Bible canon, it would be absolutely imprudent, irresponsible and unwise for any reformer—ancient or modern—to declare that the Hand of God was or has been utterly absent in the assembly of the Bible canon. It is, after all, primarily the books of *Matthew, James, Jude*, parts of *Revelation* and even parts of Luke's own *Acts of the Apostles* that indeed confirm the original unchanging standard of God's TRUE Law. It has also been in the consistent standard outlined by the content of these first century books that we have been able to see and measure many of the profound contradictions of other writings included in the Bible canon by Rome.

CHAPTER 6

❖

BROKEN DREAMS & SHATTERED BELIEFS

I shall be telling this with a sigh
Somewhere ages and ages hence:
Two roads diverged in a wood, and I –
I took the one less traveled by,
and that has made all the difference.[49]

Growing up as a sixth-generation Adventist, I took great pride in the fact that I was an integral part of the *Remnant Church*, the church that would *finish the work* so that Yeshua could come sooner. I had chain-referenced my Bible from the time I was in academy,[50] and could quote multiple Scriptural passages to defend my beliefs. But now, I just couldn't explain away or ignore the fact that the very founda-

---

[49] The Road Not Taken, Robert Frost
[50] Private Adventist high schools are referred to as *academies*.

tion of my faith, the *Word of God*, had some truly troubling holes in it.

The facts were irrefutable: the Reformers had *changed* the infallible and inspired Bible, modern *corrections* were being made that changed long-held doctrine (or at best made the tradition Biblically unsupportable), and Christianity couldn't even get God's own name right within the Scriptures. It didn't make any sense! I finally had to face the fact that the doctrine of Biblical inerrancy (along with total inspiration and infallibility) was a bold-faced lie.

I cared very deeply about my faith and realized that in order to follow God in truth, I needed to know exactly where my doctrines had come from and why. I continuously and earnestly prayed to God that He would show me HIS TRUTH, no matter how hard it might be to face. There were so many times that I cried on my knees, struggling with God over what I had just discovered. Still, through the tears I kept repeating, "Show me YOUR truth, Father, please, show me YOUR truth!"

I felt like I was wandering in a vast desert of broken dreams and shattered beliefs. When I looked around, it seemed like the road I had chosen was not only less traveled, but was also overgrown with useless rituals, heathen practices, and various other skeletons of doctrinal detritus.

Then there was the issue of my rapidly sinking self-esteem. I had always judged my perceived value by what I could contribute to others. The songs I had written, the programs I had produced, and the music I had played that had brought people closer to God; all of these things defined my value, in my own eyes and, I felt, in the eyes of God. If I was *not* doing all of these things, what good was I, really? So I was discovering new truths about God—how was I personally contributing to the good of His Church? Furthermore, would expressing my concerns accomplish more harm than good if my words of doubt caused others to also question what they had been taught?

The times I had felt closest—and the most valuable—to God were those times when I was writing music. Now, I not only didn't know what to write about, but many of the songs I had already written contained doctrine I was now questioning or even flat-out rejecting. My spiritual self-esteem plummeted to sub-oceanic depths. I grieved for the loss of community I experienced because I was too uncomfortable to even go to church. And even worse, I grieved for the loss of my spiritual self-worth, now that I wasn't visibly contributing to the edification of God's people.

I not only felt invisible to my fellow Christians; I felt invisible to God.

It was too late now to wish that I had never undertaken this journey to find out more about the history of my beliefs. I couldn't close Pandora's box, couldn't un-ring the bell, couldn't unlearn what I taken from the *Tree of Knowledge*, and couldn't go back and choose to take the road that actually had familiar people on it. But I sensed deep down that in spite of some intermittent turmoil and sadness, I needed to continue bravely down this new road, leaving no stone unturned and no fact unchecked. The difficulty and loneliness would all be worth it if I could really get to know the loving God that Yeshua talked about.

Upon further scrutiny, it became apparent that Christianity itself seems to be changing. There seems to be an increasing trend to present only a *relevant, seeker-sensitive* pop Christianity that is heavy on the warm comfy feelings and light on one's personal responsibility to obey God's TRUE instruction.

This troubling trend was aptly illustrated in an interesting sermon transcript/article in the *Adventist Review* online.[51] The article, entitled *Crossing Over,* was all about inspiring believers to step out in faith, take a chance, and leap off the proverbial bridge of faith to reach one's own personal Promised Land. The hip young speaker was very engaging, and he shared some interesting stories and motivational suggestions.

I'm all for stepping out in faith, following God's leading, and taking chances, so I read the transcript with interest. My curiosity was particularly piqued as I read the following selection of the article. The speaker began quoting from Joshua chapter 1.

> Wow, where were we? Back to Joshua. God says to the people, "Be the new generation. Be the people who God calls to cross. Go across. Don't be the old people, the old generation that died in the wilderness. Don't say it can't be done. Don't say that isn't where God wants us."
>
> Verse 5. God says, "No one will be able to stand up against you all the days of your life. As I was with Moses, so I will be with you; I will never leave you nor forsake you."
>
> If you are following along, verse 6, prepare to jump: "Be strong and courageous."
>
> Verse 7: "Be strong and very courageous."
>
> Verse 9: "Have I not commanded you? Be strong and courageous. Do not be terrified; do not be dis-

---

[51] http://www.adventistreview.org/article.php?id=117

couraged, for the Lord your God will be with you wherever you go."

I don't know about you, but I find it curious if someone jumps over or skips all around a text while they are making their point. I had to see what was in verse eight. Was it insignificant? Irrelevant? Uninspiring? Unnecessary? Or was it merely superfluous to the point being made?

> Do not let this Book of the Law depart from your mouth; meditate on it day and night, so that you may be careful to do everything written in it. Then you will be prosperous and successful.

Far from being superfluous or irrelevant, the skipped text appears to be what the entire promise of the rest of the passage hinges on! Let's compare it to a contract to buy a house.

> "Go ahead. Buy it!"
> "You just need to sign on the dotted line."
> "It will be *great* owning a house!"
> (Skipping over the section that says my responsibility is to pay X amount of dollars per month for the next 30 years for the privilege of homeownership.)
> "Wow, you really need to take this chance. Isn't it awesome?"

By avoiding Joshua 1:8, the speaker essentially promised *all* of the benefits with *none* of the responsibility!

Because of the independent and self-focused mindset of today's *don't fence me in* generation, and also realizing that *you need to obey God's law* doesn't play well with Gen-X or Gen-Y Christians, many of today's Christian leaders just gloss over or even completely disregard the fact that our Heavenly Father actually expects obedience from those who would claim His promises. The fault doesn't lie only with the leadership; it also reflects on the rest of us who expect—no, demand—miracles while refusing to entertain the notion that some responsibility for obedience lies with us.

A few years ago I saw an advertisement for a "Just Claim It!" international SDA Youth Prayer Conference. I recall being stunned by the motto, which read something like this:

> If my people, who are called by my name, will humble themselves and pray... then will I hear from heaven... and will heal their land.

What was in the ellipses? The text of Scripture, unedited, actually goes like this:

> If my people, who are called by my name, will humble themselves and pray *and seek my face and turn from their wicked ways,* then will I hear from heaven *and will forgive their sin* and will heal their land.[52]

Once again, our own personal responsibility to *turn away from our sin* has been left out in favor of *just claiming* all sorts of promises and blessings.

The Psalmist spoke so glowingly of the gift of God's TRUE Law. What will it take for our generation to see our Father as someone that we need to obey *because* He has authority over

---

[52] 2 Chronicles 7:14

us? When will we submit to His instruction, embrace our responsibility for obedience to our Maker and grow up as believers? Lastly, when will we see the Eternal One's TRUE Law for what it is—a gift to make our lives better?

The Law of the Lord has been written and stored
in the hearts and the minds of His children
So blessed will be they who would walk in its way
for its statutes bring life-giving freedom

It's holy and right; it's a clear blazing light
that shines down on the land of each nation
Its justice excites us; its teachings invite us
to share it with all of creation

Sacred legacy
Ancient code; Heaven's key
Eternal Covenant of TRUTH...
His Law IS

My soul will awaken; I will not be shaken,
AHEYEH in His glory is with me
His Name is my treasure; His precepts, my pleasure,
His promises comfort and keep me

Sacred legacy
Ancient code; Heaven's key
Eternal Covenant of TRUTH...
His Law IS[53]

---

[53] BEAUCHAMP, Serena, *His Law Is*, ©2010

CHAPTER 7

❖

ETERNAL COVENANT OF TRUTH

A *Jew and a Christian were arguing about the ways of their religion. The Jewish man said, "You people have been taking things from us for thousands of years; the Ten Commandments, for instance."*

The Christian replied, *"Well, it's true that we took the Ten Commandments from you, but you can't actually say that we've kept them!"*

Many Christians will chuckle at the above joke, realizing that it is humorous because there is some truth in it. And the point is very valid—if you line up a *New Covenant Christian* and a Jew and ask them the first text that comes to mind when you mention *God's Law,* their answers will likely be worlds apart. The Jew will probably give you a text like this one; "The law from your mouth is more precious to me than thousands of pieces of silver and gold."⁵⁴ The *New Covenant Christian,* on the other hand, will very likely quote the following text; "Anyone who tries to please God by obeying the Law is under a curse."⁵⁵ Adventist Christians and to an extent Reform and Conservative Jews tend to ride the fence on this one—*God's Law* is classified according to whether it is the *Ten Commandments* or the *Jewish Ceremonial Law,* and the *Ten Commandments* portion (as well as any *relevant* additional Torah instruction) is extolled and upheld.⁵⁶

Where did Yeshua fall within this spectrum of understanding and belief? Rather than promoting the multiple and unending list of commandments extolled by the religious leadership, historical records preserved through time⁵⁷ indicate that Yeshua upheld a simpler, *reformed* version of God's TRUE Law. Yeshua was never wishy-washy in his teachings: "If you want to have eternal life, you must obey (God's) commandments."⁵⁸ His counsel was simple and completely consistent with the latter prophets.

As a Jewish rabbi, Yeshua kept the Sabbath and instructed everyone to do the same.⁵⁹ What Yeshua came against with regard to the Sabbath is the militant demands that the

---

⁵⁴ Psalm 119:72

⁵⁵ Galatians 3:10a CEV

⁵⁶ Except for select few of the Levitical passages, such as the one regarding homosexuality. That one is still considered to be valid to most Adventists and to conservative Christianity in general.

⁵⁷ The Clementine Homilies are one such source.

⁵⁸ Matthew 19:17b

⁵⁹ Within Acts 15, James, the brother of Jesus, clearly instructs the Gentiles to enter the synagogue with their Jewish brethren on the Sabbath to learn the Law, saying, "It is my judgment, therefore, that we should not make it difficult for the Gentiles who are turning to God.... For Moses has been preached in every city from the earliest times and is read in the synagogues on every Sabbath."

priesthood had made regarding how the Sabbath should be kept. Yeshua offered that, "The Sabbath was made for man, not man for the Sabbath."[60] In other words, the Sabbath was intended to be a joyous event each week! It was never intended to be laden with all of the man-made rules and *mitzvah* (laws) that turned the Sabbath into an unbearable yoke of slavery—which is exactly what the Pharisees and Sadducees had done to this weekly day of rest, relaxation and joy.

Growing up in a conservative Adventist environment, our family followed our own unwritten version of the *Adventist Talmud* on Sabbath. For example, we could play with other Adventist kids on Sabbath (*Bible tag*, etc.) but not with the *non-Adventist* kids next door. We could wade into the water at the beach if we were fully dressed (and it was sort of okay or at least forgivable if you accidentally fell in) but we couldn't dress as if we were *intentionally* going swimming. We could go for a walk, but not ride our bikes. There were even certain foods that weren't really considered appropriate Sabbath fare—hot dogs, pizza, burgers, and other such *fun* foods.

Despite these unwritten and sometimes nonsensical regulations, I realized deep in my heart that the Sabbath was special. Indeed, God has always affirmed via the prophets that His Sabbaths are important to Him and His people.

> I gave them my laws and teachings, so they would know how to live right. And I commanded them to respect the Sabbath as a way of showing that they were holy and belonged to me.[13] But the Israelites rebelled against me in the desert. They refused to obey my laws and teachings, and they treated the Sabbath

---

[60] Mark 2:27 / "The Sabbath was made to meet the needs of people, and not people to meet the requirements of the Sabbath." –NLT

> like any other day. Then in my anger, I decided to destroy the Israelites in the desert once and for all.[61]
>
> Her priests do violence to my law and profane my holy things; they do not distinguish between the holy and the common; they teach that there is no difference between the unclean and the clean; and they shut their eyes to the keeping of my Sabbaths, so that I am profaned among them.[62]

While God said that His people were to keep His Sabbaths holy, and while the Almighty One can be seen clearly chastising the elders and leaders for not keeping them, the debate among Christians of different denominations rages on. The *New Covenant Christian* will base his argument upon Paul's counsel in Romans 14.

> One man considers one day more sacred than another; another considers every day alike. Each of them should be fully convinced in their own mind.[63]

In Luc's long-ago *Bapticostal* past, he quoted this specific verse many times in his arguments with Adventists regarding the Sabbath. He would emphasize how Adventists were applying an *unhealthy focus* on Sabbath observance, in direct contention to what Paul had said! He would gleefully crow that within these very same verses Paul was calling these compassionate vegetarian believers *weak in their faith*. After years of prayer and study and long after he had lost contact with the Adventist family he had so unmercifully heckled as a

---

[61] Ezekiel 20:11-13 CEV
[62] Ezekiel 22:26
[63] Romans 14:5

kid, he finally realized that the Sabbath was indeed a blessing and not a burden for the people of God.

The average Christian of any denomination is bound to have noticed that there are some very marked differences in what Yeshua the Messiah taught about the TRUE Law of God and what Paul of Tarsus counseled. Yeshua said,

> Do not think that I have come to abolish the Law or the Prophets...[64]

...while Paul demands that Yeshua abolished the Law saying,

> ...by abolishing in [Yeshua] flesh the law with its commandments and regulations...[65]

Yeshua's answer to the question of how one was to enter into eternal life was quite simple:

> And, behold, one came and said unto him, "Good Master, what good thing shall I do, that I may have eternal life?" And [Yeshua] unto him, "Why callest thou me good? There is none good but one, that is, God: but if thou wilt enter into life, keep the commandments."[66]

---

[64] Matthew 5:17
[65] Ephesians 2:14-15 CEV
[66] Matthew 19:16-17 KJV / Take note here that Yeshua corrected the man for calling Yeshua *good*. Most modern translations of this passage skew the translation so as to make it more palatable to Christian sensitivities regarding the assumed perfection of Yeshua. If the laity discovers that Yeshua wasn't perfect (i.e. good), then whole act of his *sacrifice* is moot. As such, most modern translations massage (twist) the translation of this verse, moving the *subject* of the verse off of Yeshua and refocusing the subject onto a manufactured subject of what is good in and of itself, such as, like *"Why do you ask me*

Paul's answer was markedly different than that of Yeshua. Rather than elevating God's TRUE Law, Paul offered that the Law of God is moot for salvation.

> I do not set aside the grace of God, for if righteousness could be gained through the law, Christ died for nothing![67]

I studied these passages deeply, prayerfully and at length and found the discrepancies—the contradiction—troubling. How could I go about reconciling these two contradictory viewpoints? Clearly, I would have to *pick and choose* the counsel that I felt was most correct and sort of disregard the other as much as possible. It was not an ideal solution, but it seemed to be the only possible way to deal with the fact that Yeshua and Paul were really not at all in agreement with each other.

---

about *what is good?*" However, the revisionism doesn't really make any sense because Jesus immediately follows up the thought by saying, *"There is only one who is good, God."* The subject of the thought of the underlying Greek is not *what* is good, but rather *who* is good! As such the true and correct translation in this case does indeed come from the KJV and also YLT.

[67] Galatians 2:21

PART II
THE HEART OF THE MATTER

CHAPTER 8

❖

TRYING TO MAKE GOD HAPPY

My daughter Ana came running into my office one day, just itching to get her younger brother, Alex, in trouble. "Mommy, Alex just hit me!" she tattled. Fortunately for Alex, he had been quietly drawing in the next room this whole time and I knew it. Ana was caught in a lie and it wasn't the first time.

I realized that I really needed to drive the point home with Ana about how serious it was to break God's law. Figuring that if it worked in the olden days when Jewish priests were in charge of religion it could work now, I sent Ana outside to get her favorite cat, Harley. He innocently sauntered in and rubbed against me, delighted to be receiving attention. Because he trusted me, he didn't even struggle when I tied him down to the kitchen island. I took a deep breath, instructed Ana to hold him tightly so he couldn't escape, grabbed my sharpest kitchen knife, and quickly slit his throat before I lost my nerve.

As he gasped and took his last breath, his life-blood running down the island to the floor, I dropped to my knees with a sobbing Ana and approached the Throne of Grace. "Oh Father, please forgive Ana for her sin. Help her not to lie in the future. Thank You for Your blessings. Amen."

I then discussed with my daughter how important it is to always tell the truth. I don't think that she got much of it—she was way too distraught at the fact that I had just killed noble Harley because *she* had been naughty in telling a little lie. But I felt pretty positive about the fact that I had illustrated God's plan of salvation to her just like they had done it in Bible times. Ana was no longer oblivious to the cost of sin.

We celebrated my daughter's spiritual breakthrough by inviting the rest of the family over and holding a feast. After that, we assembled a makeshift altar in the back yard and burned Harley's lifeless body as an offering to God. As the smoke from our sacrifice ascended to heaven, we were quite certain that if certain Bible accounts were any indication, God likely smelled the pleasing aroma and said in his heart, "Never again will I curse this family because of the sacrifice that they have offered."[68] [69]

---

[68] *God's blessing* given here is based on the accounting given of Noah after the flood found in Genesis 8:20-22. "Then Noah built an altar to the LORD and, taking some of all the clean animals and clean birds, he sacrificed burnt offerings on it. The LORD smelled the pleasing aroma and said in his heart: 'Never again will I curse the ground because of man, even though every inclination of the human heart is evil from childhood. And never again will I destroy all living creatures, as I have done.'" The story is accepted by Christianity as God's honest truth – but is it really? The discerning Christian or Messianic believer should seriously question the motives and inner thoughts that the unknown author has assigned to our compassionate Creator!
[69] DISCLAIMER: This story is a fictionalized account offered for the purpose of showing in real-world, modern vernacular just what it is that we in Christiani-

If you actually believed this fictitious story for even one second, you are very likely overcome with shock and horror about how unbelievably pagan and evil I am to even think about this type of scenario, much less write about it as if it happened. Good! Keep that feeling, because you know what? I have no doubt that you would have felt the *exact same way* if you had observed any of the sacrifices that took place in Bible times! If you were an actual spectator at just one of these abominable animal sacrifice *worship services,* watching it firsthand, you would know instantly in your compassionate heart that such an act was not in any way fulfilling the will or desire of the Eternal One.

One softhearted friend confided to me that she thinks she might have just killed herself if she had lived back in Bible times and had been forced to sacrifice animals. I completely understand her point, and am quite certain that a god you *honor* by sawing into the neck of a helpless animal is not a god that I want to be worshiping. However, this horrific action was carried out millions of times in both paganism and in Judaism with the priestly directive, "This is what God wants and demands—blood sacrifice!"

We in Christianity have indeed distanced ourselves from the horrific reality of such a monstrous teaching about God. In doing this, we have totally sanitized what people taught and did *in the name of God* and subsequently wrote into the ancient Scriptures as being *inspired truth.* Furthermore, when we are confronted about the illogicality of such a doctrine, we justify our beliefs by saying, "God made the Israelites go through the horror of sacrifice so they would realize how heinous their sin was." Sounds like sage advice—until you

---

ty say that God *wanted* when He supposedly *required* blood sacrifices. Harley is alive and well at the time of this writing.

confront the dismal, bloody reality of what you are really saying *God* wanted.[70]

Christendom as a whole has become very accustomed to ignoring an obvious disconnect between *our* definition of love and *God's* definition of love. We somewhat obliviously and self-righteously cite John 3:16 as the ultimate example of love:

> For God so loved the world, that he gave [sacrificed, murdered] his only begotten Son, that whosoever believeth in him should not perish, but have everlasting life.

We define our spiritual self-worth with the thought, "Yeshua loved me so much that he was willing to die for me! That is the ultimate love!" And indeed, self-sacrifice for the benefit of others *is* the ultimate act of love. But that's not what John 3:16 is all about. It's about a god who demands a *perfect* human blood sacrifice in order to forgive us, His sinful and presumably wretched children.

While we comfort ourselves with the selfless personal sacrifice of Yeshua, we don't really allow ourselves to question the motivation of a *god* who requires either animal sacrifice or even worse, human blood sacrifice in order to forgive us in the first place! For one reason, our Church teaches that even questioning such a horrific character trait would be an affront to God! Who wants to do that? But in reality, questioning such character is not so much question-

---

[70] If you have doubts about this, do a YouTube search on "sheep" and "sacrifice". You can observe actual religious rituals where people are killing sheep as a sacrifice. It is pretty horrifying.

ing God—it is merely questioning those who have brought us this blood-drenched *gospel* in the first place.

At the dedication of Solomon's Temple, so many sheep and cattle were sacrificed that "they could not be recorded or counted."[71] At times in Israel's violent past, the bloodlust of these fervent believers would escalate to the point that merely shedding the blood of an innocent animal was not enough, so they would offer up their very own children—again, something God had specifically prohibited! So egregious was the carnage that the hand of God brought destruction to Solomon's Temple. When the Israelites rebuilt their Temple once again, blood sacrifices resumed because that was the sin that had been passed on to the priesthood from their fathers. Once again, history repeated itself as the sins of the fathers were passed on to their children through the "lying pen of the elders".[72] History would again repeat itself via the lie of the written word.

In first century Jerusalem before the destruction of the second Temple, the blood of innocent animals ran so thickly from the temple altar that there were literally rivers of blood gushing from what was supposed to be God's *House of Prayer* but was in fact nothing more than a butcher shop of epic proportions! The Jewish historian Josephus wrote of this wholesale slaughter around the time of the destruction of the second Temple:

> So these high priests, upon the coming of that feast which is called the Passover, when they slay their sacrifices, from the ninth hour till the eleventh, but so

---

[71] 1 Kings 8:5
[72] Jeremiah 8:8; Ezekiel 18:1-4 illustrates that the children are not guilty of the sins of parents, but in fact inherit their parents' sinful habits.

that a company not less than ten belong to every sacrifice, (for it is not lawful for them to feast singly by themselves), and many of us are twenty in a company, found the number of sacrifices was *two hundred and fifty-six thousand five hundred*; which, upon the allowance of no more than ten that feast together, amounts to two million seven hundred thousand and two hundred persons that were pure and holy ...[73]

Various historians have noted that the impact and intensity of this collective sacrificial carnage was mind-numbingly stunning. So intense was the slaughter by the priests that a veritable river of blood ran out the back of the temple and into the Kidron Valley. One need necessarily ask: Was such a brutal slaughter of the innocent really the mechanism of forgiveness of a compassionate and loving God—the very same God who is mindful and cares about the fall and death of a single sparrow?[74]

We need to analyze what our doctrines are actually communicating. On the one hand, *people*, created beings, can forgive others if those who have wronged us repent of their actions and apologize. Yet, on the other hand, we believe that our even more loving Heavenly Father, *our Creator*, cannot forgive that easily—He somehow *must have blood!*

How come we in Christianity never stop to ask ourselves why we call this kind of Sovereign Monarch *loving* and *perfect* when we can apparently forgive more easily than we believe He can?

Again, to raise such questions is not to question God Himself, but rather to question a religious institution that

---

[73] Josephus (c. 37- c. 100 AD), *War*, vi. 9,3. ii. 14,3
[74] Matthew 10:29

has perpetrated and propagated a terrible error about what our own Creator is really like. Because of Christianity's insistence on this requirement of blood, our heavenly Father's reputation is being sacrificed on the altar of the Bible.

CHAPTER 9

❖

PAGANISM'S DARK INHERITANCE

Let us rewind for a moment and examine how the practice of sacrifice really took root for the children of Abraham. After 400 years of living with the Egyptians, the Israelites had fully assimilated into Egyptian society and were now, for all intents and purposes, culturally Egyptian. During the long centuries of living among the pagan mystery religions of Egypt, the Israelites had become completely convinced that the only way to effectively worship one's god was to offer blood sacrifices. By bringing this heinous practice out of Egypt with them, they were attempting to honor their Creator in the way all their Egyptian friends honored their gods; despite the fact that they were repeatedly instructed by Moses not to do so.

Could these simple people, who had been slaves for as long as they could remember, adequately understand Moses' instruction regarding how God really wanted to be worshiped? Maybe; maybe not. They were, in a spiritual sense, children. They needed to get to know the difference between the vile, pagan, and bloodthirsty gods of the Egyptians, and the compassionate God of their forefathers.

Sadly, this lesson was not easily learned. The early Israelites were given a choice: obey God's clear instruction that was simple and uncomplicated enough to be *already* written in their hearts and minds, or disobey God's TRUE Law and get kept out of the *Promised Land*.[75] Willful and disobedient, they chose the latter path. Their initial disobedience led them to wander around the wilderness for 40 years. Their persistent disobedience led to repeated exile from their beloved homeland. It led to eventual destruction of their Temple not just once, but twice. It even resulted in the eventual destruction of Jerusalem itself!

The Israelites' extended sojourn in the land of Egypt not only built sacrifice into the framework of the priesthood, but also ushered in another bloody ritual that was woven into the very fabric of Judaism itself. This pagan custom was the ancient practice of circumcision. Although most Christian or Messianic believers think that this practice started with Abraham[76] as an exclusive sign of his *covenant* with God, historical records indicate that circumcision was being performed in pagan Egyptian ceremonies at least 500-600 years before the time of Abraham. In addition, some of the

---

[75] Deuteronomy 30:11-20

[76] Abraham was thought to live sometime between 1637-1976 years BCE. Sixth Dynasty (2345-2181 BC) tomb artwork found in Egypt is thought to be the oldest documentary evidence of circumcision; with the most ancient possible depiction being a bas-relief from the necropolis at Saqqara (ca. 2300 BC). See *The Travelers' Key to Ancient Egypt* by John Anthony West, p. 187-88, for a description of the Saqqara artwork. Additional information taken from: http://www.1902encyclopedia.com/C/CIR/circumcision.html on 7/24/12.

bodies that have been exhumed in Egypt from 4000 BCE show evidence of circumcision.[77]

The primal practice of circumcision had substantial religious significance for the ancient Sumerians and Egyptians that related to their Sun-god.

> There was a myth common to Egypt and Phœnicia, though not of very ancient date in its extant Egyptian form, which seems to bring circumcision into connection with the Sun-god. In the *Book of the Dead*, chap. xvii., we read of the " blood which proceeded from the limb of the god Ra, when he wished to cut himself," which the late Vicomte de Rougé interpreted, with much plausibility, of circumcision (*Revue archéologique*, nouveau série, i. 244). And in a fragment of the Philonian Sanchoniathon (*Fragmenta Historicorum Graecorum*, ed. Müller, iii, 568, 569), we find a similar tale of El circumcising his father Uranos, or, according to another version, himself, and the blood flowing into the springs and rivers.[78]

It is notable that the Israelites, who as we have discussed were culturally Egyptian by the time of the Exodus, loyally and even fiercely adopted circumcision as a sign of their *covenant* with God. But was it, really? The compassionate believer in the One True God needs to ask him or herself: *Do I think that the same God who admonished* do not cut your

---

[77] Discussion of the history of circumcision in Egypt and pictures of the pictorial depictions of such were found at
http://www.nocirc.org/symposia/second/larue.html on 7/24/12.
[78] See previous 1902 encyclopedia article.

bodies for the dead[79] *and strongly condemned those who burned their children in the fire as offerings to Ba'al*[80] *would really be honored by watching the priests of Israel, the presumed spiritual leaders, ritualistically cut into the sexual organ of a helpless child?*

It is a tragic and shameful fact that for millennia, countless numbers of powerless and innocent children have had all manner of cruel rituals perpetrated on them in the name of religion. To help illustrate this fact, let us fast-forward about 3300 years to the 1970s and consider the story of a very dear friend of mine, Shaynie Anderson.[81] Shaynie's mother was a devout Protestant woman who took her children to Church every Sunday. In Sunday School, Shaynie learned all the traditional Bible stories that earnest Christian children learn about. She heard about how the Israelites were miraculously brought out of Egypt, and how they offered constant animal sacrifices to show their love for God. She then learned about how Yeshua was the final *atoning sacrifice* that finally *satisfied God's wrath* over the sinfulness of His children. One of her most distinct memories was of singing this perky, catchy worship song as she took Communion:

> *Sons of God hear his holy word;*
> *gather 'round the table of the Lord.*
> *Eat his body; drink his blood.*
> *and we'll sing a song of love.*

---

[79] Leviticus 19:28

[80] Jeremiah 19:5, Ezekiel 20:31

[81] *Pseudonym.* Actual name withheld for purposes of safety. Look for Shaynie's story, which will be told in greater detail in my upcoming book, *Monsters In Your Head.*

Allelu, allelu, allelu, alleluia![82]

On Sunday night, everything would change for little Shaynie. Her father would take her to another type of worship service, a secret one this time. Week after week she was forced to participate in the *other* family religion – generational Satanism. In these gatherings, the Bible stories about blood and sacrifice came alive in graphic, gory detail as Shaynie was forced to sacrifice both animals and humans to Satan in order to garner power from him. Blood, paganism, darkness – she experienced it all. Although she survived these heinous experiences, the trauma from these events haunts her to this day.

This background gave Shaynie a much more authentic perspective of what paganism at its ugly, bitter core, is actually like. It also gave her a very mixed-up view of what God really wants from His children, and how God wants to interact with her specifically.

Deep in her heart, Shaynie longed to overcome the dreadfulness of her past; so as an adult, she tried her hardest to reach out to God in the best way she knew how. Part of her recovery process consisted of learning more about God so she could become a better Christian, while another equally important part was to try to overcome all of the satanic triggers and flashbacks and memories that haunt her on a daily basis.

I met Shaynie many years ago while working in a psychiatric treatment center. She was a scared and traumatized adolescent, and I was a young and compassionate psychiatric nurse. Shaynie was beginning to have terrifying flashbacks of

---

[82] ©James Thiem, 1966

memories that had previously been deeply repressed, and would spend long hours restrained or locked in a seclusion room as she mentally relived these terrifying memories. I would spend countless hours holding her in a basket hold; trying my best to offer any comfort I could to this terrified child with the bloodcurdling memories. "I've got you," I would whisper while rocking her back and forth. "You're safe."

Many of my fellow staff members on the Adolescent Unit did not want to be around as Shaynie relived her flashbacks, because the events she was relating were so shockingly violent. I began to have symptoms of PTSD[83] myself as I struggled to mentally cope with the horrors that I had heard so vividly described. The experience did not come without significant emotional cost, as there were many nights that I had to sleep with a nightlight on because the mental pictures racing through my head after hearing about these events were so intense and chilling.

Although we were extremely different and came from backgrounds that were worlds apart, Shaynie and I somehow bonded and became very dear friends. Staff members and patients are not supposed to keep in touch after a patient has been discharged from a psychiatric hospital, but Shaynie did not want to lose my friendship and tracked me down years later, miraculously locating me where I was working in a different hospital, in a different state, at a time when she really needed help and support!

Our friendship became very precious to both of us, and I have long considered Shaynie *family*. Although I have never once regretted our bond, it has at times been extremely difficult to behold the utter pain and agony that is left behind

---

[83] Post Traumatic Stress Disorder

after a human being has survived the worst kind of horrible, pagan rituals. While trying my best to be supportive and comforting, I have also tried to help her Shaynie see that her loving heavenly Father is not anything like her violent earthly father.

On the flip side, looking at Christianity through the eyes of someone who grew up in what is essentially a *pagan mystery religion* has helped me see Christianity and the Scriptures from a decidedly different perspective, from the perspective of someone who has personally experienced many of the sacrificial rituals written about in the *Old Testament*.

As Shaynie has diligently tried to become a more authentic Christian, she has run into some distinct challenges. One of these challenges relates to the fact that although many people have pushed her to just *accept Christ's sacrifice,* they refuse to look at this blood atonement issue from her perspective.

From where Shaynie sits, how is the theology behind Christianity and early Judaism really any different from the paganism she was raised with? After all, when she was involved in the satanic cult, many blood sacrifices were offered, both human and animal. Her father made *her* offer up blood sacrifices, and innocent babies were frequent targets! The cult's reasoning was that the more innocent and perfect the victim was, the more the sacrificial offering would appease and please Satan, and the more power would be given to the cult.

Christianity looks at Yeshua in the exact same manner. We believe that it wasn't until orthodox Christianity's *god* was placated and appeased with the blood of *his own son Yeshua* that he was willing to forgive us sinners! Now, because of this magical *blood sacrifice,* our god is *pleased* with us and will accept us into his fellowship!

The blood of animals or humans atones for the adherents of Satanism, and the blood of animals or Yeshua atones for the adherents of Christianity. In Satanism, the participants *literally* eat the flesh and drink the blood of the slain victims; while in Christianity, the participants *symbolically* eat the flesh and drink the blood of Christ in Communion. We also sing about eating Yeshua's body and drinking his blood—cannibalistic practices—and don't think twice about it. One good example of this is a praise song I wrote that stated,

> *Take, eat, this is my body that was broken for you*
> *Broken for you...*
> *Take it and eat, take it and eat*
> *Spiritual manna and the bread of life...*

Many people—including me—found the song to be very inspirational! [84]

Catholicism takes it one step further. The doctrine of Transubstantiation states that those participating in *Holy Communion* are actually eating Yeshua's literal body and drinking his literal blood, i.e., making this so-called blessing a somehow holy form of cannibalism.

Even worse, we teach / brainwash / indoctrinate our children to do likewise, just like the Satanic cult did with Shaynie. In Satanism, the children and believers are literally washed in the blood of a lamb (or other animal or human

---

[84] I eventually rewrote the lyrics to be more descriptive of God's actual Character: "Love, love, love one another just as God has loved you, tender and true. Love, love, love one another, for your sister and brother need to see God in you."

victim); in Christianity we are symbolically "washed in the blood of the Lamb."[85] We rejoice about this experience and sing songs about it; and we teach our children to do the same from the time that they are very young. To illustrate this point, consider the lyrics of another of my original praise songs:

> *Wash me in the blood of the Lamb*
> *Wash me in the blood of the Lamb*
> *I know my heart is blackened with sin's dark stain*
> *So please wash me in the blood of the Lamb*

We sang this chorus many times in my church. At one point I was annoyed because one of the worship leaders said we should avoid singing blood-type songs in our outreach or contemporary services because they are not *seeker-sensitive* to the *unchurched*. I thought at the time that she was compromising her principles because she didn't want to give these seekers the really important information!

Realizing that it can be difficult to make these *unchurched* seekers accept and embrace such bloody doctrines, Christian leaders wrap these concepts in pretty words and soft melodies, presenting them in songs like this one written by a Christian pastor entitled, *Jesus, Thank You*. The lyrics read,

> *The mystery of the cross I cannot comprehend*
> *The agonies of Calvary*
> *You the perfect Holy One, crushed Your Son*
> *Who drank the bitter cup reserved for me*

---

[85] Revelation 7:14

Your blood has washed away my sin, Jesus thank you
The Father's wrath completely satisfied, Jesus, thank you
Once your enemy, now seated at your table
Jesus, thank you

By your perfect sacrifice I've been brought near
Your enemy You've made Your friend
Pouring out the riches of Your glorious grace
Your mercy and your kindness know no end

Your blood has washed away my sin, Jesus thank you
The Father's wrath completely satisfied, Jesus, thank you
Once your enemy, now seated at your table
Jesus, thank you[86]

Through artful words and compelling melodies we deeply sanitize the repulsive act of human sacrifice; keeping our personal distance from it while surrounding it with all kinds of warm, loving feelings. By doing this, we remove the sheer horror of what it is we are pretending the Church has demanded God somehow needs before He can forgive us!

In Satanism, the power is all purchased with blood. Christianity is no different. How many times have you sung enthusiastically at the top of your lungs:

Would you be free from the burden of sin?
There's power in the blood! Power in the blood!
There is power, power, wonder working power
in the precious blood of the Lamb![87]

---

[86] SCZEBEL, Pat, © 2003 Integrity's Hosanna! Music (ASCAP)/Sovereign Grace Worship (ASCAP).

What Christian, current or former, hasn't been inspired by this enthusiastic Gospel song?

What can wash away my sin?
Nothing but the blood of Jesus!
What can make me whole within?
Nothing but the blood of Jesus!

How precious is the flow
that makes me white as snow?
No other fount I know;
Nothing but the blood of Jesus![88]

We preach that God is a God of love, but to someone like Shaynie who grew up intimately acquainted with paganism, the *God* of Christianity looks like a god of bloodlust and violence just like all the rest! The only difference is that at this point in time, Christianity's rituals are symbolic. Satanism's rituals are literal.

Once we analyze it from both sides, it is easy to see what the traditions and customs of Christianity might look like to someone who has grown up in paganism. It is true that there are many, many Bible verses calling for blood; however, there are also many verses condemning blood and showing what God really desires from His children—repentance. It all comes down to which verses you choose to believe truthfully reflect the real character of the God you worship; the passages that reflect a bloodthirsty god, or the ones that speak of a merciful and compassionate one?

---

[87] JONES, Lewis E., *Power In The Blood*, 1899
[88] LOWRY, Robert, Nothing But the Blood of Jesus 1876

I believe that the TRUE Character, the TRUE Word of God is simply this:

> I want your constant love, not your animal sacrifices. I would rather have my people know me than burn offerings to me.[89]

And in Isaiah 1:11-13,

> Your sacrifices mean nothing to me. I am sick of your offerings of rams and choice cattle; I don't like the blood of bulls or lambs or goats. Who asked you to bring all this when you come to worship me? Stay out of my temple! Your sacrifices are worthless, and incense is disgusting. I can't stand the evil you do on your *New Moon Festivals* or on your *Sabbaths* and other times of worship.

And in First Samuel 15:22,

> To obey is better than sacrifice.

If we continue searching the Scriptures, we find that,

> This is what the Lord of Heaven's Armies, the God of Israel, says: "Take your burnt offerings and your other sacrifices and eat them yourselves! When I led your ancestors out of Egypt, it was *not* burnt offerings and sacrifices I wanted from them. This is what I told them: 'Obey me, and I will be your God, and you will

---

[89] Hosea 6:6 GNT; Jesus also quotes this passage in Matthew 9:13, 12:7

be my people. Do everything as I say, and all will be well!"⁹⁰

God said through the prophet Isaiah,

> This is the one I esteem: he who is humble and contrite in spirit, and trembles at my word. But whoever sacrifices a bull is like one who kills a man, and whoever offers a lamb, like one who breaks a dog's neck; whoever makes a grain offering is like one who presents pig's blood, and whoever burns memorial incense, like one who worships an idol. They have chosen their own ways, and their souls delight in their abominations.⁹¹

Did God really allow or bless the practice of sacrifice in the first place?

> God looks down from heaven on the entire human race; he looks to see if there is even one with real understanding, one who seeks for God.⁹²

---

⁹⁰ Jeremiah 7:21-23 NLT; NOTE: Take careful notice that the NIV deliberately mistranslates this passage by inserting a word that does not exist within the Hebrew. The NIV renders the passage adding the word "just" into the passage, which completely changes the meaning from the original thought and context of the underlying Hebrew. This *sectarian bias* in the NIV's translation is part of the problem with Christian translators who try to push the simple Hebrew into a decidedly Christian mold in an effort to water down Hebraic passages that would naturally destroy a cherished but highly errant doctrine that have either contradictory or absolutely no real support within the Scriptures.
⁹¹ Isaiah 66:2-3
⁹² Psalm 53:2 NLT

Throughout time, there have been people like Shaynie who have longed to draw near to God while being surrounded by horrible pagan practices. The early Israelites were no different. Through all of the chaos and tumult of the pagan practices instituted by a corrupt priesthood, there still remained those whose hearts drew near to God. In return, the God of their forefathers drew near to them. These righteous individuals inherently knew that God was a God of love and compassion; not a god of bloodlust and violence. Did they know everything there was to know about God, or have every doctrine correct? No! But they lived their lives as best they could amidst the evil that was taking place all around them.

WHAT CAN WE LEARN FROM ISRAEL'S FAILURES?

From Israel's failures we can learn a very valuable lesson. We need to realize that the Presence of God drawing near to us is not actually validation and verification that what we believe about God is 100% true. God's Spirit and approval is not tied to the rightness of our beliefs, but to the purity of our hearts and the fruits of our actions.

Understanding God's relationship with us is most easily understood by looking at our relationships with our children. How many times will we tell an eager, trusting child, "Yes sweetie, that picture you have drawn of me is beautiful!" when it is merely a few crayon scribbles that don't resemble us at all?

At the time, we reward our children with pats and accolades because of their heartfelt efforts. We kindly realize that they can't handle the truth; which is, that their depiction of us is no more accurate than if they drew a three-headed horse and called it Mommy! However, their hearts are pure and they are offering us the best that they have, so we reward their efforts with hugs and affirmations.

In like manner, our best efforts at reaching out to God and portraying God to others will always fall far short of what God is actually like. We might not realize that our very actions or most cherished doctrines may repulse God, like the practice and thought of sacrifice clearly did in Israel's day and continues to do in our day. But God judged the Israelites—and continues to judge us—on the purity of our hearts, not on the accuracy or truthfulness of our various, cherished doctrines.

> AHEYEH detests the way of the wicked, but he loves those who pursue righteousness.[93]

---

[93] Proverbs 15:9

CHAPTER 10

❖

YESHUA THE JEWISH REBEL

There is really one primary reason, one primary plan, one primary purpose Jesus came to suffer and to die. That's why He came. Bethlehem only happened so Calvary could happen. He was only a baby so He could be a man and die. He only lived in order to die.

Those soft baby hands, fashioned by the Holy Spirit in Mary's womb were made in order that nails might be driven through them. Those chubby feet, pink and unable to walk, were one day to walk a hill and be nailed to a cross. That sweet head with sparkling eyes and eager mouth was formed in order that some day men might crush into a crown of thorns. That tender body, warm and soft, wrapped in swaddling clothes would one day be ripped open by a spear to reveal a broken heart and that's exactly why God made that body. Jesus was born to die."[94]

---

[94]http://www.gty.org/Resources/Sermons/1204_Why-Was-Jesus-Born 7/21/10

When you study the issue of sacrifice carefully, it is easy to conclude that sacrifices were definitely offered by the Israelites as part of their worship. However, when you read the latter prophets, you begin to realize that these horrific sacrifices were certainly not something that our Creator, the God of Abraham, required or even wanted! And once you come to this realization, then the mainstream Christian and Messianic message that *Yeshua was born to die*[95] makes little if any God-given sense whatsoever.

We have become so accustomed in Christianity to thinking of Yeshua only in terms of what we think he was—*an Atoning Sacrifice who was Born to Die*—that we all but forget to focus on what he called himself, what he believed, and what he taught. Rather than appreciating him for the amazing reforming evangelist and prophet that he was, we simply relegate him to *martyred god* status.

I really think that we as Christian or Messianic believers have it all backwards! So for a moment, rather than focusing on what we believe Yeshua *was*, let us pay a bit more attention to his absolutely transformational message. What issues was he passionate about? What did he fight about with the religious leaders? What kind of God did he worship?

Yeshua haMaschiach was, first and foremost, a Jewish reformer. He was a rebel of sorts; contradicting the priests and leaders, calling the Pharisees *white-washed tombs*, a *brood of vipers*, and attacking the swindling sacrificial racket they had going on in the Temple. In general, he did whatever he needed to do in order to get his message of hope and peace to

---

[95] The ministry organization Amazing Facts has reprinted part of Ellen White's *Desire of the Ages* and renamed it, *Born To Die*. Part of the promotional text for this book exhorts, "For the first time, you'll understand the timing of His birth and why He was truly born to die."

the Jewish people. Above all, he wanted his Hebrew brothers and sisters to see God's TRUE Character the way he saw it; not through the power-hungry eyes of the self-serving spiritual leaders of the day.

The reformed faith that Yeshua preached in the first century was well in line with what the prophets themselves were attempting to teach centuries before. Yeshua's message was a transformed faith in our Creator, AHEYEH, that stood against practices that the priesthood itself had conditioned the people to accept and believe via their altered version of the Torah.

The prophets are indeed on record within the Bible as saying that the written Law handled by the priesthood did not accurately reflect what God had originally said.[96] Furthermore, these prophets admonished that the priesthood had *deliberately altered God's TRUE instruction* to suit the pagan traditions earlier leadership had inserted into the Scriptures. These corrupt religious leaders were deliberately altering the Scriptures to the point where the Torah was no longer an accurate depiction of God's TRUE Word.

It is remarkable how history consistently repeats itself. What the priesthood did to Judaism is the exact same thing that the Roman Catholic Church did to Christianity via nothing more than altering the written word that was supposed to represent the TRUE Word of God.

---

[96] Jeremiah 8:8, Isaiah 1, Hosea 6:6, Ezekiel 18

This "Jewish Messiah" Thing Ain't Gonna Fly In Rome...

First-century Rome was a highly anti-Semitic society and would remain so for centuries. After Jerusalem became a province of Rome in 40 BCE, numerous uprisings and unrest from the Jewish province would become an almost incessant thorn in the side of the Roman Empire. After three major wars beginning in 66 AD and ending in 135 AD with the literal burning to the ground of Jerusalem and enslavement of much of the Jewish population, Rome had had enough of the so-called *Jews*. There is no shortage of Roman writings detailing the disdain Rome had for the *accursed Jews*, mostly because of Israel's deep patriotism and spirit of independence.

Yet, ironically enough, belief in the teachings of a certain Jewish *Mashiach* or *Anointed of God* who had been executed in 30 AD would grow incessantly among the people everywhere. These *Christians*, followers of this *Christ*, came from all walks of life and cultural backgrounds. Their writings would thus reflect some, if not much, of their own culture and their own version of the *Christ* they followed. Hellenized (Greek) Christians, Gnostic Christians, Jewish Christians, Roman Christians and everything and everyone in between would begin to write their own versions of who Yeshua was and what this Messiah meant to them within their cultural world.

These early Christians invented their own themes and stories about Yeshua and his Apostles, thus creating all manner of writings; many of which were simply myth based on the teachings and ministry of the real man. The writings were numerous, but lacked any kind of real authenticity or standard of fact. One might attempt to glean the facts about a real event by validation via numerous different sources, but even this would not be able to achieve any factual basis since the sources of the stories and events may have simply been replicated from a manufactured single source to begin with. Indeed, this is one of the very difficult issues facing modern scholars today, when they are attempting to authenticate various events of history from multiple written sources.[97]

By the middle of the second century, numerous versions of differing *Gospel* accounts and other writings about Yeshua could be found throughout the Roman Empire. Christianity was growing more and more popular, even within the city of Rome itself. The Jews had solidified a kind of Scriptural *kanon*, a standard by which to measure the truth of one's beliefs, yet nothing really existed for the Christians.

One of the first people to propose and solidify a Christian canon of Scripture was a man by the name of Marcion.[98] A textbook example of an anti-Semitic *Christian*, Marcion of Sinope was a wealthy 2nd-century merchant who joined the church in Rome circa 140 AD, and is credited with creating the first *New Testament* canon (Bible). Marcion's canon included most of the Pauline epistles we have today and about two thirds of the Gospel of Luke, which Marcion had heavily edited to removed any references to Yeshua's Hebraic (Jewish) family or associations. Paul's letter to the Galatians became the centerpiece of the Marcion canon and the basis for much of his core doctrine.

---

[97] EHRMAN, Bart, *Jesus, Interrupted: Revealing the Hidden Contradictions in the Bible (And Why We Don't Know About Them)*, 2010, Section 4, Who Wrote the Bible, pp. 101-138

[98] EHRMAN, Bart, Lost Christianities: The Battles for Scripture and the Faiths We Never Knew, 2005, p. 109

At some point, Marcion and the Roman church leadership had a falling out (ostensibly because of his editorialization of the Gospel of Luke; but more likely because Marcion's popularity was beginning to overtake Rome's own leadership!) and Marcion was expelled from the church in Rome as a *heretic*. However, he continued to attract a large group of followers, called Marcionites, the size of which rivaled the Church in Rome. Marcion's *denomination* survived well into the fourth century.

Although the influential Church leaders in Rome would later reject Marcion himself, his anti-Semitic teaching and Pauline theology were highly popular with the Roman people. Marcion unquestionably had a deep influence on proto-orthodoxy's earliest beginnings.

One of the central pillars of so-called Marcionism was the rejection of Yeshua's own *Jewishness*, and the recasting of Yeshua's teachings as being not culturally Hebraic or *Jewish Christian*, but rather more culturally *Gentile Christian*, much more Hellenist and Greco-Roman. This *Jewish-less* version of Christianity was much more palatable to the Gentile populous of Rome, and the Gentile Empire at large.

As a result of this Marcion-Pauline theology, this new *Gentile Yeshua*—a kind of fantasy Yeshua that had no factual basis in history—would eventually became the *Messiah of choice* for the modern Christian Church and even Messianic congregations today.

Marcion's recasting of the Jewish Messiah did not stop with his lineage and culture. Marcion also deprecated the *Tanakh*, which we know today as the *Old Testament*, and relegated it to the trash bin of history as entirely uninspired junk. Marcion went so far as to assert that the God of the *Tanakh* was not at all the same one found within Paul's writings; and that Yeshua was in fact a completely different *God* to be worshiped.

In his book *The Goodness of God*, author Troy Edwards makes the following observations by quoting other Christian authors such as John Bright and Marvin Wilson:

> If Marcion subscribed to any part of this Gnostic teaching then it would seem convenient for him to have the OT done away with which proclaims God as the creator of this world. Bright goes on to say that, 'This strange doctrine logically led, and in fact did lead, to a drastic devaluation of the Old Testament.' Some may read this and say that they would never fall into the type of error that Marcion advocated. Yet, if you have relegated the Old Testament to a place inferior to the New Testament, then you have given yourself over to the same spirit of error as this man [Marcion]. If you believe that certain promises and moral teachings have no place with the New Testament believer then I am afraid that you have, without realizing it, embraced Marcionism:
>
> ...for there is—if I know the situation at all—not a little neo-Marcionism in our churches. It has no official standing—indeed, under that name it scarcely exists at all—but it is unofficially present nonetheless: call it a practical Marcionism, an implicit Marcionism, an inconsequent Marcionism, or what you will. That is to say, there are people who never heard of Marcion and who would be horrified to learn of the company they are in but who nevertheless use the Old Testament in a distinctly Marcionist manner. Formal-

ly, and no doubt sincerely, they hail it as canonical Scripture; but in practice they relegate it to a subordinate position, if they do not effectively exclude it from use altogether.[99]

Dr. Marvin R. Wilson, author of *Our Father Abraham*, also agrees with Mr. Bright that neo-Marcionism [modern-Marcionism] has crept into the present day church:

> Though often cunningly concealed, in today's Church rather strong vestiges of Marcionism have survived. But we are polite. Hardly aware of its subtle presence, we do not call it 'neo-Marcionism,' 'heresy,' or 'anti-Judaism.' Nevertheless, in our concerted effort to be 'New Testament' believers, we have too often unconsciously minimized the place and importance of the Old Testament and the Church's Hebraic roots. At worst, many so called Bible-believing Christians have become de facto 'quarter-of-the-Bible' adherents (the New Testament has 260 chapters compared to the Old Testament's 929 chapters); at best, they rely on a 'loose-leaf' edition of the Old Testament (i.e. they select only a few portions of the Old Testament), in addition to the New Testament. This selectivity has had the effect of neglecting the totality of written revelation, severing the Hebrew roots of the Christian faith, and thus eroding the full authority of the Holy Scriptures.[100]

---

[99] BRIGHT, John, *The Authority of the Old Testament*, 1975, Baker Book House, Grand Rapids, MI, p. 60
[100] WILSON, Marvin R., *Our Father Abraham*, www.messianicmoments.com / Notes: Marvin R. Wilson is the Harold J. Ockenga Professor of Biblical and

When Luc and I first started dating, he admitted that he had always scoffed at Sabbath keepers. I did not want to marry a *non-Adventist,* so I worked really hard to show him from the Bible why he should keep the Sabbath. When he finally came to the conclusion that the Fourth Commandment was a valid one, he started saying to his friends back home, "I keep the Jewish Sabbath." I cannot tell you how much that irked me! It wasn't the *Jewish* Sabbath; it was the *Adventist* Sabbath! If he was going to be a proper Adventist, he really needed to get that straight!

It took me a long time to realize that instead of feeling any kinship with the Jewish people, I had grown up feeling like I needed to distance myself from them. Deep in my heart, I felt like God was looking down on the Jews. Adventists were His *new* chosen people, and I wanted no association whatsoever with the group of people that had gone down in history for *killing Yeshua.*

My life and actions pretty much illustrated Dr. Wilson's point. In Marcion-like fashion, many Christians still seek to divide the Hebrew Messiah and his teachings from his deeply Hebraic culture—and all for the sake of some good old-fashioned Roman anti-Semitism that now lives on within the pages of our own Bible! It is a deeply seeded but usually subtle anti-Semitism that is still very much alive and well

---

Theological Studies at Gordon College in Wenham, Massachusetts. He received his Ph.D. in the field of Semitic Studies at Brandeis University under Professor Cyrus Gordon. Wilson served for eight years as a translator and editor of the New International Version of the Bible, and also contributed notes to two books in the NIV Study Bible. Four of his books deal with the relationship between Christianity and Judaism. Wilson has authored or edited seven books, including Our Father Abraham: Jewish Roots of the Christian Faith, www.hebroots.org

within many circles of Christianity—and especially Adventist Christianity—even today.

Although many Christian denominations openly love the Jewish people, it is only because they believe that the Jews are God's chosen people who will somehow bring about the return of Yeshua. Even so, most of these Christian denominations all but completely strip Yeshua of his Jewish heritage. Any mention of Yeshua's *Jewishness* is often met with everything from, "Wow, I didn't know that!" to outright disdain and rebuke for even bringing it up. Messianic congregations will embrace Yeshua's Jewish culture and customs – but will still consider Yeshua to have the same *atoning* purpose as their Christian neighbors.

CHAPTER 11

❖

WILL THE REAL CHRISTIANITY PLEASE STAND UP?

After researching the history of both Judaism and Christianity, it became clear that there were quite a few things that had been left out of my Bible classes. For one thing, I had never been told that one of the results of Christendom's Marcionist-like historical revisionism has been the emergence of two competing histories of Christianity. One version is decidedly orthodox, supported by Roman Catholic / Protestant tradition which is validated by the Roman Catholic Bible canon. The other is simply a historical version supported by both canonical (Biblical) and non-canonical historical documents from the first through fifth centuries; much of it from the annals of Rome and the early Catholic Church's own records.

In order to get anywhere close to the truth, one needs to study *both* of these versions of history, not just the orthodox revisions that were handed down to Protestantism from Catholicism. The problem is that most Christians are not encouraged or in some cases even allowed to study the real historical record of Christianity. Even when we do study any unbiblical early Christian writings, it is with a deep bias that demands that the Bible alone is the infallibly inspired Source that is automatically free from error and therefore, to be believed at all costs. There is just no way a non-canonical source is ever allowed to supersede a *New Testament* one, no matter how deep and credible the historical source and no matter how factually unassailable the evidence!

The problem with this culturally Christian paradigm is that the Bible becomes not just another historical witness, but the *only* historical witness Christians are allowed to view as authoritative. We never even realize that there is a deeply rich and historical record of Yeshua outside of the Bible's orthodoxically selected and edited Gospels and epistles; a history which reveals a Messiah quite different than what has been offered to us through our Roman Catholic approved version of *Scripture*.

Facts the Bible Left Out

Reviewing the factual history of Yeshua and studying the reformed Jewish message that he taught reveals that he held to the following general doctrines:

First: Historically, and like the latter prophets before him, Yeshua taught against the sacrificial system that had been put in place by Rabbinical Judaism since before the

Diaspora.[101] Because of this, many Christian and even secular scholars note that Yeshua may have been an *Essene*.[102] The *Essenes* did not participate in Judaism's sacrificial system or beliefs. In the non-extant (extinct) *Gospel of the Hebrews*, the early (Roman Catholic) Church historian Epiphanius quotes Yeshua as saying:

> I have come to end the sacrifices and feasts of blood; and if you do not cease in offering and eating flesh and blood, the wrath of God shall not cease from you; even as it came to your fathers in the wilderness, who lusted for flesh, and they ate to their content, and were filled with disease, and the plague consumed them.[103]

However, because of a firm, man-made Roman Catholic tradition, this historical document observing that Yeshua stood against blood sacrifice—and declaring that God did not require blood sacrifice—has never gotten communicated to everyday Christian or Messianic believers. It is obvious that if the documented evidence ever becomes well known that historically Yeshua stood *against* the Temple sacrifices, it would be utterly illogical to think and believe that Yeshua would teach that he himself was to *become* a human blood sacrifice to the God of the Hebrews.

---

[101] The *Diaspora* refers to the dispersion of the Jews outside the geographical location of Israel, beginning with the Babylonian exile.

[102] *Essenes* are the group of people who collected the Qumran library, i.e. the Dead Sea Scrolls.

[103] Epiphanius quoting the words of Jesus the Messiah within *The Gospel of the Hebrews* [also known as *The Gospel of the Ebionites*)

SECOND: Yeshua practiced and taught what he considered to be the TRUE Commandments and instructions of God—and these TRUE laws *did not* include blood sacrifices. The latter prophets (Isaiah, Jeremiah, Hosea, et. al.) railed incessantly against the sacrificial system! Yeshua was yet another one in a long line of *prophets* who did likewise.[104]

Upon careful examination, it becomes evident that there are two competing versions of God's Word and Character in the *Old Testament* Scriptures. Not surprisingly, this very same issue of two competing gospels is happening within the *New Testament* as well. The version of God that has been brought to us by the priesthood makes Him out to be a bloodthirsty monster that continuously demands all manner of blood and animal deaths. The *other* version of God, as related by the latter prophets, shows that our Creator does not now and has in fact never in the past demanded, required or even desired any kind of blood sacrifice to atone for the sins of His people!

This understanding is well illustrated in other early Christian documents, such as Clementine Homilies:

> Then said Simon: 'I understand that you speak of your Yeshua as Him who was prophesied of by the scripture. Therefore let it be granted that it is so. Tell us, then, how he taught you to discriminate the Scrip-

---

[104] Indeed, Jesus refers to himself as a prophet within the Gospels when he stated, "Prophets are respected everywhere except in their own hometown and by their relatives and their family." Mark 6:4 GNT. It is the belief of many that Jesus was the long-awaited prophet Moses prophesied about: "AHYH said to me: "What they say is good. I will raise up for them a prophet like you from among their brothers; I will put my words in his mouth, and he will tell them everything I command him. If anyone does not listen to my words that the prophet speaks in my name, I myself will call him to account." Deuteronomy 18:17-19

tures.' Then Peter: 'As to the mixture of truth with falsehood, I remember that on one occasion He [Yeshua], finding fault with the Sadducees, said, "Wherefore ye do err, not knowing the true things of the Scriptures; and on this account ye are ignorant of the power of God." But if He cast up to them that they knew not the true things of the Scriptures, *it is manifest that there are false things in them*. And also, inasmuch as He said, "Be ye prudent money-changers," it is because there are genuine and spurious words [written within the scriptures].

And whereas He said, "Wherefore do ye not perceive *that which is reasonable in the Scriptures?*" He makes the understanding of him stronger who voluntarily judges soundly. And His sending to the scribes and teachers of the existing Scriptures, as to those who knew the true things of the law that then was, is well known. And also that He said, "I am not come to destroy the law," [Matthew 5:17-20] and yet that He appeared to be destroying it, is the part of one intimating that the things which He destroyed did not belong to the law. And His saying, "The heaven and the earth shall pass away, but one jot or one tittle shall not pass from the law," intimated that the *things which pass away before the heaven and the earth do not belong to the law in reality*. Since, then, while the heaven and the earth still stand, *sacrifices have passed away*, and kingdoms, and prophecies among those who are born of woman, and such like [kingdoms, prophecies and laws that were merely man-made], as not being ordinances of God.'[105]

The Clementine Homilies offer additional insight into whether sacrifices were ever ordained by God in the first place. When referring to the episode in the desert where the Israelites demanded meat and God responded by sending quail, they explain:

> But that He is not pleased with sacrifices, is shown by this, that those who lusted after flesh were slain as soon as they tasted it, and were consigned to a tomb, so that it was called the grave of lusts. He then who at the first was displeased with the slaughtering of animals, not wishing them to be slain, did not ordain sacrifices as desiring them; nor from the beginning did He require them. For neither are sacrifices accomplished without the slaughter of animals, nor can the first-fruits be presented.[106]

THIRD: Since, according to Yeshua, the sacrificial system as written within the Torah[107] is not truly part of the TRUE Law and Commandments of God, it becomes axiomatically obvious that these books of the Bible have been meddled with; edited by unscrupulous Jewish men down through the

---

[105] Clementine Homily 3 XLIX-LII; emphasis supplied
[106] Clementine Homily 3 XLV
[107] In Judaism, the *Torah* consists of the first five books of the Bible, also called *the books of Moses*. The *Torah* is considered to be the most sacred Scriptures in Judaism. Judaism refers to the entire *Old Testament* as the *Tanakh*.

centuries to support whatever doctrines they wanted the people to believe.[108]

Such an observation is not just some hypothetical supposition but was confirmed by God, speaking through the prophet Jeremiah. God said:

> How can you say 'We are wise for we have the Torah of AHYH,' when the lying pen of the scribes [elders, leaders] has handled it falsely?[109]

There is an ancient Hebraic understanding that goes along with what both Yeshua and Jeremiah proclaimed, that is:

> God's TRUE Laws and Commandments are eternal; they do not change just as God does not change.

God's past is just as infinitely long as His future will be. God does not need to change![110] He knows His Creation and His created children whom He has made. He has put in place His TRUE Law and instruction that reflects who He is. He has no need to update His Word or His Character to accommodate man's whims and failings.

The Clementine Homilies illustrate a historical understanding that the earliest Judeo-Christian believers knew regarding what Yeshua taught about the Law: What God did not actually *plant* as everlasting will eventually be *uprooted*

---

[108] One must keep in mind that the Jewish priests made their living through the institution of sacrifices. Putting them in charge of *Scripture* is a bit like letting the American Beef Association dictate the contents of the USDA food pyramid!

[109] Jeremiah 8:8

[110] Malachi 3:6

and done away with. The prime example is that the Temple and the sacrificial laws are no longer with us. Ergo, these systems and laws were not eternal and as such were not actually inspired of (planted by) God in the first place! In fact, we can agree that it has been the very hand of God that has done away with and *uprooted* the falsehoods of the past via the destruction of the Temple, the disbanding of the priesthood and even the destruction of the nation of Israel for a time! Sacrifices have totally passed away from our worship of God in both Judaism and, by extension, Christianity.

Of course, we in Christianity or Messianic Judaism have our own standard excuse for why there are no longer sacrifices being offered. Our claim is, "God sacrificed Yeshua on the cross as my once-and-for-all-time sacrifice! Because of Yeshua's death on the cross, God doesn't need any more sacrifices."

The problem with this feel-good but factually vacuous reasoning is that according to the latter prophets, God never asked for blood sacrifices to begin with! It's not part of His Character to even *ask* for such a heinous thing as an animal blood sacrifice, let alone demand a human one!

God said through the prophet Jeremiah,

> Thus says AHYH of hosts, the God of Israel, "Add your burnt offerings to your sacrifices and eat flesh. For I did not speak to your fathers, or command them in the day that I brought them out of the land of Egypt, concerning burnt offerings and sacrifices. But this is what I commanded them, saying, 'Obey My voice, and I will be your God, and you will be My people; and you

will walk in all the way which I command you, that it may be well with you.'[111]

As an important side note: Earlier we discussed how modern Christian scholars sometimes deliberately alter the translation of Biblical text as the means to provide support for cherished doctrine(s). Jeremiah 7:21-23 is such a text. Jeremiah 7:21-23 completely destroys the notion that God ever required or commanded sacrifices. But take note that the translators of the NIV deliberately mistranslate this passage by inserting the word *just* into their import of the text, in order to completely change the meaning of this passage.

The word *just* and the *thought-for-thought* context of the passage is *not* part of the underlying Hebrew. The NIV is the *only* major serious translation that inserts this wholly Christian sectarian bias into the simple Hebrew of this text. This further illustrates how the Bible is *still* being edited and mishandled by the *lying pen of the scribes*. It is still being groomed and changed by people who have a doctrinal agenda they want to maintain, even in the modern era.

---

[111] Jeremiah 7:21-23 NASB

CHAPTER 12

❖

I Don't Want Your Bloody Sacrifices!

So silently the lamb awaits his final destiny
He soon will be a sacrifice,
he'll have no chance to flee
His blood will pour so freely
and so quickly to the ground
His heart will cry for justice; but alas it won't be found

The temple courts are noisy as the priests rush all around
It seems like they've forgotten this is AHEYEH'S holy ground
The money has been offered, and the lamb will now be slain
His blood will flow across the feet of butchers bringing pain

They tell us God is angry; that His heart is filled with grief
They say this crimson sacrifice will bring Him sweet relief
They say that the Eternal One cannot forgive our sins;
Unless we have an offering of blood, we won't be cleansed

> *Our Father up in Heaven has been slandered and defamed*
> *He does not want a sacrifice; and blood won't hide your shame*
> *His mercy has no limits, and His love will not depart*
> *He's promised His forgiveness to the true, repentant heart*[112]

WHAT DOES SACRIFICE LOOK LIKE FROM GOD'S PERSPECTIVE?

Have you ever been rather absent-mindedly traveling along a long stretch of highway when you notice a really interesting billboard ahead of you that makes a pointed religious statement and is then signed, —*God*? It might say something like,

> *What part of THOU SHALT NOT did you not understand?*
> *—God*

> *Need Directions? —God.*

> *Will The Road You're On Get You To My Place? —God*

And then there is one of my favorites:

> *That 'Love Thy Neighbor' thing—I meant that. —God*

If you look carefully, you can find quite a few of these billboard-type sound bites in Scripture, especially when it comes to the subject of sacrifice.

> *To do what is right and just is more acceptable [to me] than sacrifice. —God*[113]

---

[112] BEAUCHAMP, Serena, *The Sacrifice* 2012

> *Your sacrifices do not please me. —God*[114]

> *I desire mercy, not sacrifice. —God*[115]

> *[I] detest the sacrifice of the wicked, but the prayer of the upright pleases [me]. —God*[116]

In a nutshell,

> *I don't want your bloody sacrifices! —God*

God's outright condemnation of sacrifice is evident in a multitude of Scripture texts—but Christianity's leadership rarely points out these particular texts. Obviously, to do so would utterly destroy the foundational beliefs of what Christianity has mistakenly thought our Creator is like, and instead would make us aware of the fact that God has never desired sacrifice to begin with.

Realizing that more study was needed about the issue of sacrifice, I decided to look into Judaism's own history and seek out the thoughts and teachings of its most respected minds—much like a Christian would want to study the perspectives of well-respected Christian scholars such as Martin Luther or A.W. Tozer. How had the past scholars of Judaism dealt with the sacrificial contradictions?

One of Judaism's most esteemed Jewish scholars was Rabbi Moshe ben Maimon, who lived in the middle ages. He was also known as Maimonides, but is more commonly

---

[113] Proverbs 21:3
[114] Jeremiah 6:20
[115] Hosea 6:6
[116] Proverbs 15:8

referred to as *Rambam*. *JewFAQ.org* discussed the issue this way:

> Some would say that the original institution of sacrifice had more to do with the Judaism's past than with its future. Rambam suggested that the entire sacrificial cult in Judaism was ordained as an accommodation of man's primitive desires.
>
> Sacrifice is an ancient and universal human expression of religion. Sacrifice existed among the Hebrews long before the giving of the Torah. When the laws of sacrifice were laid down in the Torah, the pre-existence of a system of sacrificial offering was understood, and sacrificial terminology was used without any explanation. The Torah, rather than creating the institution of sacrifice, carefully circumscribes and limits the practice, permitting it only in certain places, at certain times, in certain manners, by certain people, and for certain purposes. Rambam suggests that these limitations are designed to wean a primitive people away from the debased rites of their idolatrous neighbors.[117]

In other words, Rambam concedes that Judaism inherited blood sacrifice from its idolatrous (pagan) neighbors and that the God of the Jews never intended for such rites to be included as part of His worship. This is wholly in agreement with the latter prophets.

The second century Christian writer, Clement, brings up a similar point very early in Christian history. He adds to that

---

[117] JewFAQ.org/qorbanot.htm on 8-31-06

understanding by intimating that Yeshua himself was the one ordained to correct the people's understanding regarding sacrifice:

> When meantime Moses, that faithful and wise steward, perceived that the vice of sacrificing to idols had been deeply ingrained into the people from their association with the Egyptians, and that the root of this evil could not be extracted from them, he allowed them indeed to sacrifice, but permitted it to be done only to God, that by any means he might cut off one half of the deeply ingrained evil, leaving the other half to be corrected by another, and at a future time; by Him, namely, concerning whom he said himself, 'A prophet shall the Lord your God raise unto you, whom ye shall hear even as myself, according to all things which he shall say to you. Whosoever shall not hear that prophet, his soul shall be cut off from his people.[118]

This explanation certainly makes sense, but even that may not tell the whole story. Contrary to the above explanation and in Moses' defense, Torah writings indicate that the elders of Israel and even some of Moses' own family members were periodically working against him; subverting his authority and going so far as to permit and even promote sacrifice and idolatry. The latter prophets, however, indicate that Moses himself did not actually instruct the people to worship God via sacrifices. The Jeremiah passage we looked at previously

---

[118] Deuteronomy 18:15, 18-19; Acts 3:22-23. Recognitions of Clement, Book 1, Chapter XXXVI, Allowance of Sacrifice for a Time

clearly states that God's TRUE Law that Moses gave did *not* include any kind of sacrifices.

> I gave your ancestors no commands about burnt offerings or any other kinds of sacrifices when I brought them out of Egypt. But I did command them to obey me, so that I would be their God and they would be my people. And I told them to live the way I had commanded them, so that things would go well for them.[119]

However, the thought that another great prophet would come along to help rid the people of this evil in their midst was undoubtedly comforting for God's righteous children. These believers knew that the atrocities being perpetrated on God's creation needed to be stopped, and sooner rather than later! This prophecy was fulfilled when the false belief that God needed or even desired sacrifice was corrected by the later prophets Isaiah (Chapter 1), Jeremiah (8:8), and Ezekiel (Chapter 18). Perhaps not so ironically, these books also appear to have been meddled with, if the conflicting accounts one finds of *God wants sacrifice / God detests sacrifice,* sometimes only a couple of verses away from each other, are any indication. And it is a shameful blot on Israel's history that all of these prophets were harassed and persecuted at the hands of an evil and bloodthirsty priesthood.

---

[119] Jeremiah 7:22-23 GNT

CHAPTER 13

❖

MIDNIGHT IN THE GARDEN OF GOOD & EVIL

It is at this point that you are very likely reaching for whatever story you can think of to somehow prove that God indeed instituted sacrifice as the ultimate expression of His love and holiness. Thinking sequentially, you are headed straight back to what appears to be the very first sacrifice within the Scriptures. After all, God Himself sacrificed animals to atone for the sin of Adam and Eve, right?[120]

Here again is where our desire to support the doctrine that we know and believe in overrides our ability to identify the truth and translate the Scriptures properly. Many people within both Orthodox Judaism and Christianity attempt to press Genesis 3:21 into a kind of sacrificial mold in which it does not actually belong. Keep in mind that the ancient Hebrew was an incredibly simple language and is therefore

---

[120] Genesis 3:21

many times easily susceptible to misguided and false interpretation by scholars translating it with a presumptive sectarian bias.

In discussing when animal sacrifices might have originated, A. J. Fecko observes:

> There are also the renderings of the Targums. The Targums are Aramaic interpretive renderings of the Hebrew Scriptures. Such versions were needed when Hebrew ceased to be the daily language of the Jewish people. In Synagogue services the reading of the Scriptures was followed by a translation into the Aramaic vernacular of the populace. Targums on [the topic of Adam and Eve being clothed by animal skins] are:
>
> P.S. Jonathan: And the Lord God made garments of glory for Adam and for his wife from the skin which the serpent had cast off (to be worn) on the skin of their flesh, instead of their (garments of) fig leaves of which they had been stripped, and he clothed them.
>
> Onkelos: And the Lord God made for Adam and his wife garments of honor for the skin of their flesh and He clothed them.
>
> Neophyti: And the Lord God made for Adam and for his wife garments of glory, for the skin of their flesh, and he clothed them. This suggests another possibility. That it simply means that the garments were made for the skin of Adam and Eve.

Also, the root of the Hebrew word, "Owr", modified only by more recent vowel points has the meaning of bare or naked, while "coat" is more literally a covering and therefore the passage might be a "cover of nakedness". But, regardless which solution is the right one, there's no suggestion of an animal sacrifice or killing in this passage.[121]

If we read the passage more closely in its original Hebrew, we discover that God merely *clothed* Adam and Eve's *skin*, nothing more. It is only because we want to assume that God desired sacrifice and then clothed Adam and Eve with animal skins that we come away with a mistaken translation of God's Word; a misunderstanding of His Character. Indeed, we have seen the Scriptures written by the prophets where God warns us that He abhors sacrifice! If God has said He abhors sacrifice, then He is not going to be sacrificing animals to clothe Adam and Eve, right?

If you still feel that God taught Adam and Eve to kill/sacrifice, you need to tell me if the following scenario rings true. The Creator of all life sits down and starts to instruct Adam and Eve about how they should act after they have disobeyed and lied about it.

> "Adam, Eve," He begins. "Now that you have officially *fallen,* I'm going to give you some house rules for living. Let's start with *Thou shalt not murder.* That's a really important one."

---

[121] FECKO, A.J., When Did Animal Sacrifices Begin? All-Creatures.org/discuss/whendid.html on 07/28/07

Adam, wanting to make up for the fact that he feels bad for lying to Father: "What does *murder* mean, Father?"

> God: "Well, watch this. I'll show you. Have you ever seen blood? Silly me, of course not, so I'm going to show you! I'm really kind and loving, and *because* I'm so kind and loving, I want you to stab and kill an animal—*just like this*—every time you do something that offends me. This will *appease* me and teach you to be sorry for your actions."

Adam and Eve are gasping and crying on the ground. They literally cannot take comprehend what is going on because they are innocent as newborn babies and are having a hard time even processing the fact that an innocent lamb is bleeding out onto the ground because they *disobeyed* and *lied about it*. Seemingly callous to their pain, God continues.

> "Then, you can be reminded of your disobedience every time you wear the clothes I will make for you out of these animal skins. Furthermore, even though I have instructed you to eat only fruits, grains, and nuts, we don't want this all this good *meat* to go to waste! Now pass the barbecue sauce, please."

It's utterly preposterous, isn't it? Is this what you really think of God?

But what about Cain and Abel?

The story of Cain and Abel is an account that has been drummed into the fabric of our belief system for millennia.

We are taught from childhood that God told Cain and Abel to offer animal sacrifices, and then Cain screwed up by offering something that didn't include blood. That's how it is, period, end of story. Right? God said it, I believe it, and that settles it for me!

The discerning reader might stop to consider that once again, the priesthood of Israel was intimately involved and ultimately benefited by the strength of the belief that *you must bring God blood sacrifices!* We are never allowed to even entertain the question; did God really require a blood sacrifice from Cain and Abel, or did he merely ask to be remembered by the bringing of offerings?

There is an early Christian book entitled *The Conflict of Adam and Eve* that contains some Jewish legends found in early rabbinical writings. This book states that it was Cain and not Abel that brought the animal sacrifice. Apparently Cain was angry with his parents because they wanted his sister Luluwa to wed Abel instead of Cain, who wanted to marry her himself.

> Upon learning this, Cain... went to Eve, his mother, and beat her, and cursed her, and said to her, "Why are you planning to take my sister to wed her to my brother? Am I dead?" His mother, however, quieted him, and sent him to the field where he had been. Then when Adam came, she told him of what Cain had done. But Adam grieved and held his peace, and said not a word. Then on the next morning Adam said to Cain his son, 'Take of your sheep, young and good, and offer them up to your God; and I will speak to your brother, to make to his God an offering of corn.' They both obeyed their father Adam, and they took

their offerings, and offered them up on the mountain by the altar.[122]

But Cain behaved haughtily towards his brother, and shoved him from the altar, and would not let him offer up his gift on the altar; but he offered his own on it, with a proud heart, full of guile, and fraud. But as for Abel, he set up stones that were near at hand, and on that, he offered up his gift with a heart humble and free from guile. Cain was then standing by the altar on which he had offered up his gift; and he cried to God to accept his offering; but God did not accept it from him; neither did a divine fire come down to consume his offering. But he remained standing over against the altar, out of humor and meanness, looking towards his brother Abel, to see if God would accept his offering or not. And Abel prayed to God to accept his offering. Then a divine fire came down and consumed his offering. And God smelled the sweet savor of his offering; because Abel loved Him and rejoiced in Him. And because God was well pleased with him, He sent him an angel of light in the figure of a man who had partaken of his offering, because He had smelled the sweet savor of his offering, and they comforted Abel and strengthened his heart. But Cain was looking on all that took place at his brother's offering, and was angry because of it. Then he opened his mouth and blasphemed God, because He had not accepted his offering. But God said to Cain, "Why do you look sad? Be righteous, that I may accept your offering. Not against Me have you murmured, but against

---

[122] I Adam and Eve 78:12-17

yourself." And God said this to Cain in rebuke, and because He abhorred him and his offering. And Cain came down from the altar, his color changed and with a sad face, and came to his father and mother and told them all that had befallen him. And Adam grieved much because God had not accepted Cain's offering.[123]

Isn't this interesting? In this accounting, Cain is the violent brother, which jives with what we see in Torah. *Cain* is the one who murders animals to offer to God, and Abel brings an offering of corn. God accepts Abel's gift and rejects Cain's bloody sacrifice.

Is this version of the story true? There is, of course, no way to be sure. However, whether we like it or not, the Cain and Abel story, as it has been related to us, *only makes sense* if we believe God *must* have blood sacrifice in order to forgive.

To the victor goes the privilege of writing history. It is an unavoidable fact that historical records are brought to us by groups of people who have certain agendas. In a society that defined itself by sacrifice, the scribes, members of the priesthood, were completely invested in showing that sacrifice was *what God required,* so it behooved them to slant the records to reflect this point of view.

There are enough Scriptures (especially penned by the latter prophets) that rebuke and come against sacrifice to illustrate that the statement *God told Cain and Abel to offer blood sacrifices* doesn't ring true or is at best contradictory; especially if we truly believe that God is the same yesterday, today, and forever!

---

[123] I Adam and Eve 78:18-28

Let me tell you a secret. From the time I was just a little girl who loved kittens and puppies and rescued crickets who had gotten trapped in the house, I was never comfortable with this *sacrifice-demanding* side of God. I could never understand why He couldn't just forgive me if I apologized, but instead, demanded that someone had to *die* because I did something wrong. I felt so guilty because I had been told that the death of Yeshua was, in fact, my fault. I was told that Yeshua had to die because of the sinful things I had done, even though I hadn't even been born at the time he died! Furthermore, every time I did a bad thing, it reminded him again of the pain and agony he suffered on the cross.

That is a lot of abusive religious guilt to load onto a small, tenderhearted child! Those intense feelings of remorse and shame were in the forefront of my mind decades later when I wrote the following song entitled, *Every Time I Fall*. The lyrics read,

Lord, I know I wasn't there at Calvary that day
The hands that cruelly scourged you weren't my own
I was not the one to turn my back to you and walk away
When you fell beneath the cross you bore alone

I was not the one to force the thorns onto your brow
As tears mixed with the blood upon your face
Though I did not pound the nails myself,
I'm guilty, even now –
For when all is said and done, this fact remains...

Every time I fall, I send you back to Calvary
Once again you feel the nails that pierced your skin
You relive the painful memory

> *of the day you bore that cross*
> *Every time I fall, oh Lord, you are crucified again...*
>
> *Every time I fall, oh Lord,*
> *You'd gladly die for me – again.*[124]

This rhetoric really makes no sense at all once logic is introduced. Does a mother only remember the pain and agony of childbirth whenever she sees her beloved child? No! It is clear that this "crucifying Yeshua anew" doctrine is yet another nail of guilt to hammer into the coffin of the Christian's self-worth and self-esteem.

As I was a kindhearted child who tried her best to obey and please her parents, this dogma of *Substitutionary Atonement* affected me a great deal. Deep down, I really didn't understand how they could proclaim that *God is love* based on this core doctrine. But what else did I have to go on?

Christianity offers its children quite a dichotomy—we tell them that God is forgiving and compassionate, but we also expect them to believe that this same loving God can't actually forgive us unless He is appeased with blood. It is a difficult doctrinal pill to swallow, and the only way it really makes sense is if you have been taught to think that way from childhood; or, if you suspend your common sense disbelief long enough to just go with it.

Ask yourself this question. Would you have survived the bloody sacrificial years of Judaism? Would your heart have become more tender and compassionate or more hardened and callous after murdering hundreds and eventually thousands of animals to *atone* for your sins?

---

[124] BEAUCHAMP, Serena, *Every Time I Fall* 1998

Because of the brutality of this atrocious doctrine, you would think that Christianity would welcome the news that God really doesn't want, need, or require sacrifice! But because we don't want to believe that we have misinterpreted the Bible—and hence the Character of God—this badly, we flatly reject the notion that our interpretations could really be this biased that we cannot see God's TRUE Character, His TRUE Word. So we fall back on Christianity's traditional interpretations and insist: "Isaiah prophesied that Yeshua would come and pay the price for my sin."[125]

The problem here is that Isaiah also prophesied against blood sacrifices![126] Once again, Christianity purposely ignores the contradiction to favor its own mistaken interpretations of Isaiah's ancient Hebrew.

ISAIAH 53 AND THE SUFFERING SERVANT

Christendom typically demands that Isaiah 53 is a prophecy of a *Messianic human sacrifice of atonement* for sin. We naturally and honestly want to infer this from Luke's statement in Acts 8,[127] although Luke never actually says that Isaiah 53 is a Messianic prophecy.

Isaiah 53 doesn't just pop up out of nowhere, but is the culmination of an impressive prophecy about Israel that begins around chapter 41 of the book of Isaiah. Within Isaiah 41-54 God discusses the events surrounding His *servant* Israel. This epic prophecy has come to be known as the *Servant Songs*.

---

[125] Isaiah 53
[126] Isaiah 1
[127] Acts 8:32-33

Because of Isaiah 53, chapters 41-54 are typically translated by Christian scholars with a decidedly *Christian* bias that assumes the *suffering servant* is Yeshua, the coming Messiah, when in fact the balance of these passages consistently refers to *the servant* collectively as Israel. At points within the *Servant Songs,* God is praising His *servant* for doing well (Christians and Messianic Jews will point out that this *servant* is naturally Yeshua), while in another passage God is chastising this very same *servant* for his willful disobedience (who is now, of course, Israel). Sometimes God both highly praises and harshly chastises His *servant* within the same chapter.

Consistent context is paramount within any translation. The flip-flopping of the context of the subject within the translation of Scripture is typically considered bad scholarship—but because the *Servant Songs* (when translated by Christians) appear to support the Christian and Messianic view of God asking for a human sacrifice, this flip-flopping of context has become *accepted bad scholarship.*

Interestingly, the Greek translation of Isaiah 53 within the Septuagint (also called the LXX) does not at all imply any kind of sacrifice of atonement for sin. Editors Bellinger and Farmer, two conservative Christian theologians note,

> The Greek version of Isaiah 53 offers the Christian exegete considerably less support than the Hebrew versions for the doctrine of atonement from sin through Yeshua's sacrificial death and resurrection.... But taken in context, the LXX translators stopped

short of seeing in the Servant's actions an atoning sacrificial death...[128]

The Jewish scholars who originally translated the Septuagint possessed the knowledge that our Father *could not possibly require a human sacrifice* when He had consistently repudiated such a pagan practice within the Law. Bellinger and Farmer go on to essentially conclude that the ancient translation of the Greek within the Septuagint must be a *biased* translation of the Hebrew.

It is interesting to note that these two Christian scholars fail to be concerned about the fact that their *own* translation of the simple Hebrew could itself be seeded with a mainstream Christian bias. This bias is in and of itself tampering with the Isaiah text by attempting to read more into the passage than is actually there when viewed from the perspective of true Hebraic thought.

Again, in Hebraic thought, human sacrifice was a direct violation of God's Law; God throughout the Scriptures literally and consistently condemns it. Therefore, God would not be inspiring Isaiah to be prophesying such for the atonement of sin—especially to *atone* for the sin of another! This is a concept that God outright repudiates via the prophet Ezekiel.[129]

To summarize: the KJV, NIV and other major translations indeed deliberately mistranslate the Hebrew of Isaiah 53 and bend its context to make it indeed sound like some-

---

[128] BELLINGER, JR, William, and FARMER, William, (editors) *Jesus and the Suffering Servant: Isaiah 53 and Christian Origins*, Trinity Press, 1998, pp. 186, 188
[129] Ezekiel 18:1-4

one is paying the price of another's sin when Ezekiel 18 utterly contradicts this possibility.

CHAPTER 14

❖

THE AKEDA CONUNDRUM

If you are like most Christian or Messianic believers, you have already thought of another Biblical example to bring home the *God demanded a sacrifice and Yeshua Was It* point. "Yeshua was the *antitype* of Isaac. God told Abraham to go and sacrifice Isaac! God told Abraham to sacrifice his only son Isaac on the altar!"

Step away from tradition from a moment and try to look at this story as if you've never heard it before. Ask yourself, "Is the Character of God really on display within this story?" If you heard what you thought was the Voice of God instructing you to go *slay your son or daughter,* would you automatically believe that it was God who was instructing you to do such a heinous thing?

Really?

Such circumstances have happened within the modern era as otherwise good Christian people have murdered their own children; wholly because they heard what they thought was the voice of God telling them to do so. Many of us are understandably shocked and horrified over such actions of these otherwise *good* Christians.

One such story is that of Deanna Laney, a highly religious Texas woman who slew two of her sons and severely injured another, all because she felt God was telling her to do so. Laney's attorney, F.R. "Buck" Files, argued that Laney believed that "the word of God was infallible. It destroyed her ability to discern the wrongness of her act."[130]

Laney herself explains, "I thought it was the Lord speaking to me, 'You're just going to have to step out in faith. This is faith. You can't see the why. You just got to obey'... It was like, I had been given the instructions, and it was a matter of obeying or disobeying."[131]

While we in Christendom repeatedly *sanitize* the story of God telling Abraham to sacrifice Isaac, how can we honestly condemn Deanna Laney for acting on her faith and *obeying God* if we believe God asked the same thing of Abraham? Is there really a difference? No! There is no difference in ethical and moral behavior here. Murder is murder; it is an act prohibited by God. As such, God *would not ask anyone to murder his or her child,* even as a test.

One can easily insert a different commandment to bring this point home. Would God ask someone to commit adultery to prove his or her love for Him? Come to think of it, many people would appreciate that one. "Babe, it wasn't really cheating. God told me to go get a hot young honey on the side to prove my love for Him!" Ridiculous, isn't it?

Can we really believe it was somehow okay for Abraham to (attempt to) slay his son as a human sacrifice just because

---

[130] CNN.com/2004/LAW/03/29/children.slain/index.html on 09/17/06
[131] CourtTV video of Deanna Laney's testimony dated 12/15/03

this event was written into the Torah and later canonized into the Protestant Bible?

What Christian and most Messianic believers are never told, mostly because we aren't familiar with traditional Judaism, is that this episode within Torah creates a huge contradiction and conundrum for Judaism's ostensive belief in the inerrancy of Torah. Jewish scholars have been well aware of this rather glaring contradiction for centuries.

This event within Torah is known as the *Akeda* or *Binding of Isaac,* and is considered by the majority of Jewish scholars to be Judaism's most ethically troublesome passage. On the one hand, Torah is considered utterly infallible and without error; on the other hand, God *will not void His Covenant* by asking man to violate His commands. Period.

Christian scholars, on the other hand, all too easily dismiss the deep contradiction in the story without realizing the discordant issues the *Akeda* represents to mainstream Christian *soteriology*[132] and the Character of the Eternal One.

Rashi, a Hebrew acronym for Rabbi Shlomo Yitzchaki, or Rabbi Shlomo Yarchi, (circa late eleventh century), was the author of the first comprehensive commentaries on the Talmud and Tanakh. Rashi was very highly respected then and in the present:

> Acclaimed for his ability to present the basic meaning of the text in a concise yet lucid fashion, Rashi appeals to both beginning students and learned scholars. His commentaries, which appear in all printed editions of the Talmud and Torah (especially the Chumash), are

---

[132] *Soteriology*—the branch of Christian theology that deals with salvation as the effect of a divine agency (i.e. forgiveness through the sacrifice of Jesus Christ)

an indispensable companion to both casual and serious students of Judaism's primary texts.[133]

Part of Rashi's commentary on Genesis 22 includes the following:

> Said Rabbi Abba: Abraham said to Him, "I will explain my complaint before You. Yesterday, You said to me (Genesis 21:12): 'for in Isaac will be called your seed,' and You retracted and said (Genesis 22:2): 'Take now your son.' Now You say to me, 'Do not stretch forth your hand to the lad.'" The Holy One, blessed be He, said to him (Psalm. 89:35): "I shall not profane My covenant, neither shall I alter the utterance of My lips." When I said to you, "Take," I was not altering the utterance of My lips. I did not say to you, "Slaughter him," but, "Bring him up." You have brought him up; [now] take him down."[134]

Realizing the incredible contradiction the *Akeda* creates, many Jewish scholars argue that God had never actually asked Abraham to *sacrifice* his son because of the Law that forbade human sacrifice; but believe instead that God had instructed Abraham to *"alah* for a sacrifice on the mountain." These scholars argue that the word *alah* had two meanings and could be taken one of two ways by Abraham. It could mean to *take him* [Isaac] *up* onto Mount Moriah, or to *burn*

---

[133] Adapted from Wikipedia.com, "Rashi", 9-11-06 Wiki uses as a source Chaim Miller's article "Rashi's Method of Biblical Commentary" found on chabad.org, which is a web site for Jewish history.

[134] Gen. Rabbah 56:8, Judaica Press, Complete Tanach with Rashi's Commentary on Genesis (Bereishit) 22.

him as a sacrifice on the mountain. It seems to have been a kind of test for Abraham—*What would Abraham believe God was really asking of him?*

Having come out of a deeply pagan culture, Abraham must not have stopped to really think that the God he had been worshiping all these many years was not like the harsh and bloodthirsty pagan gods who demanded human sacrifice. Obviously, Abraham must have taken God's statement to mean that he was supposed to offer his son in the fire. Clearly, it is argued, Abraham was misunderstanding God's character *and* His Law. Citing Rashi, these Jewish scholars, much more in concert with and attuned with God's Word (His Character) than today's Christians generally are, correctly assert that God could not have actually asked Abraham to slaughter his son, because *God would never ask anyone to do something contrary to his own law.*[135]

Christianity, with its peculiar contradictory soteriology (forgiveness through the breaking of God's Law) to uphold, doesn't agree with this Jewish understanding. Christian and Messianic believers teach that they have a much more advanced understanding of this event, because Abraham offering his son as a *sacrifice* was a *type*[136] that pointed forward to its *antitypical* fulfillment in God offering His own son, Yeshua, as the final atoning sacrifice for our sin.[137]

---

[135] Psalm 89:34 in the Christian Bible & Psalm 89:35 in the Judaica Press Complete Tanach.

[136] "A type is a shadow cast on the pages of Old Testament history by a truth whose full embodiment or antitype is found in the New Testament revelation" (Wick Broomall, Baker's Dictionary of Theology, p. 533).

[137] Yet no one ever promotes the thought that the sacrifice of Isaac was in any way an atoning sacrifice for the sins of Abraham, so even that comparison falls flat!

But now we must face an unavoidable situation: the Christian and Messianic version of God's Character, His Word, utterly contradicts God's Law. We believe on the one hand that "God would not ask us to do something that is totally against His Law". But we also believe that God did the *exact opposite* in His dealings with Abraham by asking Abraham to do something that drastically went against God's own commandment.

Worse still is the implication that if the Most High so despised sacrifices—especially human sacrifice—then He would not have made Yeshua any kind of sacrifice on the cross! Again, this essentially amounts to *forgiveness through the breaking of God's Law*.

What Christian and Messianic believers are generally not taught in Bible class or Torah study or church is that this *human sacrifice for the sins of the world* concept comes straight out of the ancient tenets of a long-dead and originally Persian religion.

Historically, the concept and dynamic of a *human sacrifice by a god-man (part god, part human) who is murdered to atone for the sins of humanity* and then *resurrected and ascends into heaven* has a well-established pagan precedence from ancient Persian-Greco-Roman mythology. It comes from the religion called Mithraism.

CHAPTER 15

❖

MITHRAISM: A CONVENIENT TEMPLATE

After the first century, various groups of Christianity borrowed many of their practices and traditions from Greco-Roman paganism. For example, in the fourth century, the Roman Catholic Church changed the day of worship from the seventh day to the first day of the week to coincide with the popular *Dies Solis* (Sun's Day) pagan worship day.[138] Most Christian denominations still worship on this day even though it was a direct import from pagan Roman culture and not original to Christianity.

The two religions of Mithraism and Christianity were considered by many to be contemporaries of each other. In fact,

---

[138] BACCHIOCCHI, Samuele, *From Sabbath to Sunday*: A Historical Investigation of the Rise of Sunday Observance in Early Christianity, Bacchiocchi, 2008, p. 12, 250, 337

Mithraism was one of Christianity's major competitors in the Roman Empire. Indeed, the French historian Ernest Renan once declared that 'if Christianity had been stopped at its birth by some mortal illness, the world would have become Mithraic.' No doubt Renan's statement is somewhat exaggerated. Nevertheless, Mithraism and Christianity were in many respects sister religions. Arising at the same time and spreading in roughly the same geographical area, Mithraism and Christianity embodied two responses to the same set of cultural forces. The study of Mithraism therefore provides us with insight into 'the road not taken' by Western civilization nearly two thousand years ago–insight, that is, into an unrecognized part of who we are today.[139]

Tenets of Mithraism were also imported into Christianity very early, as early as the middle part of the first century. Part of the Mithraic communion ritual reads:

> He who will not eat of my body and drink of my blood, so that he will be made one with me and I with him, the same shall not know salvation.[140]

Compare this with John 6:53-54, where Yeshua is said to have repeated this theme:

---

[139] ULANSEY, David, The Origins of the Mithraic Mysteries: Cosmology & Salvation in the Ancient World, Oxford University Press 1991, 168 pages, pp. 3-4

[140] VERMASEREN, Maarten Jozef, *Mithras, The Secret God*, Barnes & Noble, 1963, 200 pages, p. 104

> ... Except ye eat the flesh of the Son of man, and drink his blood, ye have no life in you. Whoso eateth my flesh, and drinketh my blood, hath eternal life; and I will raise him up at the last day.

Isn't it deplorable how both religions incorporated cannibalizing or pretending to cannibalize one's *god* as part of their worship?

Martin Luther King, Jr. wrote extensively about the stark similarities between Christianity and the pagan religion of Mithraism:

> Originally Mithra was one of the lesser gods of the ancient Persian pantheon, but at the time of Christ he had come to be co-equal with Ahura Mazda, the Supreme Being. He possessed many attributes, the most important being his office of defender of truth and all good things... He hears all and sees all: none can deceive him. [Footnote: Cumont, Mysteries of Mithra, pp. 2, 3.]
>
> Tarsus, the home of Saint Paul, was one of the great centers of his [Mithra's] worship; and there is a decided tinge of Mithraism in the Epistles and Gospels. Such designations of our Lord as the Dayspring from on High, The Light, the Sun of Righteousness, and similar expressions seem to come directly from Mithraic influence." [Footnote: Weigall, op. cit., p. 129.]
>
> Again tradition has it that Mithra was born from a rock, "the god out of the rock." It must also be noticed that his worship was always conducted in a cave. Now

it seems that the general belief of the early church that Jesus was born in a cave grows directly out of Mithraic ideas. The words of St. Paul, "They drank of that spiritual rock... and that rock was Christ" also seem to be a direct borrow from the Mithraic scriptures.

The Hebrew Sabbath having been abolished by [proto-Roman Catholic] Christians, the Church made a sacred day of Sunday, partly because it was the day of resurrection. But when we observe a little further we find that as a solar festival, *Sunday was the sacred day of Mithra*; it is also interesting to notice that since Mithra was addressed as Lord, Sunday must have been "the Lord's Day" long before Christian use. [Footnote: Ibid., p. 137.] It is also to be noticed that our *Christmas, December 25th, was the birthday of Mithra*, and was only taken over in the Fourth Century as the date, actually unknown, of the birth of Jesus.

To make the picture a little more clear, we may list a few of the similarities between these two religions: (1) Both regard Sunday as a holy day. (2) December 25 came to be considered as the anniversary of the birth of Mithra and Christ also. (3) Baptism and a communion meal were important parts of the ritual of both groups. (4) The rebirth of converts was a fundamental idea in the two cults. (5) The struggle with evil and the eventual triumph of good were essential ideas in both religions. (6) In summary we may say that the belief in immortality, a mediator between god and man, the observance of certain sacramental rites, the rebirth of converts, and (in most cases) the support of high ethical ideas were common to Mithraism as well as Christianity. In fact, the comparison became so evident that many believed the Christian movement itself became a mystery cult. "Jesus was the divine Lord. He too had found the road to heaven by his suffering and resurrection. He too had God for his father. He had left behind the secret whereby men could achieve the goal with him." [Footnote: Enslin, op. cit., p. 190.][141]

Historian Franz Cumont elaborates,

> The struggle between the two rival religions was the more stubborn as their characters were the more alike. The adepts of both formed secret conventicles, closely united, the members of which gave themselves the name of 'Brothers.' The rites which they practised offered numerous analogies.... Their conceptions of the world and of the destiny of man were similar. They both admitted the existence of a Heaven inhabited by beautified ones, situate in the upper regions, and of a Hell peopled by demons, situate in the bowels of the earth. They both placed a Flood at the beginning of history; they both assigned as the source of their traditions a primitive revelation; they both, finally, believed in the immortality of the soul, in a last

---

[141] From Martin Luther King Jr. in a paper entitled, *The Influence of the Mystery Religions on Christianity*. King wrote this paper for the course "Development of Christian Ideas". Stanford.edu/group/King/publications/papers/vol1/500215-The_Influence_of_the_Mystery_Religions_on_Christianity.htm; quoted on 09-17-06

judgment, and in a resurrection of the dead, consequent upon a final conflagration of the universe.

We have seen that the theology of the Mysteries made of Mithra a 'mediator' equivalent to the Alexandrian Logos. Like him, Christ also was an intermediary between his celestial father and men, and like him he also was one of a trinity. These resemblances were certainly not the only ones that pagan exegesis established between the two religions, and the figure of the tauroctonous god reluctantly immolating his victim that he might create and save the human race, was certainly compared to the picture of the redeemer sacrificing his own person for the salvation of the world.[142]

While some of this may come across as shocking or even totally unbelievable, the history is factually unassailable; so much so that some Christian leaders are now preaching that "Satan established the pagan religion of Mithraism centuries in advance of Yeshua to unseat the faith of Christians who would come later." This is a severe leap of logic to make, yet for many believers it is far more preferable to make that leap than to acknowledge how many of Christianity's most precious doctrines come straight out of a mystery religion that was very popular in the home town of the Apostle Paul, who many consider to be the Father of Christianity.

---

[142] CUMONT, Franz Valéry Marie, *The Mysteries of Mithra*, Forgotten Books, 1956, 239 pages pp. 119-120

PART III
UNMASKING PAUL

CHAPTER 16

❖

THE FATHER OF CHRISTIANITY

There is no other person in the Bible that is so extolled, appreciated, and quoted as much as Paul of Tarsus. Hundreds of books have been written about his life. Thousands more have been written exploring his writings. Entire doctrines have evolved because of the counsel set forth in his letters. His influence has been so strong that Paul might rightly be called the Father of Christianity.

Like any other strong personality, Paul has also had his share of critics. He is a very polarizing character and while the majority of Christians consider his writings to be sacred, many believers–especially Messianic Jews–quietly cringe when certain passages in his letters are brought up. In fact, his writings alone have been responsible for splitting Christian churches and even entire denominations.

Adventism itself has something of a love/hate relationship with Paul. He is a huge force in the New Testament, and his letters are lauded and memorized. Yet there are some singular incongruities in Paul's writings that traditional Adventism attempts to discretely ignore. Interestingly, these *problem passages* are the first texts quoted by someone who has left Adventism; in fact, these letters and passages from Paul are generally cited as the main reason for their exit from Adventism! I have personally seen multiple friends leave the Adventist Church, basing their actions and beliefs exclusively on Paul's writings.

As soon as Luc and I discovered that there were some discrepancies in the Scriptures, we began an intensive study of Paul's writings in search of answers to our ever-increasing list of doctrinal questions. Our study and investigation of Paul was uneventful until one day when Luc began combing through Paul's letter to the Galatians. Luc typically couldn't get enough of Galatians, but oddly enough on this particular day, instead of sharing inspirational nuggets of his reading with me he turned and said with a frown, "This book is making me really uncomfortable."

"Why?" I asked, puzzled. I couldn't comprehend his remark. Galatians is part of the Bible! How can you be *uncomfortable* with part of the Bible? Furthermore, Luc was a former Bapticostal. He was well aware that Galatians contains the most important and definitive chapters of Paul's counsel! What could possibly make him uncomfortable about Galatians? After all, nowhere else in Paul's letters do you see him so passionate, so vehement, and so on fire for his beliefs!

"Well," Luc began, "Galatians 1:8 is making me uncomfortable. Listen."

> But even if we or an angel from heaven should preach a gospel other than the one we preached to you, let him be eternally condemned![143]

I had heard this verse a hundred times, and it had never bothered me. To the contrary, I just figured it meant Paul was super-passionate and confident about his beliefs. I just wished I was that sure of my beliefs myself! Why was Luc not in agreement?

"I've just been reading the book of Jude," he continued. "Jude says,

> In the very same way, these dreamers pollute their own bodies, reject authority and slander celestial beings.[144]

"In saying what he does in Galatians 1, Paul seems to be *slandering God's celestial beings*, God's angels," Luc stated worriedly. "I think this might be what Jude was talking about when he warned against those who slander celestial beings."[145]

---

[143] Galatians 1:8 NIV 1984

[144] Jude verse 8 NIV 1984

[145] Jude, who is called Jude Thaddeus by many historians, is thought to be the brother (some always emphasize "half" brother) of Jesus as well as being one of the Apostles and a member of the leadership of the *Jerusalem Church*. Historians and scholars are well divided on whether or not Jude was actually the brother (some say twin brother) or nephew (a son of James) of Jesus.

The book of Jude has been a disputed book since its canonization by the Roman Catholic Church. Most well studied historians and Bible scholars, including the Reformers, do not believe the book of Jude was actually written by Jude, but rather is yet another pseudepigraphical (i.e. the book is written, *forged*, in the name of an apostle) work similar to that of the books of Peter. However, whether or not the book of Jude was actually written by Jude, the

Slandering Celestial Beings

Additional study into Hebraic culture and beliefs revealed that the above passage is indeed deeply alarming to the Hebraic mindset. Such a comment within the Hebrew culture exhibits a lack of consideration and a real carelessness in one's core understanding of God's Character and the Nature of God's Holiness.

Having been immersed in Jewish culture, Paul knew that among the Jewish Christians, such a comment would be highly inflammatory if not outright sacrilegious. Why? Because in Jewish understanding, the Law of God was delivered through the mediation or agency of heavenly messengers. We see this Hebraic understanding being communicated by the Apostles, the unknown author of the book of *Hebrews*, the historian Josephus, and even Paul himself.

Stephen's speech in the book of Acts affirms this Hebrew understanding.

> This is the same Moses whom they had rejected with the words, 'Who made you ruler and judge?' He was sent to be their ruler and deliverer by God himself, through the angel who appeared to him in the bush. He led them out of Egypt and did wonders and miraculous signs in Egypt, at the Red Sea and for forty years in the desert...

---

book does clearly demonstrate some version of period Christian thought—Christian thought that is not at all flattering toward Paul. In this small but significant book, the author of the book of Jude gives a powerful warning about false prophets and their false teachings. In a side-by-side comparison, Jude's describes many tenets of Paul's personal characteristics ominously well.

> He (Moses) was in the assembly in the desert, with the angel who spoke to him on Mount Sinai, and with our fathers; and he received living words (from the angel) to pass on to us.[146]
>
> Was there ever a prophet your fathers did not persecute? They even killed those who predicted the coming of the Righteous One. And now you have betrayed and murdered him—you who have received the law *that was put into effect through angels but have not obeyed it*.[147]

The very Pauline author of the book of Hebrews states,

> For if the message *spoken by angels* was binding, and every violation and disobedience received its just punishment, how shall we escape if we ignore so great a salvation?[148]

Josephus, the first-century Jewish historian, is another witness that clarifies the period understanding of God's Law being delivered through the mediation of angels. He states,

> And for ourselves, we have learned from God the most excellent of our doctrines, and *the most holy part of our law, by angels* or ambassadors.[149]

---

[146] Acts 7:35-38
[147] Acts 7:52-53
[148] Hebrews 2:2-3
[149] Antiquities XV

Paul's own words verify this understanding. He taught, "The law was put into effect *through angels* (or an angel) by a mediator."[150]

How could Paul write Galatians 3:19 and still say what he said in Galatians 1:8?

> But even if we *or an angel from heaven* should preach a gospel other than the one we preached to you, let him be eternally condemned![151]

It was very troubling to realize that either Paul really didn't understand this Hebraic concept or he simply felt free to condemn and slander the celestial beings that were and are commissioned by God to bring vital messages to His children. The interaction with God via a heavenly messenger is a solemn and holy circumstance and event when it happens. It is nothing to be trifled with lightly. Yet Paul was in effect saying,

> 'Even if a commissioned messenger of God Himself were to come down from Heaven and give you a Gospel different that the one I am preaching to you may this messenger of God Himself be eternally damned!' (Or, "May this angel of God 'go to hell!'" in our vernacular.)

In making this comment, Paul categorically sets himself and his gospel as being *above* that of God and His Heaven. Not

---

[150] Galatians 3:19 NIV 1984
[151] Galatians 1:8 NIV 1984

only does Paul take a stand against the Law of God but against the messenger who delivered it as well!

This was beyond discouraging. How had I never noticed this before? I realized that some further study of Galatians was needed—maybe I could find something else to help encourage me in my quest for Truth. Yet as I pondered these things in my heart and mind, I had no idea of the much darker discoveries that awaited me.

CHAPTER 17

❖

A LIVING CRUCIFIX

In chapter 6 of Galatians as Paul is about to close the letter, he makes a peculiar and very interesting declaration. In this declaration, he emphasizes something he wants the readers in Galatia to remember about himself; something they have indeed *already seen* in Paul. Paul is emphatic in his point:

> But God forbid that I should boast except in the cross of our Lord Yeshua HaMaschiach, by whom the world has been crucified to me, and I to the world. ... From now on let no one trouble me, for I bear in my body *the marks* of the Lord Yeshua.[152]

This is a very curious passage. What does it mean to *bear in your body the marks of Yeshua?*

---

[152] Galatians 6:14-17 NKJV (emphasis provided)

Within the Greek, the specific word-for-word translation of the last part of this sentence is,

> ...ego bastazo en mou soma *s*tigma kurios Iesous.

This sentence translated word-for-word into English is,

> ...I bear in my body [the] *marks* [of the] Lord Yeshua (*Jesus*).

The word *stigma* appears only once within the entire New Testament and is used only by Paul to denote a very specific kind of *sign* or *mark*—a religious mark, in fact.

In the Greek language, the true and full meaning of *stigma* is so much more than a mere *mark* or brand—it has a deep religious and spiritual meaning and significance as well. Galatia's *spiritual father* is in actuality issuing a stern warning to his churches, admonishing them,

> Leave me alone! Don't mess with me; I have the religious brands, the wounds (cuts), the bodily imprints of Yeshua HaMaschiach himself, upon me![153]

If we take Paul's commentary in the Greek language at face value, and also take into account the mimicking of Christ that was apparent within the ministry of his distinctive gospel message, it becomes well apparent that the *illness* Paul had

---

[153] Galatians is not the only witness where Paul discusses the fact that he *carries around Christ's death* in his body. Consider 2 Corinthians 4:10 where he exhorts the Christian to be "Always carrying around in (our/the) body the death of Jesus so that the life of Jesus may also be revealed in our body."

while he was in the company of the people of Galatia was indeed a supernatural condition known as *stigmata*.

WHAT ARE STIGMATA?

Stigmata are a very real condition where the *wounds of Christ* that Yeshua received during his crucifixion supernaturally appear, to varying degrees and at different times, on the *stigmatic* or *victim*. In essence, mysterious deep wounds appear in the palms/wrists, feet/legs, side, and/or on the brow of the victim. The wounds are real and they bleed just like any other wound. They heal very slowly, if at all.

Most Protestants are completely unaware of stigmata, but within Roman Catholic circles, this condition has historically been considered to be a form of high blessing as one is physically, not just emotionally or spiritually, *sharing* in the suffering tortures of Christ, as well as sharing in what is believed to be the redemptive nature of Christ.

In his book, *They Bore the Wounds of Christ: The Mystery of the Sacred Stigmata*, Catholic author Michael Freze states:

> Paul responds literally to the words of our Lord to take up His cross and follow Him if he is to remain a true disciple. Because he [Paul] offers himself up voluntarily and unconditionally to atone for sinners, he becomes one specially marked by God to be His victim for others—to help Jesus carry His unending Cross for humanity: 'Now I rejoice in my sufferings for your sake, and in my flesh I complete what is lacking in Christ's afflictions for the sake of his body, that is, the church' (Col 1:24). Paul puts 'on the Lord Jesus Christ' (Rom 13:140, 'conquering evil with good' (Rom

12:21), and does so out of love and compassion for sinners everywhere:

> Even if I am to be poured as a libation upon the sacrificial offering of your faith, I am glad and rejoice with you all (Phil 2:17).

> I appeal to you therefore brethren, by the mercies of God, to present your bodies as a living sacrifice, holy and acceptable to God, which is your spiritual worship (Rom 12:1).

> Now I rejoice in my sufferings for your sake... (Col 1:24).[154]

Freze also notes,

> In general, those who sacrifice themselves for the sake of sinners are called victim souls. These souls help atone for our sin in union with Christ. ... They are free to reject the role of victim, because God wants the consent of His chosen ones first before He assigns them to this supernatural task. ... Once the soul consents, however, God is free to do whatever He wills with the person who will be His redemptive helper... usually, however, the chosen ones freely offer their sufferings up to God with the specific intention of making atonement or expiation for their own sin, or for the sins of others. ... With some of these servants, God answers their prayers and offerings and takes

---

[154] FREZE, Michael, *They Bore the Wounds of Christ: The Mystery of the Sacred Stigmata,* Our Sunday Visitor Publishing, 1989 350 pages p. 40

them at their word. In even fewer cases, God sometimes chooses to unite them even more intimately with the Son on the Cross; hence, they become stigmatists—true victims of divine love who offer their lives for the ransom of many.[155]

The Passion of the Christ

Like many Protestants, I originally had no idea what *victim souls* or *co-redemption* or even *stigmata* were. I did not become familiar with this condition until Mel Gibson released his blockbuster movie, *The Passion of the Christ*. While I was researching the film to determine if it was something I should view, I discovered an interview in which Gibson talked about an old book that helped him create many of the extra-Biblical scenes within the film—scenes that were in the film but not the Gospels. This book, as it turns out, was the main source of Gibson's inspiration for the movie's many additions to the Biblical account of the crucifixion story.

Gibson recounted the story of how he discovered the source for his inspiration while browsing through his library of old books. He reached up to grab a book off the shelf and suddenly another book that was close to the one he was reaching for literally jumped off the shelf into his hand. That book was *The Dolorous Passion of Our Lord and Savior Jesus Christ*, a composition of the writings of one Anne Catherine Emmerich.

Emmerich was an Augustinian mystic, a Roman Catholic nun who lived from 1774 to 1824 in Germany. Her brief life has been described as being one of poverty, hardship, and

---

[155] FREZE p. 59

terrible suffering. She spent the final years of her life bedridden and in constant pain. During this time, she experienced visionary meditations or *visions* on the passion of Christ. These visions were recorded by the poet Klemens Brentano and published in 1833.[156]

Emmerich's life was far from being extraordinary simply because of her visions; Emmerich was also a stigmatic. To top her list of supernatural sufferings, it is said that she also levitated, many times against her will.[157]

I am not familiar with any part of the Character of God that insists on afflicting His obedient and humble children with any kind of painful wounds, crucifixion wounds or otherwise, so that we might somehow *share* in the suffering of Yeshua HaMaschiach. Indeed, Yeshua himself is telling about the TRUE Character of our heavenly Father within these verses in Matthew:

> Which of you, if his son asks for bread, will give him a stone? Or if he asks for a fish, will give him a snake? If you, then, though you are evil, know how to give good gifts to your children, how much more will your Father in heaven give good gifts to those who ask him! So in everything, do to others what you would have

---

[156] Such *visions* were quite a popular part of Christianity in the 1800s and a lot of people in Christian leadership apparently had them—including Ellen White, the popular Adventist mystic.

[157] There are no Biblical accounts that I know of where anyone was levitating under the influence of the Holy Spirit. Within the Acts of Peter, however, a non-canonical early Christian book, Simon the Sorcerer apparently levitates under the power and influence of Satan. Simon the Sorcerer will be further discussed in a later chapter.

them do to you, for this sums up the Law and the Prophets.[158]

Think about it: Which of us can imagine torturing our own children with bleeding wounds that never heal as some kind of *blessing?* True, human suffering is a fact of life, but it is not the Nature nor is it the desire of Almighty God to give his children horrific *gifts* to *reward* them for their devotion and obedience to Him!

Consider for a moment the untold amounts of pain experienced by these ostensibly blessed stigmatic mystics, and then think about whether you really think these so-called *gifts* are from a truly loving God.

What is it Like to Experience Stigmata?

In his previously mentioned book, *They Bore the Wounds of Christ,* Freze describes the well-documented experience of Louise Lateau of Belgium, 1850-83:

> Louise first began to suffer the pains of the Passion on January 3, 1868, and on every following Friday until April 24, when blood began to flow from the upper surface of the feet. On May 8, the hand wounds appeared, thus completing her stigmatization. The pain caused by these wounds became so intense that she was no longer able to attend Mass in the church; instead, Communion had to be brought to her every day in her own home. ... According to Dr. Lefebvre, Louise hemorrhaged some 800 times from the

---

[158] Matthew 7:9-12

wounds of her stigmata, which bled weekly from April 24, 1868, until her death on August 25, 1883. He even reported that on one day the blood flowing from the wounds was about 250 grams. In addition to receiving the Five Sacred Wounds, Louise Lateau experienced the crown of thorn wounds. There were 12 to 15 circular marks around the head that frequently issued forth blood.[159]

This experience sounds pretty brutal, doesn't it? Imagine going through this horrific experience every week and being told (or being brainwashed into thinking) that your experience is some kind of *blessing!*

Another famous Catholic mystic who received the so-called *blessing of the stigmata* was Therese Neumann, who was born in 1898 and lived in Germany as well. A Hindu yogi, of all people, wrote about meeting her on July 16, 1935.

During this meeting between the two mystics of different religious traditions, Mr. Yogananda inquired about her stigmata. Ms. Neumann disclosed to him that her wounds would open and bleed from every Thursday at midnight until Friday afternoon at one o'clock; causing her to lose ten pounds of her normally 121-pound weight per event.[160]

The Friday following his visit, this Hindu sage, described by Ms. Neumann as a "man of God from India", went to observe Ms. Neumann as she experienced her weekly stigmatic trance. Before entering her room, he mentally put himself into a deep super-conscious state in order to supernaturally *share* in her vision. Although I do not subscribe in

---

[159] FREZE p. 272

[160] YOGANANDA, Paramhansa; *Autobiography of a Yogi*, 1946. Online edition. Chapter 39, Therese Neumann, the Catholic Stigmatist

any way to his beliefs, I found his description of what he *saw* and purportedly experienced while in this trance to be of note:

> Just before I went upstairs to her room, I put myself into a yogic trance state in order to be one with her in telepathic and televisic rapport. I entered her chamber, filled with visitors; she was lying in a white robe on the bed... I halted just inside the threshold, awestruck at a strange and most frightful spectacle.
>
> Blood flowed thinly and continuously in an inch-wide stream from Therese's lower eyelids. Her gaze was focused upward on the spiritual eye within the central forehead. The cloth wrapped around her head was drenched in blood from the stigmata wounds of the crown of thorns. The white garment was redly splotched over her heart from the wound in her side at the spot where Christ's body, long ages ago, had suffered the final indignity of the soldier's spear-thrust.
>
> Therese's hands were extended in a gesture maternal, pleading; her face wore an expression both tortured and divine. She appeared thinner, changed in many subtle as well as outward ways. Murmuring words in a foreign tongue, she spoke with slightly quivering lips to persons visible before her inner sight.
>
> As I was in attunement with her, *I began to see the scenes of her vision.* She was watching Jesus as he carried the cross amidst the jeering multitude. Suddenly she lifted her head in consternation: the Lord had fallen under the cruel weight. The vision disappeared.

In the exhaustion of fervid pity, Therese sank heavily against her pillow."[161]

The yogi footnoted that,

> During the hours preceding my arrival, Therese had already passed through many visions of the closing days in Christ's life. Her entrancement usually starts with scenes of the events which followed the Last Supper. Her visions end with Jesus' death on the cross or, occasionally, with his entombment.[162]

It is remarkable—and very unsettling—to consider that this famous yogi claimed to *share* and *verify* Ms. Neumann's stigmatic vision. This should make any follower of the One TRUE God pause and seriously consider, yet again, if this condition really seems like a spiritual *gift* from the Eternal One? Was this Hindu yogi really blessed by God with this *shared sight* or was it possible—even probable—that demonic forces were in play?

There is another issue that discerning Christian or Messianic believers need to consider. While the Roman Catholic Church continues to officially consider stigmata to be a gift or *high blessing* from God, and historically many members of the Roman Catholic Church have observed that it seems quite obvious through the reading of Paul's letters that Paul himself could indeed have been the first recorded stigmatic, those in Roman Catholic authority seem to downplay and enigmatically dismiss without further comment this *high blessing* resting upon Paul. But if this condition is truly

---

[161] YOGANANDA Chapter 39, *italics* supplied
[162] YOGANANDA Chapter 39

God's holy mark upon an individual that allows them to actually *share in the suffering of Christ,* then why does the Church seem so unwilling to admit that this seemingly most precious honor was bestowed on their beloved apostle, Paul?

CHAPTER 18

❖

A CONSPIRACY OF SILENCE

The online Catholic Encyclopedia, available at NewAdvent.org, acknowledges that the possibility of Paul being a stigmatic has been well known for centuries, yet offers the following politically correct repudiation regarding the possibility of Paul himself being a stigmatic:

> Under any circumstances it is noteworthy that the first recorded instance of stigmata (if we leave out of account the doubtful case of St. Paul) was that of St. Francis of Assisi. Since his time there have been over 320 similar manifestations which have reasonable claims to be considered genuine.[163]

---

[163] POULAIN, Augustin, *Graces of Interior Prayer*, tr., 175. NewAdvent.org/cathen/11527b.htm

Outside of Paul, the earliest recorded accounts of stigmata began surfacing from Europeans around the early fourth century—about the same time the Roman Catholic Church was finalizing its authoritative list of orthodox books that would become the foundation for our modern Bible. One account from the late eighteen hundreds states regarding the attendees of the Council of Nicea:

> Three-hundred and eighteen bishops were assembled... At this period many individuals were richly endowed with apostolical gifts; and many, like the holy apostle, bore in their bodies the marks of the Lord Jesus Christ.[164]

The editors, Henry Wace and Phillip Schaff, are careful to relay the approved period Protestant explanation of what they felt these stigmata had to be. In the footnote to the above notation they explained,

> Cf. Gal. vi. 17. The "stigmata" here meant are the marks of persecution.

According to this publication, one of these bishops, James of Antioch, even "raised the dead and restored them to life, and performed many other wonders"; a claim that is eerily similar to those made regarding what Paul was said to have done.[165]

Despite these later Protestant claims to the contrary, it is clear that for Roman Catholic Christians in early 300 CE, the term *stigma(ta)* was indeed very well understood, used and

---

[164] SCHAFF, Phillip and WACE, Henry, *A Select Library of Nicene and Post-Nicene Fathers of the Christian Church*, Second Series; 1892; Volume 3, p. 43
[165] SCHAFF, Phillip and WACE, Henry, p. 43

applied to denote the mysterious *bleeding wounds (and pain) of Christ* that appeared on the victim. The etymology of the term hasn't really evolved at all since Paul's usage of it in c. 50 CE. And regardless of the ambiguity of what the Catholic leadership says, many Roman Catholics unofficially but firmly believe that Paul was indeed the very first recorded case of stigmata.

In his previously mentioned book, Michael Freze interviewed Father Ulrich Veh,[166] who also knew Therese Neumann personally. Mr. Freze inquired of Vey,

> You know, St. Paul once said that even though Christ died once and for all for our sins, nevertheless some souls are called to make up for what is lacking in the sufferings of Christ for His Church. Do you think it's possible that St. Paul might have been a stigmatist himself?

Father Veh replied,

> Oh yes, I do believe that. At the end of the letter to the Galatians, Paul had said that he bore in his body the marks of Christ. You can think otherwise, but Therese Neumann through her ecstasies knew that he was.[167]

---

[166] Father Veh was from the Order of Friars Minor Capuchin, an order of friars in the Catholic Church among the chief offshoots of the Franciscans.
[167] FREZE p. 301

Clearly, Ms. Neumann was highly respected by the Catholic Church,[168] and Father Veh asserted that Neumann *saw* Paul as a fellow stigmatic within her ecstatic visions. One might think that such dramatic religious *evidence* proclaimed by one of its more renowned visionary and mystic stigmatists might encourage the Roman Catholic leadership to do an about face in its downplaying of Paul's stigmata. Yet curiously, they have not done so.

In discussing the nature of stigmata, Freze writes,

> Our Blessed Lord appears to have rewarded Paul's intense desire for the Cross by making of him a living crucifix, a victim of love who follows in the footsteps of Christ. Paul himself seems to indicate that he has been given the gift of the stigmata. (Gal 6:17) If Paul was truly a victim soul, a living stigmatist, then the question must be raised: why Paul and not the Apostles John or James? Why Paul and not John the Baptist or Simeon? This remains a mystery, for God's ways are not our own.

Freze continues with his explanation:

> ...Perhaps it was because Paul was so intimately associated with the Cross of Christ and with His Passion—a choice he freely made—that God rewarded his fidelity with the most precious grace; perhaps it was be-

---

[168] A petition asking for Ms. Neumann's beautification–a high honor in Catholicism and the first step to being declared a saint–was signed by 40,000 people; showing that she is very popular with Catholic believers. Subsequently in 2005, the Bishop of Regensburg formally opened the Vatican proceedings requesting her beautification. (source: Wikipedia 2012)

cause he offered himself up voluntarily to be God's victim for sinners, to help cooperate in the plan of redemption through the Cross of our Lord. More than likely, it was a combination of the two that explains Paul's extraordinary gift. Besides, how many souls in Sacred Scripture so loved the Cross as Paul? How many would offer themselves as living sacrifices as he did? For Paul and the other victims of God's love, there is always hope and confidence in the future. They all recognize that the sufferings of this life will one day be no more, and for the sake of the Kingdom they endure, storing up treasure for their heavenly reward.

...Although we can never prove if St. Paul bore the Sacred Stigmata, the internal evidence from his own pen seems quite strong and convincing. What else could he possibly mean by 'I bear on my body the marks of Jesus' (Gal 6:17)? I must conclude privately that this indeed seems to be the case, although the Church has never formally recognized this to be so. (I didn't think she's denied it either, for that matter.) I submit to her judgment if she were to decide otherwise.[169]

There is no doubt at all that Michael Freze has a lot of love and passion for his Church! However, it is to a deep fault. Only within the twisted pagan logic of Roman Catholicism's ghastly dogma—which Protestants have to some degree abandoned—is the pain, bleeding, and terrible horrific suffering that accompanies the stigmatic condition consid-

---

[169] FREZE p. 41

ered to be a *good gift* and one who receives it to be called a *victim of God's love*. Within this supernatural condition, one is literally physically sharing in the suffering of Christ as Roman Catholics believe, and as Paul himself testifies about himself and his specific *gospel*.[170]

The orthodox Christian mind typically wants to dismiss the substantial evidence and even tradition surrounding Paul's stigmatic condition as *loose*, or merely *circumstantial* and therefore totally unsupportable. However, bear in mind that the evidence surrounding Paul's stigmatic condition is substantially more Biblically based than many other foundational doctrines of Christian faith, which have substantially less scriptural support than Paul's stigmatic condition. Christmas and Easter, for instance, are *never* mentioned within the Scriptures as festivals of AHYH, yet millions of Christians celebrate them as if God Himself had commanded them. Peter is said to have died in Rome, crucified upside down on a cross; yet this martyrdom isn't even Biblical! The only evidence for this is the non-canonical (non-Biblical) book called the *Acts of Peter*. The paying of Indulgences, praying to Mary and other saints ... this list of non-Biblical doctrines and beliefs could be easily well expanded.

STIGMATA IS NOT OF ALMIGHTY GOD

The effects of stigmata wounds are observable, documented and real. They are excruciating as the victim experiences real physical injuries and bleeding of the same types of wounds that Yeshua Himself experienced while on the cross. And

---

[170] Romans 8:17

rather than experiencing it only once as Yeshua himself did, these stigmatics typically experience it week after week!

The practice of marking one's self with wounds in worship of one's god, *stigma*, came out of the pagan religions as a means of physically marking one's flesh by cutting deep gashes that would form scars, piercing the body or carving symbols into one's flesh. The wounds would heal as large raised scars. It was a means of identifying someone with his or her spiritual god. While stigma itself can be traced to the Hellenistic (Greek) culture, such marking is a specifically prohibited act within the Law of God:

> Do not cut your bodies for the dead or put tattoo marks on yourselves. I am AHEYEH.[171]

As such, it leads one to reason that God would not be *marking* his faithful children with this *stigma* when He Himself has specifically prohibited this action within His own Law; which is a reflection of His own Character.

It is noteworthy that even devout Catholics will admit that stigmata may not be of God. Father Vey, in the previously mentioned interview about Therese Neumann, warned:

> We must be very careful when we hear the claim of a living stigmatist. Sometimes the devil can cause the wounds, so the Church must proceed with great caution.[172]

The Catholic Church clearly feels that it is in her power to determine at her sole discretion whether the horrific bleeding

---

[171] Leviticus 19:28
[172] FREZE p. 301

wounds of stigmata are a *gift from God* or are *caused by the devil;* just like she is convinced that it is up to the her to determine which writings should legitimately be considered Scripture and which writings should be considered *heretical*. Protestantism has fallen nicely in line with the Catholic Church regarding which writings are *inspired;* are today's Christian or Messianic believers willing to fall as nicely in line by letting the Catholic Church also judge whether stigmata is a *gift* or a *curse*? And if so, why would we not be willing to defer to her judgment and let her determine which saint or mystic may be truly speaking for God, and which saint or mystic may in fact be a false prophet?

If we in Christendom or Messianic Judaism are *not* willing to cede this authority to the Catholic Church, the next question we are faced with is: when it comes to mystics, visionaries, or prophets, how can you tell the gold from the dross? How can you identify a false prophet?

CHAPTER 19

❖

THE PATH OF A MYSTIC

Part of what has excited and reassured Christianity about Paul's message over the years is the dramatic, supernatural aspect of his calling. *Facts tell and stories sell* is the frequently quoted sales mantra, and Paul has one giant humdinger of a story!

Paul's fantastical, supernatural, life-changing experience happened while on the road to Damascus:

> As he neared Damascus on his journey, suddenly a light from heaven flashed around him. He fell to the ground and heard a voice say to him, "Saul, Saul, why do you persecute me?"
>
> "Who are you, Lord?" Saul asked.
>
> "I am Yeshua, whom you are persecuting," he replied. "Now get up and go into the city, and you will be told what you must do."

The men traveling with Saul stood there speechless; they heard the sound but did not see anyone. Saul got up from the ground, but when he opened his eyes he could see nothing. So they led him by the hand into Damascus. For three days he was blind, and did not eat or drink anything.[173]

Enter another apparent visionary into the story, Ananias.

> The Lord called to him in a vision, 'Ananias!'
> 'Yes, Lord,' he answered.
> The Lord told him, 'Go to the house of Judas on Straight Street and ask for a man from Tarsus named Saul, for he is praying. In a vision he has seen a man named Ananias come and place his hands on him to restore his sight.'
> 'Lord,' Ananias answered, 'I have heard many reports about this man and all the harm he has done to your holy people in Jerusalem. And he has come here with authority from the chief priests to arrest all who call on your name.'
> But the Lord said to Ananias, 'Go! This man is my chosen instrument to proclaim my name to the Gentiles and their kings and to the people of Israel. I will show him how much he must suffer for my name.'
> Then Ananias went to the house and entered it. Placing his hands on Saul, he said, 'Brother Saul, the Lord—Yeshua, who appeared to you on the road as you were coming here—has sent me so that you may see again and be filled with the Holy Spirit.' Immedi-

---

[173] Acts 9:3-8

ately, something like scales fell from Saul's eyes, and he could see again. He got up and was baptized, and after taking some food, he regained his strength.

Saul spent several days with the disciples in Damascus. At once he began to preach in the synagogues that Yeshua is the Son of God. All those who heard him were astonished and asked, 'Isn't he the man who raised havoc in Jerusalem among those who call on this name? And hasn't he come here to take them as prisoners to the chief priests?' Yet Saul grew more and more powerful and baffled the Jews living in Damascus by proving that Yeshua is the Messiah.[174]

Paul's *mystic calling* illustrates what will become a very familiar story. An ordinary but fervently religious person has a life-threatening or life-altering event, suffers a severe physical ailment that may even threaten his or her life and then, in what appears to be a supernatural intervention, is miraculously healed of this physical ailment. The devotee now has a powerful mandate to share the message of this paranormal event with everyone around them. Eventually, this individual might start his or her own church.

Paul's experience is not an atypical one, because the road to religious fervor and even grandiosity is quite often paved with mysticism and visions. The daunting task of the believer is to identify and separate those mystics who are called by God from those who are not. Let us look into this phenomena a bit further by briefly analyzing a few other famous mystics to see if they follow this same progression.

---

[174] Acts 9:10-23

We will start by looking more closely at Therese Neumann, the Catholic mystic and stigmatic mentioned in the previous chapter. At the age of 20, Ms. Neumann had an accident in which she became blind and paralyzed. Five years later after devotedly praying to a specific Catholic saint, she received her sight back. Miraculously, her paralysis was also reversed. As a bonus, she received an additional *blessing,* the *miracle* of weekly stigmata. This miracle came with an additional cost: because she could no longer eat regular food or drink regular water, she could only keep down one (*blessed*) communion wafer per day.[175]

The Hindu Yogi Paramhansa Yogananda, whose path intersected with that of Ms. Neumann in 1935, had a life-threatening experience when he was stricken with Asiatic cholera at the age of eight. While on his deathbed, so weak he was unable to physically move, he mentally bowed and showed his devotion to a deceased *Kriya Yoga* master named *Lahiri Mahasaya,* after which time his life was quite miraculously spared. He describes the event:

> I gazed at his photograph and saw there a blinding light, enveloping my body and the entire room. My nausea and other uncontrollable symptoms disappeared; I was well. At once I felt strong enough to bend over and touch Mother's feet in appreciation of her immeasurable faith in her guru. Mother pressed her head repeatedly against the little picture.
>
>   "O Omnipresent Master, I thank thee that thy light hath healed my son!"

---

[175]YOGANANDA Chapter 39

I realized that she too had witnessed the luminous blaze through which I had instantly recovered from a usually fatal disease.[176]

This incident placed the young boy firmly on a path to mysticism. Subsequently Yogananda, a very popular speaker when he came to America, was instrumental in exposing the Western world to his mystical philosophy and religion.

Joseph Smith, the founder of Mormonism who was considered to be its greatest *prophet* and mystic, lived during the religious fervor of the early eighteen hundreds. Young Joseph was about 16 years old when he became concerned about religious matters. He was especially distressed about the certainty of being forgiven of his sins. While praying his first audible prayer in a secluded grove of trees near his home, his prayer was interrupted by a *being from the unseen world* that was more powerful than any that he had encountered before.

This *spirit* apparently caused his tongue to swell up in his mouth so that he could not speak. Some of the accounts he gives describe how he was covered with a thick darkness; thinking he would be utterly destroyed.

At young Joseph's darkest and most hopeless moment when he knelt a third time to pray, he *saw a vision* where, of course, a *pillar of light* "brighter than the noonday sun" slowly descended on him. When it enveloped him, it was said to produce *a peculiar sensation*. "His mind was caught away from the natural objects with which he was surrounded, and he was enwrapped in a heavenly vision" where he *saw the Lord;* actually, *two beings* that he later attributed to be God the

---

[176] YOGANANDA Chapter 1

Father and Yeshua himself. *The Lord* gave him additional instructions at that time. Mr. Smith eventually became the founder of his own church, *The Church of Latter-day Saints,* or *Mormons.*[177]

In what is becoming a familiar refrain, let us last consider the *mystic calling* of Ellen G. White. This pioneer and founder of the Seventh-day Adventist Church is still considered to be Adventism's greatest authority next to the Bible.[178] Her *prophetic gift* was especially active in the latter eighteen hundreds.

Young Ellen suffered a terrible head injury when she was nine years old and was subsequently in a coma for three weeks. After she rather miraculously recovered, she became religiously fervent and eventually started having seemingly supernatural *visions* at the age of 17. In these numerous visions she was *taken to heaven,* presumably *saw* God our Father and Yeshua *in person,* and was subsequently *given* an enormous number of other prophetic messages, ostensibly from God, to relay to her fellow Adventist believers.

Like Paul and the Hindu sage Yogananda, Mrs. White also had a pivotal experience with a supernatural bright light that convinced her she had a heavenly calling. She described a meeting that was held at her parents' home in which she received what she felt was confirmation of her ministry:

> While praying, the thick darkness that had enveloped me was scattered, a bright light, like a ball of fire,

---

[177] SMITH, Joseph, Jr. (1832), *History of the Life of Joseph Smith*, in JESSEE, Dean C, *Personal Writings of Joseph Smith,* Salt Lake City: Deseret Book, 2002
[178] Some extremely devout Adventists will even place the authority of Ellen White's writings above that of the Bible. Instead of saying "What does the Bible say?" they instead inquire, "What does Sister White say about this?"

came towards me, and as it fell upon me, my strength was taken away. I seemed to be in the presence of Jesus and the angels. Again it was repeated, 'Make known to others what I have revealed to you.'[179]

Ellen White's *visions* were allegedly accompanied by supernatural phenomena such as apparent lack of respiration during these visions, superhuman strength as evidenced by being able to hold up a heavy Bible above her head for an extended amount of time, and other physical symptoms that were testified to by physicians in attendance. The Adventist Church that she helped found reverently considers Mrs. White's prolific writings to be completely and totally inspired by God; in fact, acceptance of the *Spirit of Prophecy* as evidenced in the ministry of Ellen White remains a fundamental belief of the Seventh-day Adventist Church.[180]

Ellen White's path to mysticism shares startling similarities with those of Paul, Therese Neumann, the Hindu Yogi, and Joseph Smith, doesn't it? The Protestant Christian will likely find it troubling that two of these mystics, Therese Neumann and Paramhansa Yogananda, both claimed to *see* and *experience*, while in a trance state, the same events of Yeshua's crucifixion. How was a Hindu yogi who believed in

---

[179] WHITE, Ellen G., *Spiritual Gifts* vol. 2, (1860), 37.

[180] Fundamental Belief number 18, *The Gift of Prophecy*:
"One of the gifts of the Holy Spirit is prophecy. This gift is an identifying mark of the remnant church and was manifested in the ministry of Ellen. G. White. As the Lord's messenger, her writings are a continuing and authoritative source of truth which provide for the church comfort, guidance, instruction, and correction. They also make clear that the Bible is the standard by which all teaching and experience must be tested. (Joel 2:28, 29; Acts 2:14-21; Heb. 1:1-3; Rev. 12:17; 19:10.)" Taken on 6/18/12 from http://www.adventist.org/beliefs/fundamental/index.html.

reincarnation, was the master of an Eastern mystery religion, and had a completely different set of scriptures, able to telepathically horn in on a vision being experienced by a Christian Catholic stigmatic? By what or whose power did he participate in her trance and vision? Was it by God's power, or the power of darkness?

Adventist readers are likely to be especially disturbed to see this meeting and unity of the minds between the Hindu sage and the Catholic mystic. But would Ellen White's own visions and trances about the Crucifixion event be out of place if she were in the company of these other mystics? Referring to her visions she clearly states, "I was shown..." and subsequently talks about *seeing* many of the very same things!

The bottom line is simply this: is the information that was *shown* via Mrs. White's visionary events significantly different than the information that was *shown* to this Catholic stigmatic and the Hindu sage? If the vision is essentially the same, thus appearing to originate from the same place, shouldn't followers of the Eternal One find this to be troubling?

It is natural to find the shared experiences of a *bright heavenly light* that is said to verify these *mystic callings* to be curious—especially in view of the fact that Paul himself warned his followers that Satan masquerades as an *angel of light*.[181] I am not saying that one should judge any individual's *mystic calling* to be false based entirely on Paul's *angel of light* warning, but on the other hand the inclusion of *heavenly light* in the supernatural calling experience should not be total

---

[181] 2 Corinthians 11:14

verification of heaven's actual involvement and endorsement, either!

In a curious reversal of events, Martin Luther, who is often called the *Father of the Protestant Reformation,* experienced a similar supernatural occurrence, but with far different results. He relates,[182]

> On Good Friday last, I being in my chamber in fervent prayer, contemplating with myself, how Christ my Saviour on the cross suffered and died for our sins, there suddenly appeared upon the wall a bright vision of our Saviour Christ, with the five wounds, steadfastly looking upon me, as if it had been Christ himself corporally. At first sight, I thought it had been some celestial revelation, but I reflected that it must needs be an illusion and juggling of the devil, for Christ appeared to us in his Word, and in a meaner and more humble form; therefore I spake to the vision thus: Avoid thee, confounded devil: I know no other Christ than he who was crucified, and who in his Word is pictured and presented unto me. Whereupon the image vanished, clearly showing of whom it came.

Having recently escaped from a religious system whose history was heavily seeded with visionaries, paranormal activities, and stigmatic and / levitating saints, Martin Luther understood that he should not let *supernatural visions* shape and define his beliefs. He realized that depending on such events to determine truth makes one extremely subject to deception; so he rebuked the phenomena as being *from the*

---

[182] LUTHER, Martin, Table Talk Section CCXXXVI

devil. Was he correct or incorrect in his actions? What would you have done?

DOES THE PRESENCE OF SUPERNATURAL PHENOMENA VALIDATE THAT THE MESSAGE IS FROM GOD?

It is remarkable that the journeys of these mystics are so extraordinarily similar in many respects. In our desire to understand the true Character of God, this leads us to a very crucial and critical question: if the pathway of a mystic is rather like that of other *visionaries*, what determines whether or not their resulting message is actually of God? Who determines if a mystic is *inspired?* Is it a given that if supernatural phenomena accompany their message, that God is the author? How about if there are additional signs, wonders, miracles, and unexplainable occurrences, such as healings and miracles? Does the presence of these phenomena verify the mystic's message?

It is obvious that not every mystic or self-described prophet in history has been working on orders from the enemy, far from it! There are many authentic prophets who have brought messages from God for people of troubled times. But what insures that a prophet's message is from God? In order to determine that, we need to ask ourselves a series of critical questions:

1. The prophets of God in the Hebrew Scriptures elevated our Heavenly Father, as did Yeshua himself.[183] Who do the mystics on *this side of the cross* edify? Upon whom is the focus of their *gospel message?*

---

[183] Matthew 5:16

2. What is the prophet or mystic saying about God and what God requires? Does this message line up with God's TRUE Torah, AHYH's TRUE instruction?

3. Is the prophet or mystic stating that our Father needs to be presented with a blood-drenched sacrifice in order to forgive His people; or like Yeshua and John the Baptist, is he or she preaching a gospel of *repentance?*[184]

4. By what means and method is the prophet or mystic getting his or her point across? Is he or she taking to heart Isaiah's instruction to *come and reason;* or inadvertently resorting to fantastical, super-naturally focused events such as stigmata or supernatural visions and paranormal phenomena in order to affirm his or her validity?

5. Does the prophet or mystic encourage you to think, study, pray, and seek out verification of their conclusions yourself, are does he or she encourage you to *simply believe* what he or she tells you?

6. Lastly, is the prophet or mystic a religious free agent, as it were, someone who has a choice in whether or not they receive these supernatural visions or stigmatic marks? Or, are they unable to free themselves from these ailments or events because a power beyond their control has been given dominion over their actual bodies?

---

[184] Matthew 3:8, 3:11; Mark 1:4; Luke 3:3

These questions will also be helpful in looking more specifically at the ministry of Paul of Tarsus. In Paul's very pivotal case, were his marks—his stigmata—really a blessing and sign of heavenly authority, as he claimed? Or were they instead part of a very real *punishment* sent by God?

CHAPTER 20

❖

PUNISHED BY GOD

Although we don't generally like to consider the issue of heavenly discipline, there are multiple occasions listed in Scripture where God brings down punishment on believers who disobey Him. One such person He chastised and punished was Paul. Paul openly admits that it was GOD who punished him with a *thorn in the flesh* for being, of all things, too boastful.

Indeed, if you consider the sum of Paul's writings, you will find a *lot* of boasting! Paul boasts about the flock *he* is shepherding, he boasts about *his* successes in the ministry, he boasts about the grand visions and revelations *he* sees that no one else does—and all of these boastful statements point back to *himself*. In the end, *he*, Paul, is really the only one being elevated in his boasts; not God and not the others Paul is leading.

As Christian or Messianic believers, we often attempt to *reframe* Paul's boastful comments by insisting that Paul was, of course, *humble,* but that he just liked to boast about his *spiritual successes* in the ministry. Upon closer scrutiny, such a thought does not really make any sense. Truly humble people do not boast, especially about themselves. Furthermore, our Father would have no reason to mete out punishment when we are being humble and acting with humility!

Yeshua said,

> So when you give to the needy, do not announce it with trumpets, as the hypocrites do in the synagogues and on the streets, to be honored by men. I tell you the truth; they have received their reward in full. But when you give to the needy, do not let your left hand know what your right hand is doing, so that your giving may be in secret. Then your Father, who sees what is done in secret, will reward you.[185]

Paul's religious boasting is what the Pharisees had been doing, and it was exactly what Yeshua had taught his own disciples not to do. In many ways, the goal is not about how big the ministry is getting, but rather how well we are personally upholding what God taught us to be and to do within His Law. The Eternal One tells us quite clearly what He thinks about hubris in the hearts and minds of His people, and what such arrogance is like from His perspective. Speaking of King Saul, Samuel wrote:

> For rebellion is like the sin of divination, and arrogance like the evil of idolatry.[186]

---

[185] Matthew 6:2-4
[186] 1 Samuel 15:23

God equates arrogance with the sin of idolatry, self-worship, and self-idolization. In other words, such idolatry is a form of worshiping one's self; a putting of one's self even before Almighty God. This kind of idolatry, self-idolization and self-worship—especially within a religious context—violates the First Commandment. We are, in essence, ceasing to put God first and have now put ourselves first; we elevate the creation above the Creator.

From the historical accounts we have available, we can extrapolate quite a number of characteristics about Paul and his ministry. It is most likely safe to say that Paul didn't just bring up his boasting out of thin air in his letter to the Corinthian church. For some very compelling reason, Paul indeed felt the need to write about this issue, and what it was that God had done to him. As such, Paul addresses the issue head on, and with all of the flair he is capable of.

Paul begins by giving us his version of the story. First, he offers that he likes to boast about his successes in the ministry. He boasts about the surpassingly great revelations that he has been receiving from God; indeed he asserts that God has taken him either bodily or in the spirit into the *Third Heaven*, which is purportedly the dwelling place of God. Paul is convinced that it is God who has been blessing him in the extreme. He concludes that *because* of his boasting about his blessings and revelations and successes, our loving Father has given him *a thorn in the flesh* to keep him humble.

Paul discloses,

> To keep me from becoming conceited because of these surpassingly great revelations, there was given me a thorn in my flesh, a messenger of Satan, to torment me. Three times I pleaded with the Lord to take it

away from me. But he said to me, 'My grace is sufficient for you, for my power is made perfect in weakness.' Therefore I will boast all the more gladly about my weaknesses, so that Christ's power may rest on me.[187]

Before we get too focused on what this *thorn* actually was, let's at least try to be as objective as possible for a moment about what Paul says and then does about this *thorn in the flesh* punishment from God.

In Paul's own words, God is chastising Paul for his boasting—his conceit. Paul is being punished, chastised, and *disciplined* by his Creator for his hubris. But rather than address his own sin and repent of the issue of hubris, Paul comes up with an unusual and even troubling response to what God has done. After acknowledging that God has indeed disciplined him, Paul's response to God's chastisement is to make an excuse and blame it on God. Paul claims that God said to him:

> My grace is sufficient for you, for my power is made perfect in weakness.

This is a ridiculous justification! God does not tell us to keep sinning so that we should use his grace, his willingness to forgive, as some kind of license to keep on sinning! This was the admonishment of the book of Jude—not to respect anyone who used God's grace as a license to continue sinning.[188]

God says through the prophet Isaiah,

---

[187] 2 Corinthians 12:7-9
[188] Jude 1:4

> ...Wash and make yourselves clean. Take your evil deeds out of my sight! Stop doing wrong, learn to do right![189]

The other very glaring issue here with regard to God's Character and God's response to Paul—and it is one that Christendom completely misses—is that *God will always forgive the truly repentant heart.* God says of Himself,

> AHEYEH, AHEYEH God, the compassionate and gracious God, slow to anger, abounding in love and faithfulness; maintaining love to thousands, and forgiving wickedness, rebellion and sin.[190]

In direct contrast to the texts discussing God's forgiving nature, Paul says that God *refused* to remove the punishment—refused to forgive him—of his boasting and hubris. Paul says that he pleaded with God three times to take the punishment/thorn away, but God flatly refused!

Now remember, Paul has clearly stated that it was *God Himself* who punished him for his boasting. In response, Paul says that that God told him that, "My grace is sufficient for you, for my power is made perfect in weakness." Unfortunately, Paul has no intention of repenting here, but says

---

[189] Isaiah 1:16 NIV 1984. Consider also Ezekiel 18:30-32 where God says, "Therefore, O house of Israel, I will judge you, each one according to his ways, declares the Lord AHYH. Repent! Turn away from all your offenses; then sin will not be your downfall. Rid yourselves of all the offenses you have committed, and get a new heart and a new spirit. Why will you die, O house of Israel? For I take no pleasure in the death of anyone, declares the Lord AHYH. Repent and live!"
[190] Exodus 34:6-7a

rather defiantly, "I will keep on boasting!" This is a conscious choice to keep on sinning!

At some point, if we continually refuse to acknowledge our sin and repent, God will indeed turn us over to our own sin.[191] God declares that He will place a *stumbling block* before all those who fail to follow His Law and Commandments and remain unrepentant in their sin.[192]

Unfortunately, Paul lands himself smack in the middle of this dire warning from the Almighty. But just what was Paul's *thorn*, his punishment that God gave him and then refused to remove?

---

[191] Ezekiel 20:21-26 (CEV) states, "But the children also rebelled against me. They refused to obey my laws and teachings, and they treated the Sabbath as any other day. I became angry and decided to punish them in the desert. But I did not. That would have disgraced me in front of the nations that had seen me bring the Israelites out of Egypt. So I solemnly swore that I would scatter the people of Israel across the nations, because they had disobeyed my laws and ignored my teachings; they had disgraced my Sabbath and worshiped the idols their ancestors had made. I gave them laws that bring punishment instead of life, and I let them offer me unacceptable sacrifices, including their first-born sons. I did this to horrify them and to let them know that I, AHEYEH, was punishing them."
[192] Ezekiel 3:20, 18:30

CHAPTER 21

❖

A Thorn in the Flesh

Over the years, many well-meaning theologians have attempted to offer what Paul's mysterious *thorn in the flesh* really was. Some have postulated that Paul had some physically debilitating handicap: poor eyesight, a wound that wouldn't heal, or epilepsy. A few more liberal souls, many of the Episcopal persuasion, have speculated that Paul was gay, and theorize that this explains his apparent self-loathing. Others simply assume and conclude that we really do not know what his *thorn* actually was.

This kind of wild speculation about Paul's *thorn* is a huge enigma in the study of the Scriptures because if we just read Paul's own words instead of trying to make assumptions, we'll realize that he is very specific about what this *thorn* was! We just need to read Paul's own words and follow them to their logical conclusion.

First, take note that what modern Christianity has traditionally called a *thorn* is not an actual *thorn* at all. The word translated as *thorn* is *skolops* in the Greek. This Greek word does not refer to a mere splinter, but rather *a large wooden pale, a pole, a pointed stake,* more like something used to anchor tents.[193] Rather than being something that might be a minor annoyance to you as you work in the garden, it is actually a very big deal! For reasons that will be made clear in a moment, Christian tradition has sought to downplay Paul's *large wooden stake* and portray it as an annoyance, just a *thorn.*

In 2 Corinthians 12:7 Paul very clearly states that because of his boasting God has tormented him with a *thorn* in his flesh. In most modern translations of the Bible we read Paul saying something like,

> ...there was given me a thorn in my flesh, a messenger of Satan, to torment me.

What usually gets translated as *messenger of Satan* is actually *aggelos satan* in the Greek. The Greek term *aggelos* simply means *messenger* or *one who is sent;* it is also the Greek root of the English term *angel.*

Angel? Yes. Angel.

We need to carefully note that the word *aggelos* can be translated into English in one of two ways depending upon the nature of the *subject* being referred to. *Aggelos* is *always* translated as *messenger* when referring to a *human* being, and *always* translated as *angel* when referring specifically to a *supernatural* being. Whether *aggelos* is translated into English as *messenger* or *angel* is entirely dependent upon the nature of

---

[193] Thayer's Greek Lexicon

the noun to which it belongs; whether physical, such as a man, or supernatural, such as a being sent from God.[194]

The term *aggelos* is a well-understood term that is used nearly 200 times in the New Testament's Greek. Paul himself uses the term *aggelos* thirteen other times within his epistles and in *all* instances he is referring to a supernatural being. He even refers to himself as an *aggelos* of God. This elevation of his own character is something that is not at all out of character for Paul; but even here the translators render the passage correctly because even though Paul is talking about himself, the subject is still an *angel sent by God.*

Now here is the problem: The *one and only time aggelos* is rendered in translation as *messenger* instead of *angel* when clearly referring to a *supernatural* subject (a supernatural being) is when the translators refer to Paul's *thorn*—Paul's *aggelos satan* that was sent by God.[195] To render the Bible

---

[194] *Aggelos* is not a difficult word for scholars to translate. It is used 186 times in the *New Testament*. There are six instances where translators consistently render *aggelos* as simply *messenger* when in reference to human subjects. When used in reference to supernatural subjects, the term *aggelos* is consistently rendered 179 times as *angel*.

There are clear examples of the consistent translation within other areas of Scripture showing the always consistent translation of the Greek within this context of to whom an *aggelos*, whether a human *messenger* or supernatural *angel*, belongs.

Mathew 25 presents such an additional example; verse 31 accurately presents the *Son of Man* appearing with his holy *angels* (*aggelos*); and likewise verse 41 also accurately presents the exact same context of the *devil* being punished with his *angels* (*aggelos*). The word translated as *angels* in Matthew uses is the exact same word Paul uses—*aggelos*—within the same supernatural context (*satan/diabolos*).

[195] In the Greek, *aggelos satan* has been traditionally and quite deliberately mistranslated within a majority of mainstream Bible versions as *messenger of Satan,* beginning as early as the first major Protestant translation, the Geneva Bible, and also within the KJV, ESV, NIV, NASB, etc.

passage to be consistent with every other use of *aggelos* within the Bible, and to correctly translate what Paul is saying, the passage should read:

> ...there was given me a large wooded stake in my flesh, an angel of Satan, to torment me.[196]

Let's not mince words here: an *angel of Satan* is by anyone's definition *a demonic spirit*, a *demon*. Period. This is no mere *thorn*, but a major ordeal! Furthermore, it is a consequence that God has *refused* to remove from Paul.

Our modern mainstream Bible translators also realize this, which is why they have attempted to water down Paul's admission with a deliberate mistranslation of Paul's words.[197] This is completely understandable. Who wants to be the popular mainstream scholar or pastor who is tasked to tell the rest of Christendom that Paul was tormented not just externally but *in his flesh* by an actual real *demon* of Satan that God refused to remove? It is therefore completely understandable to see why Paul's *punishment by God* has been completely reframed; recast as nothing more serious than a mere *thorn*.

Now, lest we believe that this phrase *aggelos satan* is being used allegorically for a physical disease or other ailment, consider that in all of these uses of the term *aggelos* within the New Testament, it is always used to denote a *being*, a *messenger*, whether physical or spiritual, and never a physical

---

[196] Other versions also footnote the translation: *or angel*.

[197] There are some other Bible translations that indeed get this translation correct. The Wycliffe Bible, an early *New Testament* translation c. 1382, and the modern Contemporary English Version (CEV) also *correctly* translate the passage as *angel of Satan!*

condition or disease. Remember, the word *aggelos* specifically means *one who is sent, a messenger*. *Aggelos* has nothing to do with infirmity or disease.

Christian scholars are not stupid people – they indeed know what *aggelos satan* means! But because Paul is a beloved canonized author within the Bible, they deal with this *problem passage* by deliberately massaging the translation of the Pauline text using a mechanism called *hermeneutics*, sometimes referred to as a *preferred, proper* or even the *accepted* hermeneutic. This *preferred hermeneutic* is simply a biased perspective that allows Christendom to prove whatever doctrine it desires using the Scriptures, no matter what the Scriptures actually say.[198]

As such, Christian scholars begin their *exegesis* (study / interpretation / translation) of the Pauline text with an *accepted* (i.e. totally biased) hermeneutic that places Paul in a hyper standing of inerrant inspiration and utter infallibility. It is this beloved hermeneutic for Paul that forces the Christian scholar to now sidestep well-known Greek meanings and definitions to downplay the egregious nature of Paul's *large wooden stake* to that of a mere *thorn;* and to also abandon clear and consistent translation of *aggelos* so that Paul's *angel of Satan* becomes merely an *evil messenger*. Furthermore, these scholars now distance themselves from their own watered-down translation and begin assigning new interpretive meanings to Paul's otherwise very clear words, "Oh, Paul's *messenger* was bad eyesight, or epilepsy," and so on.

Both Christianity and Messianic Judaism have a long history of selecting those words of Paul's that they think

---

[198] It is said that "Apologetics / Hermeneutics is Christianity's attempt at making the Scriptures say something they don't while ignoring that which they actually do."

should be taken literally and minimizing those they think should not. For example; when Paul says that *Yeshua is the end of the law*, we take these words literally and proclaim, "Yeshua abolished the Law!"[199] But when Paul says he was *tormented by an angel of Satan*, we suddenly want to take these words figuratively. So, we downplay and recast these plainly written words, as "Paul was afflicted with a mere thorn."

Was Paul's *thorn* an isolated case? Not likely. Interestingly enough, there are segments of today's Christian church that show signs of being afflicted with similar *thorns* to that which afflicted Paul. For example, consider the curious case of a charismatic South African preacher named Rodney Howard-Browne. Listen to him describe his *mystic calling* in 1979:

> Suddenly the fire of God fell on me. It started on my head and went right down to my feet. His power burned in my body and stayed like that for three whole days....
>
> My whole body was on fire from the top of my head to the soles of my feet. Out of my belly began to flow a river of living water. I began to laugh uncontrollably and then I began to weep and then speak with other tongues.
>
> I was so intoxicated on the wine of the Holy Ghost that I was literally beside myself. The fire of God was coursing through my whole being and it didn't quit... Because of that encounter with the

---

[199] Matthew 5:17-20 completely contradicts Paul here also. Jesus plainly says, *"Do not think that I have come to abolish the Law or the Prophets ..."*

Lord, my life was radically changed from that day on.[200]

After his *mystic calling*, Dr. Howard-Browne went on to establish a revival phenomenon in which *holy laughter* became the hallmark of his ministry. Based on his work and philosophy, the early 1990s gave rise to a movement known as the *Toronto Blessing;* a charismatic, Pentecostal church movement that was marked by wild and uncontrollable bouts of this *holy laughter*. Under the purported influence of *the Spirit*, worshippers would roll on the floor wildly laughing; looking to supernatural signs and wonders to convince them that the *Holy Spirit of God* was taking over their bodies and consciousness. They would speak in tongues, bark like dogs, roar like lions, and stagger like drunks *in the Spirit*. Under the *anointing* of this so-called *holy laughter*, some believers would even begin to strip their clothes off! [201]

The majority of Christians, the more conservative ones at least, will regretfully admit that the above actions are not the sign of the pure and holy Spirit of God, but in fact are an indication that current Christianity is tormented and afflicted with its own supernatural *thorns*; its own *aggelos satan*.

---

[200] HOWARD-BROWNE, Rodney M., *The Touch of God*, 1992, p. 74
[201] BURNS, Cathy, *Unholy Laughter, Part 1,* found at http://www.deceptioninthechurch.com/laugh1.htm on 7/21/12

CHAPTER 22

❖

A Tale of Two Benjamites

There is an irony and a corollary that escapes quite a few Christian or Messianic believers and even many Biblical scholars. King Saul of Israel and Saul-turned-Paul of Tarsus have some very stark similarities in their lives, not the least of which is that they share the same name.

Both Paul and King Saul also had very similar *thorns in the flesh*. Like Paul, King Saul was also arrogant and refused to listen to God. Remember, Samuel warned Saul that, "rebellion is like the sin of divination, and arrogance like the evil of idolatry."[202] Both men were also on paths of murderous behavior. King Saul was slaughtering the priests under Samuel[203] and Saul-turned-Paul was slaughtering the followers of God who had learned from Yeshua and the Twelve.[204]

---

[202] 1 Samuel 15:23
[203] 1 Samuel 22
[204] Acts 8:1, 9:1; 1 Corinthians 15:9; Galatians 1:13 & 23

Perhaps not so coincidentally, both Saul and Paul were also Benjamites, from the same tribe of Benjamin. Benjamin was the son whom Jacob "blessed" as a *ravenous wolf* and one who *devours prey.*[205] King Saul's arrogant and murderous behavior could easily be described as that of a murderous *ravenous wolf.* Later, the Prophets themselves would write of Israel's own evil leadership in the same manner, describing an evil religious leadership as roaring lions who tear and devour men as their prey.[206]

This very Hebraic imagery is lost to us within the modern world, but it was not lost to first-century believers. Yeshua also used this very same prophetic imagery when he spoke of false religious leaders (false prophets, false apostles), calling such false leaders, *ravenous wolves:*[207]

> Beware of the false prophets [leaders, apostles], who come to you in sheep's clothing, but inwardly are *ravenous wolves.* You will know them by their fruits [what they do and say; how well they uphold the Law and Commandments of God]. Grapes [truthful teachings] are not gathered from thorn bushes [dishonest teachers] nor figs from thistles, are they? ...
>
> Not everyone who says to me, 'Lord, Lord,' will enter the kingdom of heaven, but he who does the will of My Father who is in heaven will enter. Many will say to me on that day, 'Lord, Lord, did we not prophe-

---

[205] Genesis 49:27 This is not the kind of "blessing" one might expect from one's own father!

[206] Ezekiel 22:24-26

[207] Matthew 7:15 NASB Please note that once again the NIV deliberately mistranslates this passage as *ferocious wolves,* perhaps in an attempt to distance Paul from the very specific *ravenous wolf* corollary that the NASB clearly cross-references as valid!

sy in your name, and in your name cast out demons, and in your name perform many miracles?' And then I will declare to them, 'I never knew you; *depart from me, you who practice lawlessness* [void or have contempt for the Law of God].[208]

In telling this parable, Yeshua was actually warning us about whom we should look out for and avoid. In essence, Yeshua was giving us a prophecy against a *ravenous wolf*. The *ravenous wolf* corollary would not at all be at all lost on the Hebrews of the day; they would indeed be looking for a *murderous Benjamite*. And the one man who fit this lawless and murderous pattern to a *T* was indeed Saul-called-Paul of Tarsus!

Did the Holy Spirit of God reveal Paul's final punishment and ultimate downfall, and let Yeshua foresee that Paul's actions would be a veritable repeat of his own namesake, King Saul?

There are many more astonishing parallels between Saul, the first king of Israel, and Saul-turned-Paul, the Christian leader. Saul, the king of Israel from the tribe of Benjamin, was 30 years old when God selected him to lead the Hebrew people. When he was called for his mission, his heart was changed in one day and he started to prophesy. After that he was spiritually respected and revered by the people, and the saying became, "Is Saul also among the prophets?"[209]

Unfortunately, King Saul did not stay true to his calling. He "did evil in the eyes of AHYH" and was finally rejected by God when he disobeyed God's explicit commands.[210] It is

---

[208]Matthew 7:15-23 NASB Amplification supplied.
[209] 1 Samuel 10:9-11
[210] 1 Samuel 15

remarkable to note that his disobedience was tied directly to his desire to offer blood sacrifices and burnt offerings. While we only get a one-sided or groomed report of the ancient story from the book of Samuel that seems to support that Samuel was in favor of these sacrifices, take note of what Samuel tells Saul,

> Does AHYH delight in burnt offerings and sacrifices as much as in obeying the voice of AHYH? To obey is better than sacrifice, and to heed is better than the fat of rams. For rebellion is like the sin of divination, and arrogance like the evil of idolatry. Because you have rejected the word of AHYH, he has rejected you as king.[211]

Many theologians have offered that King Saul's sin was the offering of sacrifices outside the Levitical laws (Saul wasn't a Levite). However, Samuel's words leave open a much broader if not less obvious reason why God rejected Saul—because God didn't want blood sacrifice. "To obey is better than sacrifice" is consistent with what we see in the latter prophets' rejection of the priesthood's sacrificial system.

While Saul's kingdom was not taken away from him immediately, he would eventually succumb to God's punishment. The Biblical account is very clear about what happened to Saul during the final years of his reign.

> Now the Spirit of AHYH had departed from Saul, and an evil spirit *from AHYH* tormented him. Saul's at-

---

[211] 1 Samuel 15:20-23

tendants said to him, "See, an evil spirit from God is tormenting you."[212]

Apparently, this evil spirit came and went at will; only the psalmist David's music (which an alert reader of the psalms realizes are filled with lyrics about God's Character and His perfect Law) would give Saul relief from the evil spirit's influence.[213]

The length of Saul's reign remains under question by scholars. However, according to the Jewish historian Josephus, Saul reigned twenty years; eighteen while Samuel was alive and two more years after that.

Hundreds of years later, there came another great leader named *Saul*, also from the tribe of Benjamin and also around 30 years old at the time of his supposed *call from God*. Saul-turned-Paul had his life changed in one day on the Damascus road when he had his life-altering *vision*, was temporarily blinded, and became zealous for *his* gospel. This Saul also promoted blood sacrifice—human this time—as an avenue to spiritual forgiveness.[214]

The Most High God also afflicted this *Saul* with an evil spirit and this Saul, too, wanted to be rid of the demon. Saul-called-Paul begged God to remove this *stake*, this *angel of Satan*, and God refused. Paul's demon was still there, still afflicting him every so often just like King Saul. Yet Paul's *spiritual kingdom* was not taken away—not yet.

---

[212] 1 Samuel 16:14-15

[213] 1 Samuel 16:15, 23

[214] Samuel's rebuke to Saul could also very easily apply directly to Paul/formerly Saul, who, like his namesake and tribesman, so strongly promoted blood sacrifice as the way to gain God's forgiveness. See 1 Samuel 15:20-23

Like King Saul, Paul was still revered by many. However, his thinking and his judgment were now compromised by evil. Plagued by a *demon* sent by *God Almighty Himself*, Paul became firmly ensconced in the hands of Satan. And through this powerful evangelist and church planter, the enemy of God successfully created a *different Yeshua* with a *different gospel,* one that indeed came with a very *different spirit* attached to it.[215]

This parallel to Yeshua is made obvious when we begin to see how Paul likened himself to Yeshua the Messiah in numerous ways. To add emphasis and credence to Paul's anti-gospel, the enemy of God pursued a path of the miraculous with Paul. To cap it off, all of this masquerade was—and is still being—perpetrated in the name of the real *Yeshua HaMashiach.*

In Luke's *Acts of the Apostles,* Paul continually worked miracles in the name of *Yeshua HaMaschiach;* he reportedly healed people and raised the dead. Even objects that Paul touched were reportedly imbued with the power to heal. Paul took on followers called *disciples* and they were some twelve men in number![216]

Paul then specifically likened himself to Yeshua, saying about his infirmities within his letter to the Galatians:

> Even though my illness was a trial to you, you did not treat me with contempt or scorn. Instead, you welcomed me as if I were an *angel* (aggelos) *of God, as if I were Yeshua HaMaschiach himself.* What has happened to all your joy? I can testify that, if you could have

---

[215] 1 Samuel 15:22-23
[216] Acts 19:1-7

done so, you would have torn out your eyes and given them to me.[217]

Paul indeed had more than just a firm grip on the hearts and minds of these Galatian churches with his gospel up until this point in time. But note the last sentence of this plaintive passage here:

> Have I now become your enemy by telling you the truth?[218]

---

[217] Galatians 4:13-15
[218] Galatians 4:16

CHAPTER 23

❖

ABANDONED AND ALONE

At some point, the churches in Paul's home territory of Galatia and Asia Minor eventually came to see Paul and his particular version of the *gospel* in a much different light than we have been taught to see and believe today. As believers, we are only taught to think that these other churches became wayward because they rejected Paul. Because they rejected Paul, we automatically assume that these many churches throughout the region of Asia Minor and elsewhere were also rejecting the Messiah and his life-changing message of good news. But this is not the only possible scenario; there is another very valid explanation. The distress apparent in Paul's letter lets us know that the churches in Galatia had very likely started heeding the words of the Messiah and the teachings of the Apostles from Jerusalem, and as such had finally rejected Paul as being a *false christ*, a *false teacher*, and a *false apostle!*

The writer of Revelation speaks about the Church in Ephesus. John records a vision of Yeshua speaking to this church and saying,

> I know that you cannot tolerate wicked men, that you have tested *those who claim to be apostles but are not, and have found them false.*[219]

Paul visited Ephesus on two of his three missionary journeys. Ephesus was in Asia Minor and part of Paul's home territory, so to speak!

There is one final Saul/Paul parallel. We earlier discussed that according to the Jewish historian Josephus, Saul reigned 20 years; eighteen while Samuel was alive and two after that.[220] Paul wrote the book of Galatians in 53 A.D., approximately 20 years after his *conversion experience.*

By this time, Paul had been afflicted with the evil spirit from God and was clearly preaching a *different gospel.* Both men were entrusted with leading God's children. Both men betrayed that trust, disobeyed God, and were tormented by an evil spirit sent from God. Both of these great leaders lost their respective kingdoms, Saul when he was overthrown, and Paul when *everyone turned away* from him.

It seems hard to buy that all of these parallels between the two *Sauls* could simply be an amazing coincidence; and such a coincidence becomes nearly impossible to dismiss when you consider the words of Yeshua HaMaschiach. When he was asked about the end times, Yeshua answered:

---

[219] Revelation 2:2
[220] Antiquities Book 6, Ch. 14:9

> Watch out that no one deceives you. For many will come in my name, claiming, 'I am the Christ,' (i.e. God's anointed, chosen leader) and will deceive many... At that time if anyone says to you, 'Look, here is the Christ!' or, 'There he is!' do not believe it. For *false christs* and *false prophets* will appear and perform great signs and miracles to deceive even the elect—if that were possible. See, I have told you ahead of time.[221]

While we in the modern era tend to look at the above passage as referring to the actual end-of-the-world end times, we need to put the *end times* into the context and perspective of those to whom Yeshua was actually speaking. To the people of the time, Yeshua was discussing something that would happen in their lifetime, something in the very near future! After all, why would he bother telling his own disciples to watch for *false christs* (false messiahs) if the end times were to be thousands of years hence? This warning was for them during their current time period, as well as for us today!

In Paul's second letter to Timothy, we find him languishing in prison in Rome. With Paul effectively out of commission, the Jerusalem Church, founded by the Apostles who personally walked with Messiah, was now free to repair the damage wrought by Paul's other *gospel*.

Just what was this *other gospel* that Paul was preaching, and how did it stack up against the words of Yeshua and the prophets who came before him?

---

[221] Matthew 24:4-5, 23-25

PART IV
Deconstructing Paulianity

CHAPTER 24

❖

THE TRUE GOSPEL VS. THE NUGOSPEL

The central pillar of Galatians, in fact, the cornerstone of the Pauline *gospel* or *NuGospel* as we will call it, is that the TRUE Law of God is more or less moot for salvation and that *faith by itself*—and not obedience—is the only path of salvation. To Paul's way of thinking, *faith alone* is the path that was really followed by the patriarchs and prophets of the Scriptures.

Galatians 3 reveals a great deal about Paul's exclusive NuGospel. In this chapter, Paul levels a severe admonishment upon the Christians within the region of Galatia[222] who have been faithfully observing God's instruction, God's Law, as taught by the *Chief Apostles* in Jerusalem. Within this section of his letter, Paul builds his case to dispense with obedience

---

[222] This region comprised about one third of Asia Minor and included the cities of Antioch in Pisidia, Derbe, Iconium, and Lystra.

to God's TRUE Law and demands that the first-century believers accept *faith alone* in (Paul's version of) the Messiah for justification and deliverance from sin.

Paul begins his dissertation by using Abraham as his primary example of *faith*. Paul eloquently asserts his reasoning that because Abraham had *faith*, all who have *faith* like Abraham are therefore children of Abraham and will, like Abraham, be saved. Paul says in verses 6-9:

> Consider Abraham: "He believed God, and it was credited to him as righteousness." [Gen. 15:6] Understand, then, that those who believe are children of Abraham. The Scripture foresaw that God would justify the Gentiles by faith, and announced the gospel in advance to Abraham: "All nations will be blessed through you." [Gen. 12:3; 18:18; 22:18] So those who have faith are blessed along with Abraham, the man of faith [i.e. belief].

But what kind of *faith* [belief] was it that Abraham actually had? Was it an empty faith of belief alone? Or perhaps it was a faith of non-obedience? To answer that question, we need to look back at God's conversation with Abraham's son Isaac in Genesis 26:

> [I, AHEYEH] will confirm the oath I swore to your father Abraham. I will make your descendants as numerous as the stars in the sky and will give them all these lands, and through your offspring all nations on earth will be blessed, because Abraham obeyed me and

kept my requirements, my commands, my decrees and my laws.[223]

By reading the actual text itself, it becomes obvious that God blessed Abraham and his descendants and indeed the whole earth because Abraham had obeyed God and faithfully observed God's instruction, His TRUE law. It is this *faithful obedience* that Paul now comes vehemently against in Galatians 3!

Paul uses Abraham as his *witness* by taking what was written about Abraham—and what Abraham actually did within his faithful relationship with Almighty God—to weave a distorted description of who Abraham actually was, and what actions Abraham was indeed blessed for.

Lifting some additional misquotes from the Hebrew Scriptures, Paul begins to chastise and berate those who feel called to observe the TRUE Law of God:

> All who rely on observing the law are under a curse, for it is written: "Cursed is everyone who does not continue to do everything written in the Book of the Law."[224]

While totally ignoring the fact that Abraham obeyed God in faithfulness to achieve (earn, merit, work) his righteous standing with God, Paul asserts that all who rely on their obedience to God's TRUE Law for their salvation are under some kind of *curse* of this Law. To uphold his reasoning, Paul quotes Deuteronomy 27:26, which says,

---

[223] Genesis 26:3b-5
[224] Galatians 3:10 quoting Deuteronomy 27:26

> Cursed is everyone who does not continue to do everything written in the Book of the Law.

Never has the TRUE Law of God been misconstrued by any God-fearing son or daughter of Abraham to be a curse! There are dozens of passages in the Psalms and other parts of Scripture where David and the Prophets are calling the TRUE Law of God *perfect*[225] and praising God for his Law. As David says,

> How I love your Law![226]

As another witness in the New Testament, James says,

> But the man who looks intently into the perfect law that gives freedom, and continues to do this, not forgetting what he has heard, but *doing it*—he will be blessed in what he does.[227]

How can these men of God speak this glowingly about a *curse?* Was David really saying to God in Psalm 119, "How I love your *curse?*" Was James really offering that God's *perfect curse* gives man his freedom?[228]
    Is the TRUE Law of God Really a *curse?*

---

[225] Psalm 19:7
[226] Psalm 119
[227] James 1:25
[228] For the record, we can also conclude that Paul is not meaning the oral laws of the Scribes and Pharisees here (i.e. the Talmud) because Paul is indeed quoting Torah (the Law) directly.

It is beneficial to look at Paul's quote from Deuteronomy 27:9-26 in its full context in order to understand what the author is really saying:

Then Moses and the priests, who are Levites, said to all Israel, 'Be silent, O Israel, and listen! You have now become the people of AHYH your God. Obey AHYH your God and follow his commands and decrees that I give you today.'

On the same day Moses commanded the people: When you have crossed the Jordan, these tribes shall stand on Mount Gerizim to bless the people: Simeon, Levi, Judah, Issachar, Joseph and Benjamin. And these tribes shall stand on Mount Ebal to pronounce curses: Reuben, Gad, Asher, Zebulun, Dan and Naphtali. The Levites shall recite to all the people of Israel in a loud voice:

'Cursed is the man who carves an image or casts an idol—a thing detestable to AHYH, the work of the craftsman's hands—and sets it up in secret. ...

Cursed is the man who dishonors his father or his mother. ...

Cursed is the man who moves his neighbor's boundary stone. ...

Cursed is the man who leads the blind astray on the road.

Cursed is the man who withholds justice from the alien, the fatherless or the widow. ...

Cursed is the man who sleeps with his father's wife, for he dishonors his father's bed. ...

Cursed is the man who has sexual relations with any animal. ...

Cursed is the man who sleeps with his sister, the daughter of his father or the daughter of his mother. ...

Cursed is the man who sleeps with his mother-in-law. ...

Cursed is the man who kills his neighbor secretly. ...

Cursed is the man who accepts a bribe to kill an innocent person. ...'

Take note that none of these things are *curses* but are, in fact, *instructions* on how to live in harmony with one's family and fellow human beings! Finally we come to Paul's convenient misquote from Torah.

'Cursed is the man who does not uphold the words of this law by carrying them out. Then all the people shall say, 'Amen!'

In context, God is not at all calling His TRUE Law a *curse* to those who attempt to abide its tenets. Instead, the real *curse* is on all who do these sinful and detestable things! Paul is quoting the words of Torah way out of context to make an erroneous and unfounded point.

The primary theme within these scriptures is that the man who obeys God's TRUE Law will have life![229] By reading the original writings in context, it is easy to determine that the TRUE Law of God itself is not at all a *curse*. Abiding God's TRUE Law is a blessing that, as James says, gives a man freedom.

Sin, or disobedience to God's TRUE Law, is the real curse.

Paul's insistence that we do not need to be held accountable to God's instruction is indeed seductive, but it leads to bewilderment in the mind of the reader who is trying to make all of the writings of Scripture fit together. When a Seeker of TRUTH starts looking closely at the writings of Paul in an effort to find answers to doctrinal discrepancies, an unsettling thought may start to tickle the corners of the mind. You start to question yourself, 'Have I had it wrong this whole time? Have I been focusing on the wrong thing? Is it really as simple as somehow drumming up enough *faith* and not worrying if my actions fall short of God's righteousness? Do the commandments of God have any authority over me, or am I somehow insulting God and trying to *work my way to heaven* by attempting to follow them?'

Considering the teachings contained in the book of Galatians, it is easy to understand why most self-proclaimed *Former Adventists*[230] will declare that Galatians is the book

---

[229] Nehemiah 9:29

[230] *Formers* or *Former SDA* is what a large number of people who have left the Adventist Church will affectionately call themselves. A large number typically end up in some type of *non-denominational* or *New Covenant Christian* Church. Others have embraced Catholicism or will become Baptists, etc.

that has set them free from the *curse* of the law, and led them out of Adventism into the shining light of Paul's *New Covenant Theology.*

CHAPTER 25

❖

THE NEW COVENANT CONTRADICTION

Recently I came across an article online that was directed specifically at confused and questioning Adventists. It instructed the bewildered reader, "If you are confused about the Gospel message in any way, study exclusively from the books of Paul for one month!" The author claimed that this activity would put to rest any doubts you may still have about the fact that the *Law of God* is no longer binding or applicable for you.

Interestingly, the technique seems to work. When Protestants who have previously exalted and endorsed God's TRUE Law begin to study only from Paul's epistles, their priorities begin to shift. They quickly lose respect for the authority of God's instruction and begin to look at God's Law as a curse rather than a blessing. As a result, they soon hurry to the nearest *New Covenant* Christian church, proclaiming joyfully to all their friends; "We are no longer *under the law!*

Paul said so!" Without considering the *Old Testament* directives or even the words of Yeshua that support the authority of God's TRUE Law, the argument is over before it has even begun.

While all Christian and Messianic believers consider the *New Covenant* to be a foundational tenet of both ancient and modern Christianity, most Christian believers are not aware that the *New Covenant* doctrine that defines Christianity is the exclusive invention of Paul of Tarsus, and is a fundamental part of his select *NuGospel*.

Paul's NuGospel states, in a nutshell, that God no longer *sees* you as a sinner, because when God looks at you all he sees is Yeshua, who presumably died in your place. What you do doesn't matter; the God of the Universe who knows all and sees all somehow doesn't *see* your sins. In fact, you no longer will be held accountable for your own sins, because Yeshua *paid it all* when he died on the cross.[231] Because Yeshua paid God's *blood price* for all past and future sins, man no longer needs to worry about his actions. He just has to *believe* that Yeshua is Lord and that *Yeshua paid the price for his sins,* and he will be *saved*.

Perhaps the most remarkable problem with this belief is that while God specifically and in no uncertain terms strictly prohibits human sacrifice as murder within His TRUE Law— Paul's *New Contract* (i.e. New Covenant, New Testament) gospel is all about God somehow demanding the blood of a human sacrifice to *atone* for the sins of the world!

Loosely based on a complete misinterpretation (or misappropriation) of Jeremiah 31:31, Paul's *New Covenant,*

---

[231] This is a common refrain in Christian doctrine and music. How many of us are not familiar with the song, "Jesus paid it all. All to Him I owe. Sin had left a crimson stain; He washed it white as snow." (Elvina Hall, 1865)

which is the basis of Paul's *NuGospel* and stars his *NuYeshua*, is designed to be an all-powerful mechanism within Paul's theological repertoire that literally gives him the power and authority to up-end and utterly denigrate the Law of God. Ironically, Paul totally misinterprets Jeremiah's discussion of the *renewed covenant* in Jeremiah 31:31 that was *specifically* meant for Israel and Judah, and reinterprets it to instead apply to Christian Gentiles.

The basic premise of Paul's NuGospel is that the Jews, who were under the *Old Contract* (Old Covenant, Old Testament) failed to follow the law perfectly to the letter. Therefore, God is said to have rejected them. Instead, He has chosen to pour out His blessing of a *New Covenant* on the Gentiles. (Is it any wonder now where Marcionism got its foundations and why Marcion included only the Pauline books as part of his original canon?)

Furthermore, according to Paul, because asking people to keep God's TRUE Law and instruction didn't work, God just threw that whole requirement out. This serves to illustrate that [Paul's] God makes really big mistakes; but at least He can learn from them. Now, God *rewards* Gentiles for doing exactly what the Jews did in the first place—disobeying God's instruction. Apparently Gentiles are no longer *under* the law—they are *above* it!

Here is where traditional Adventists as well as Messianic believers tend to get into hot water with other Evangelical Christian fundamentalist groups. Adventists feel that they need to keep the Ten Commandments and even believe that in the end times, commandment keeping will be a deal breaker that will define and separate the people of God. Messianic believers go a step further and try their best to keep as many of the 613 other laws found in Torah as they can.

On the other hand, Christians who subscribe to Paul's *New Covenant Theology* feel that it is personally insulting to God if you try to keep the commandments, especially the Fourth Commandment which refers to the Sabbath. Keeping the Sabbath Commandment will get you charged by these *New Covenant* adherents with trying to *work your way to heaven*. You will get called *legalistic* and a *Judaizer*, which is the ultimate slur that one Christian can call another Christian.[232]

This *we should not be legalistic* policy is sometimes taken to ridiculous lengths. I have known former Adventists who, in order to prove that they are no longer trying to gain favor with God (or *work their way to heaven*) by presumably being vegetarian, will actually force themselves to start eating meat. It is as if they believe that exhibiting compassion toward God's living creatures is in some way "working your way to heaven!"

Another important factor in the popularity and acceptance of Paul's NuGospel relates to how God Almighty is unfairly portrayed as a rule-mongering, sometimes vindictive tyrant who cannot even *look* upon sin. This notion is supported by taking a statement from the prophet Habakkuk way out of context. We quote,

---

[232] Messianic believers are all too familiar with being called "Judaizers" because of their differences with other Christians. Since Yeshua himself was a Commandment-keeping Jew, they do not generally consider this to be an insult.

> You are of purer eyes than to behold evil, and cannot look on wickedness.[233]

Far too often we fail to finish reading the next part of the verse!

> ...Why do You *look* on those who deal treacherously, and hold Your tongue when the wicked devours a person more righteous than he?

By simply finishing out the verse, we have negated our original point that God *cannot look upon sin*. To the contrary, we have discovered that God does indeed "look on those who deal treacherously."

Habakkuk is very prophetic, but his writing itself is also very poetic, rich with imagery and filled with allegorical uses of speech. We need to keep in mind that during his poetic rant, the prophet isn't establishing a Character trait of God. Rather, he is lamenting in an allegorical way about how a holy God has to deal with man's terrible sin. Later in the same chapter, Habakkuk uses allegories of wicked fisherman catching the righteous in nets and sacrificing them. Did unrighteous people really catch men with hooks and nets to sacrifice them? No! It is a poetic allegory!

When Habakkuk offers that AHYH cannot look upon sin, he is merely bemoaning the fact that he knows that God does not like to abide the sin of man; and he feels strongly that God should not have to look upon and deal with the sin of mankind. The prophet knows that God does actually see His children and their actions; and he also knows that God

---

[233] Habakkuk 1:13 NKJV

delivers chastisement and even capital punishment to those who sin against Him (remember the flood; and Sodom and Gomorrah?). Habakkuk is ultimately discouraged, as I am sure we all are, because God seems to take so long to right the wrongs of the wicked! So the prophet is beseeching God, 'Why are You *tolerating* all this sin?' In other words, "Why can't you *do* something about these wicked people?"

Nevertheless, this "sinners in the hands of an angry God" depiction is one thing that makes Paul's *no responsibility* NuGospel so attractive. Who wouldn't appreciate being skipped over when it comes to the *accountability* portion of God's judgment? However, this woeful variation of the gospel is not the Gospel that Yeshua himself, a Jew, taught! Yeshua upheld the Jewish belief that you need to obey and follow God's TRUE Law, and love and honor God.

The differences between Paul's NuGospel and the TRUE Gospel that Yeshua and the Apostles taught have not been lost on Biblical scholars down through the ages. Most mainstream Christian scholars will endeavor to explain away Paul's multi-layered differences as *later revelation* within the context of this *New Contract* (New Covenant, New Testament) doctrine.

While we in Christendom are told by Yeshua to "establish the truth on the witness of two or three" which is a concept that comes straight out of Hebraic law, the only foundation for Christendom's version of or interpretation of the *New Covenant* is Paul and Paul alone.[234]

It was this authentic Hebraic perspective that indeed presented Paul and his Gentile-centric Hellenistic NuGospel

---

[234] Since the author of the book of *Hebrews* is unknown, in fact many scholars believed for centuries that Paul had indeed written it; it cannot be validated as any kind of additional historical witness.

with its most formidable challenge. On the one hand, Paul is claiming that he is a Jew, a Hebrew, and a *Pharisee's Pharisee*. He even name drops that he has studied under Gamaliel; perhaps one of the finest Hebraic scholars of the time.

On the other hand, Paul's Jewish brethren are successfully opposing him and his NuGospel every step of the way. Because of his distinctly *unJewish* message, Paul is having a lot of difficulty convincing people that he really is a Jew with Jewish upbringing and beliefs. Paul now needs a way to somehow convince these Gentiles who have been instructed by *real* Jews that *his* NuGospel is really based, however loosely, in Judaic ancestry and true Hebraic thought.

Paul's *New Covenant Theology* is also supported by the mysterious and unknown author of the book of *Hebrews*. For many centuries, because of the deeply Pauline themes within the book, it was more or less automatically assumed by most learned scholars that Paul himself had written Hebrews. However, the general consensus of Christian scholars today is that Paul himself probably did not write *Hebrews*, but someone very close to him most likely did.[235]

---

[235] Luther felt strongly that Apollos, an understudy of Paul's, had written the book. Tertullian believed that it was Barnabas who may actually have written the book. (The Daily Bible Study Series, The Letter to the Hebrews, William Barclay, Introduction, pp. 7-9) Enigmatically, the book doesn't at all mention who has written it, which has added to the controversy of whether or not it should have been included for canonization within the Roman Catholic Bible. Indeed, many, many books, letters, epistles and other early Christian writings did not make canonization because primarily their *authorship*, among other secondary criteria, could not at all be proved—even if only through tradition! If Apollos wrote the book, which is highly likely, then Apollos could likely not use his name. A man named after a Greek pagan god would not be inspiring to the Messianic (Jewish) Christian peoples who sought to distance themselves from anything even remotely idolatrous.

E.F. Scott notes that the book of *Hebrews* is the "riddle of the New Testament." William Barclay notes,

> When [the book of Hebrews] was written, to whom it was written, and who wrote it are questions at which we can only guess.... It was not until the time of Athanasium, in the middle of the fourth century, that Hebrews was definitely accepted as a New Testament book, and even Luther was not too sure about it. It is strange to think how long this great book had to wait for full recognition.[236]

While Barclay has a problem with understanding why this *great book* had to wait so long for *full recognition*, other scholars do not harbor his perplexity. One of the main reasons why the author of a book needs to be known is so that we can authenticate the book's time of writing. An unknown author leaves the book open to a terribly late authorship that may have been well outside of the first century. In other words, a book written in the second or early third century qualifies to be *Scripture* about as much as the writings of Tertullian, Martin Luther, Ellen White or Dwight Moody would be considered *Scripture*.

Another unsettling problem is that Barclay and other theologians, both ancient and modern, all too easily dismiss as a mere footnote the vehement historical disputing of this

---

A renowned German scholar named Harnack postulated the notion that Aquila and Priscilla, two people mentioned within Luke's book of *Acts*, may have actually written the book of *Hebrews*. It was written at a time when women were not allowed to teach, and the absence of the name of the author might attest to such an anonymous authorship.

[236] BARCLAY, William, *The Daily Bible Study Series*, The Letter to the Hebrews, Introduction, p. 5

book on their way to espousing their love and adoration for it as a supposed pillar and mainstay of *Christian* theology. Clearly, for such a deeply polarizing and disputed book, it was only a pillar of theology for a particular sectarian fraction of period *Christians*—namely the Pauline ones. The rest of the period Christians considered the book of *Hebrews* to be an outright fraud.

In the end, all of us are essentially forced to observe the same thing: no one really knows who wrote the book of *Hebrews*; or as Origen offers, "...only God knows for sure."

I recently asked the question in a discussion on Facebook, "Who is the author of Hebrews?" The general consensus of the two (only two!) Christians responding to the discussion was, "It doesn't matter if we know who wrote the book of Hebrews, because we KNOW who the Author is." There were warm fuzzy kudos and pats on the proverbial back and that was the end of it. The illogic of the comments made still astounds me; this defense is the epitome of *circular reasoning!* This unknown authorship should throw us into deep suspicion about the origin and content of the book of *Hebrews*, yet somehow, it escapes any and all scrutiny by the vast majority of today's Christian and Messianic believers because it is in the Bible—placed there under deep dispute by the period leadership of the Roman Catholic Church.

In spite of the heavy opposition to the book of *Hebrews* from the ancient Church even well into the fourth century and beyond, the book was likely added to the Roman Catholic Church's Bible because it indeed provided badly needed support for Paul's singular "NuGospel". Because this mysterious book was eventually canonized into the Bible, man was able to falsely make the pagan assertion that his god required sacrifice—human sacrifice!—as the means of atonement for sin.

CHAPTER 26

❖

EATING FOOD SACRIFICED TO IDOLS

Luc and I traveled through quite a spectrum of beliefs as we sought to find a doctrinal center during our years of intensive study and searching. A year or two into our journey we tentatively started to embrace a more literal form of Messianic Judaism, keeping as many of the 613 laws in Torah as we could. Luc stopped cutting his hair and grew a beard. I started being mindful of mixed fabrics and making sure every single bit of leavening was removed from the house at Passover time. I'll never forget little five-year-old Alex's annoyance at going a whole week without any leavened bread as he snapped after being faced with yet one more peanut butter and jelly wrap, "I'm tired of quesadilla! I want sammich!"

We celebrated all of the *Holy Day Feasts,* and tried to stay away from as many customs with pagan roots as possible. We really enjoyed some of the new traditions we were finding, and I have to admit I learned to make really yummy challah bread![237]

The downside of this equation was that we were also very challenging to be around, because our belief system was not very tolerant of the customs of others. We would not allow any candles on our birthday cakes because of their origins in pagan custom, and at one point we threw out all of our beautiful Christmas tree decorations. We kept our kids home from school on Valentine's Day because we did not want them to participate in a day honoring a Catholic saint. Looking back, I think we were a bit difficult for our families to live with during that time period, as they didn't agree with the changes we were making and became more and more concerned about where we would end up religiously speaking.

Despite the fact that others felt we were swinging a bit far over toward the *fanaticism* side, we tried really hard to understand how to apply the laws that seemed to be more culturally focused toward the customs of the time. One *law* that we really struggled with understanding was the oft-repeated admonition about *not eating food sacrificed to idols*. "What does that mean?" we wondered. "If an unbeliever owns a restaurant and has a statue of Buddha in their restaurant, does that mean I am *eating food sacrificed to idols* if I go eat there?"

For years, we avoided going to our favorite Thai restaurant because of the little statue of Buddha they had sitting on their wall. We hated no longer being able to enjoy their

---

[237] We no longer participate in traditional "Holy Day" Feasts because they are so focused on blood and sacrifice! Beau now cuts his hair and shaves, and we try to look at the 613 laws a bit more in the context of our particular culture. Although we may not be leading Davidic dances around the house, we still enjoy Jewish music and a tasty loaf of challah!

delicious yellow curry and crispy egg rolls, but really felt that we had no choice in the matter.

After performing quite a bit of additional research, we learned that in Ezekiel's day, there were multiple mountain temples dedicated to pagan gods, where all manner of sacrifices were offered (including human sacrifices). The meat of these sacrifices was not wasted; it was sold in restaurant-like fashion at the temple itself. God calls people who were eating at these places *unrighteous* and *sinners*.

In the reality of twenty-first century America, our favorite Thai restaurant was far from being a temple where all sorts of pagan sacrifices had taken place. Rather, it was an establishment where your food was prepared to order while you waited. Finally satisfied that there was indeed a significant difference, we happily resumed our patronage of the little eatery with the delicious food.

Although this issue of *eating food sacrificed to idols* doesn't seem relevant to today's Christian believer, this concern was quite a big problem for ancient Israel. The Israelite system of worship run by the priesthood was based on sacrifice, which is also how the opposing *false gods* were worshiped. There was an ongoing battle to see how far you could go in participating in the rituals taking place that were dedicated to other gods. If you married wives from other countries like Solomon did, your problems were exponentially compounded, as these wives and concubines would often bring their own pagan gods and worship customs with them, and then expect *you* to participate in the worship of *their* gods as well as your own.

This issue remained a problem in Yeshua's era and even beyond. For example, when Paul visited the Apostles in Jerusalem, the well-known Jerusalem Council, led by James and Peter, took action on some issues that had come up regarding the necessity of Gentiles learning and keeping the TRUE Law of God. After much discussion, filtered by Luke, the final decision came down from James. James proclaimed:

> It is my judgment, therefore, that we should not make it difficult for the Gentiles who are turning to God. Instead we should write to them, telling them to *abstain from food polluted by idols*, from sexual immorality, from the meat of strangled animals and from blood. For Moses [meaning the TRUE Law of God] has been preached in every city from the earliest times and is read in the synagogues on every Sabbath.[238]

This decision, made by Yeshua's brother James and the Apostles of the Jerusalem Council, is also repeated by Luke six chapters later:

> As for the Gentile believers, we have written to them our decision that they should *abstain from food sacrificed to idols*, from blood, from the meat of strangled animals and from sexual immorality.[239]

Jumping forward in time we see John, the author of Revelation, writing to the various churches. Within this book, John records a vision of Yeshua speaking to several of the churches where Yeshua admonishes not one but two of the churches for eating food offered to idols. John writes:

> To the angel of the church in Pergamum write: ...Nevertheless, I have a few things against you: You

---

[238] Acts 15:19-21
[239] Acts 21:25

> have people there who hold to the teaching of Balaam, who taught Balak to entice the Israelites to sin by *eating food sacrificed to idols* and by committing sexual immorality.[240]

And again,

> To the angel of the church in Thyatira write:... Nevertheless, I have this against you: You tolerate that woman Jezebel, who calls herself a prophetess. By her teaching she misleads my servants into sexual immorality and *the eating of food sacrificed to idols.*[241]

So now we have numerous witnesses, Ezekiel, James and Peter (via Luke), and John, all saying to *abstain from food offered to idols*. There is complete unity of thought and belief regarding this fundamental difference between paganism and Judaism. Furthermore, *sexual immorality* is generally mentioned along with the *eating food sacrificed to idols* issue; these two issues seem to be somehow inextricably linked within the ancient mindset.

However, we do not see this same unity of counsel from the prolific pen of Paul. Instead, Paul decides to promote a different message than that which has been reflected by the consensus witness of the prophets and those who actually walked with Yeshua. Paul in no uncertain terms declares,

> So then, about eating food sacrificed to idols... *(really long rationalization here)*... But food does not bring us

---

[240] Revelation 2:14 NIV 1984
[241] Revelation 2:18, 20

near to God; we are no worse if we do not eat, and no better if we do.[242]

Paul cements his opposing perspective with,

> As one who is *in the Lord Yeshua,* I am fully convinced that no food is unclean in itself.[243]

We need to understand that the ones who actually followed Yeshua and were taught personally by him for more than a year are saying the exact opposite! This is not some translation issue or difference of doctrinal perspective here. There is a clear and deep contradiction in counsel.

I once posted a simple poll question on a Christian Internet message board: "Is it okay to eat food offered to idols?" A plethora of argumentative statements quickly ensued, and the moderators all too quickly closed the discussion thread down; primarily, in my opinion, because it brought up so much dissention over how Paul differed from other apostles and writers. People could not agree to discuss the issue in a civil manner, and they were decidedly not ready to hear that Paul's counsel was different from that of many other witnesses.

The bottom line from God is—don't eat food offered to idols. Period. Paul's contradictory counsel, meanwhile, is essentially, "There's really no such thing as unclean food, it doesn't matter one way or the other what you do."

This issue of Paul teaching the exact opposite of the Prophets and the Apostles has not been lost on Bible schol-

---

[242] 1 Corinthians 8:1,8
[243] Romans 14:14

ars. The *Quest NIV Study Bible* states within its margin study notes:

> Did Paul later change the prohibition about foods polluted by idols?... Paul declared such meat acceptable for consumption (1 Cor.8:8)... [244]

We need to take a step back and think about this issue for moment. Despite what the editors of the *Quest Study Bible* have noted, did Paul, a preacher who came along hundreds of years later, really have the power to override Ezekiel, a prophet who wrote an established part of the Scripture that Yeshua used? How about James, and Peter, and the author of Revelation? Revelation was written 40 years after Paul's letters to the Corinthians! It seems that far too many Christian scholars just jettison the consistent witness of every other Scriptural authority on this issue—just so Paul's counsel can appear to be correct and infallible!

If all of these witnesses—before, during and after Paul—are upholding this prohibition as valid, and if we are listening to Yeshua's own counsel that the truth is established on the witness of two or three,[245] then Paul has absolutely no authority whatsoever to contradict them. It is *Paul* who is clearly in the wrong here.

This issue of eating food sacrificed to idols may not be particularly relevant to us in our *non-sacrificing* society, but it speaks volumes about the discrepancies between what Paul

---

[244] *NIV Quest Study Bible*, Zondervan Publishing, Grand Rapids, Michigan, published 2003, p. 1587

[245] Matthew 18:16; See also that this Law of multiple witnesses is based in Torah, Deuteronomy 17:6 & 19:15; Paul himself even notes the Law of multiple witnesses in 2 Corinthians 13:1 & 1 Timothy 5:19

taught, and what the Jewish Messiah taught via the Prophets and to the Apostles in Jerusalem.

CHAPTER 27

❖

GOING ROGUE

Paul's writings reveal a very different *Yeshua* than the one brought to us by other first-century books. Significant by their absence, we may note that the *words of Yeshua* are conspicuously missing from the thirteen Pauline epistles. Albert Schweitzer, the German theologian and missionary notes:

> Where possible Paul avoids quoting the teaching of Jesus, in fact even mentioning it. If we had to rely on Paul, we should not know that Jesus taught in parables, had delivered the Sermon on the Mount, and had taught His disciples the 'Our Father' [the Lord's Prayer]. Even where they are specially relevant, Paul passes over the words of the Lord.[246]

---

[246] SCHWEITZER, Albert, *The Mysticism of Paul the Apostle*, 1931, p. 171

This issue indeed lends substantial merit and credence to the fact that compared to Yeshua's personal disciples, Paul may have really known very little about the actual life and ministry and teachings of the historical Yeshua. Other renowned philosophers and theologians have also noted this about Paul, including the English politician and philosopher Jeremy Bentham, who wrote in 1823, *Not Paul But Jesus*,

> It rests with every professor of the religion of Jesus to settle with himself, to which of the two religions, that of Jesus or that of Paul, he will adhere.[247]

It is helpful to understand that there were a vast number of non-proto-orthodox (i.e. early non-Roman Catholic) Christians who followed the teachings of Yeshua and the Apostles that categorically rejected Paul's NuGospel. The reason these early Christians abandoned Paul was because Paul wasn't teaching the same Gospel message as that being taught by the Twelve.

Another interesting issue we see with Paul is that he wasn't teaching with the Messianic Authority and credentials of the *Jerusalem Church*. To the uncritical or unlearned eye, it indeed appears that Paul has been accepted as part of the *Jerusalem Church*. The book of Acts, written by Paul's Gentile traveling companion Luke, presents Christendom with exactly this carefully molded perspective.[248] Luke, the only known Gentile to have been canonized within the Bible, is

---

[247] BENTHAM, Jeremy, *Not Paul But Jesus*, Harvard Divinity School, Cambridge, MA, 1810, p. xvi

[248] *Acts* isn't really *"The Acts of the Apostles"*; it is mostly *"The Acts of Paul"*. Literally half of the book is devoted not to the Acts of the Twelve, but exclusively to the Acts of Paul.

careful not to write about Paul in any way that might show any controversy between Paul and the *Jerusalem Church*. He is light on the hard facts—in fact, he carefully omits them—where the true Judaic perspective might cast doubt onto his dear friend Paul.

These issues with Luke essentially running interference for Paul have not gone unnoticed by mainstream Christian and secular scholars and historians:

> ...the purposes of the book of Acts is to minimize the conflict between Paul and the leaders of the Jerusalem Church, James and Peter. Peter and Paul, in later Christian tradition, became twin saints, brothers in faith, and the idea that they were historically bitter opponents standing for irreconcilable religious standpoints would have been repudiated with horror. The work of the author of Acts was well done; he rescued Christianity from the imputation of being the individual creation of Paul, and instead gave it a respectable pedigree, as a doctrine with the authority of the so-called Jerusalem Church, conceived as continuous in spirit with the Pauline Gentile Church of Rome.[249]

It is very important for Orthodox Christianity to have Paul perceived as being in complete agreement with Peter and James and the rest of the Apostles, because without the esteemed and distinguished support of the *Jerusalem Church* and the Apostles who actually walked with Yeshua, Paul's NuGospel becomes a completely rogue one.

---

[249] MACOBY, Hyam, (Christian / Jewish / Talmudic scholar) *The Mythmaker*, (Christian / Jewish / Talmudic scholar), Weidenfeld and Nicolson, London, 1986 p. 139

This issue becomes much more obvious when we see Luke's adroitly worded facts about when Paul visits the Apostles in Jerusalem. Luke frames the story this way:

> [The Apostles] said to Paul: "You see, brother, how many thousands of Jews have believed, and all of them are zealous for the law. They have been informed that you teach all the Jews who live among the Gentiles to turn away from Moses.... What shall we do? They will certainly hear that you have come, so do what we tell you. ... Then everybody will know there is no truth in these reports about you, but that you yourself are living in obedience to the law. [250]

While Luke indeed attempts to mitigate this *lawless* issue by showing that Paul underwent a Temple ritual showing him to be a *Lawful Jew,* the accusation that Paul is teaching contrary to the Law of God is quite serious and troublesome to the TRUE Law-abiding Jewish Apostles. Despite what some in traditional Judaism have asserted, the TRUE Law of God is equally applicable for both Jew and Gentile alike. After all, why would God give his helpful instructions of obedience and righteousness to some of His children and not all of them?

THE SUPER APOSTLES VERSUS PAUL

To make the situation even more remarkable, Paul admits that there are *Super Apostles* that have been preaching a *Yeshua* and a *spirit* and a *gospel* that is different than the one

---

[250] Acts 21:20-24

he originally delivered to the church in Corinth. Paul admonishes,

> But I am afraid that just as Eve was deceived by the serpent's cunning, your minds may somehow be led astray from your sincere and pure devotion to Christ. For if someone comes to you and preaches a *Yeshua* other than the *Yeshua* we preached, or if you receive a different spirit from the one you received, or a different gospel from the one you accepted, you put up with it easily enough. I do not think I am in the least inferior to those *super apostles*.[251]

Paul himself is adamant that there are indeed *two different gospels, two Yeshuas,* and *two different spirits* being preached about here. Paul has one spirit and these *Super Apostles* have another. There is Paul's NuGospel that his group had preached to the Gentiles in Corinth, and then there is this *other* gospel, with *another* Yeshua and *another* spirit, that is being preached by these *Super Apostles*.

But just who are these so-called *Super Apostles* that Paul is complaining about? The Greek phrase *lain apostolos* is what gets translated into the phrase *super apostles* in the NIV. The King James Version renders the same phrase as *chiefest apostles*. Breaking it down, the Greek word *lian* essentially means: superlative, well-known, renowned, great, preeminent, exceedingly, beyond measure.[252] To make it even more superlative, Paul prefaces the phrase *lian apostolos* with the Greek term *hyper*, which most of us recognize already as meaning *very, intense, extreme*. So, would you like to guess

---

[251] 2 Corinthians 11:3-5
[252] Thayer's Greek Lexicon, "lian"

whom these *hyper lian apostolos,* these extremely renowned apostles, really are?

That's right! Paul's own words clearly illustrate that these *Chiefest Apostles* were by anyone's honest definition James, Jude, Peter, John and the rest of the renowned Apostles in Jerusalem. The competing gospel that Paul is denouncing in 2 Corinthians is in fact the TRUE Gospel that Yeshua Ha-Maschiach instructed his Twelve Apostles to preach to all the nations.

Bible scholars recognize that this passage paints Paul in a really bad light, and so they have attempted to water down, ignore or simply recast Paul's words in order to make it *look* like Paul is somehow not in dispute with the renowned *Super Apostles*. One of the mechanisms some scholars have used to distance Paul's divisive comments about the renowned *Super Apostles* is to attempt to paint these respected apostles as nameless, faceless, *Judaizing* interlopers. This makes it easier for the average Christian believer to hate these *Judaizers*. However, the NIV Study Bible's commentary illustrates that Paul was disputing not with some renowned pagan Gentile teachers who had somehow infiltrated the church, but rather with other *Messianic Jews* who were preaching a different message than the one Paul himself was preaching:

> 11:4 a Jesus other than the Jesus we preached. They presented a Jesus cast in the mold of Judaistic teachings (Paul's opponents were Jews; see v.22...)

> 11:5 those "super-apostles." Paul's sarcastic way of referring to the false apostles who had infiltrated the Corinthian church and were in reality not apostles at

all, except in their own arrogantly inflated opinion of themselves.[253]

Another mechanism used within the scholastic debate hinges on who Paul's group actually was. Paul says (translated),

> For if someone comes to you and preaches a 'Yeshua' other than the 'Yeshua' *we* preached... you put up with it easily enough. I do not think I am in the least inferior to those super apostles.[254]

Other scholars insist that Paul was simply saying that his skills in teaching were not inferior to the renowned *Super Apostles* in Jerusalem that Paul was part of, and that Paul was simply cementing his position among them. In this creative interpretation, Paul is essentially telling the Corinthians, "Hey, I'm part of the *Super Apostles*, and have taught you just as well as Peter, James and John would have. Yet you're still putting up with this other gospel... ?"

This exegetical argument is ridiculously weak, contextually speaking, because just a few verses later Paul very heavy-

---

[253] *The NIV Study Bible*, 10th Anniversary Edition, Zondervan Publishing, 1995, pp. 1,775

[254] *Vine's Expository Dictionary of New Testament Words* notes the translation of *lian*: Chief, Chiefest, Chiefly: "chiefest" (huper, "over," lian, "exceedingly, pre-eminently, very much"), is used in 2 Corinthians 11:5; 12:11, of "Paul's place among the Apostles."

However, we should be quick to note that there is a deep contradiction here from other Christian scholars, such as the IBS/NIV, who have charged that Paul was belittling these "super apostles" and not defining his own position among them. Either way, this passage presents a deep problem for mainstream Christianity; which is attempting to both distance Paul and include him among the Chiefest Apostles.

handedly admonishes and even slanders these same *Super Apostles* by saying,

> And I will keep on doing what I am doing in order to cut the ground from under those who want an opportunity to be considered equal with us in the things they boast about. For such people are false apostles, deceitful workers, masquerading as apostles of Christ. And no wonder, for Satan himself masquerades as an angel of light. It is not surprising, then, if his servants also masquerade as servants of righteousness. Their end will be what their actions deserve.[255]

Did Paul just call the *Super Apostles* servants of Satan? Yes, he did! So, clearly, he would not be associating himself with such people, even though this is how the scholars of *Vines* (see footnote 248) have attempted to explain the passage.

What is all too clear here is that Paul has some deep disputes with these so-called *renowned* and *preeminent* chief *Apostles of Yeshua*. We can attempt to parse and spin and remold Paul's words all we like, but in the end, we cannot escape the fact that Paul is having a very ugly dispute with some very prominent *apostles*. Furthermore, he does not appear to be winning the contest, since the church in Corinth has actually abandoned both Paul's NuYeshua and his Nu-Gospel.

Paul's second letter to the church in Corinth was written circa 55 AD, only four or five years after the Council of Jerusalem we read about in the book of Acts. The reputation of the Apostles who had walked with Christ himself was

---

[255] 2 Corinthians 11:12-15

indeed *renowned* at this period of time within this region. We have no historical or Biblical record of any other competing *Chiefest Apostles* to substantiate that Paul was talking about anyone other than these most esteemed and very well known *Apostles of Yeshua* in Jerusalem.

To get a better understanding and corroboration of this issue of just who Paul is comparing himself with in 2 Corinthians, we can look at Paul's other epistles to see that 1) he has some big personal/religious problems with the Apostles in Jerusalem and that 2) he is continually comparing himself to these same *Super Apostles*.

The first thing any student of human nature realizes is that anytime someone says "I am not in the least inferior to so-and-so", that the person is *really* feeling inferior to so-and-so and is speaking out of a deep-seated sense of insecurity. This is one thing that makes Paul's statement here in 2 Corinthians so interesting—why is he acting so defensive when comparing himself to these *Super Apostles*?

CHAPTER 28

❖

CLASH OF THE TITANS

One of the most mysterious yet influential members of the *Jerusalem Church* was James. Most Christian or Messianic believers have not been taught why James is noteworthy; however, his role in early Christianity was extraordinarily significant. James was called *James the Just, James the Righteous, James of Jerusalem,* or *James the brother of the Lord.* Believed to be the actual brother of Yeshua, he was the leader of the Christian movement in Jerusalem for decades after Yeshua's death. He is also said to have been one of the first people Yeshua appeared to after his resurrection.[256]

---

[256] The *Gospel according to the Hebrews*, which Origen often uses, tells, regarding the resurrection of the Savior: "Now the Lord, when he had given the linen cloth unto the servant of the priest, went unto James and appeared to him (for James had sworn that he would not eat bread from that hour wherein he had drunk the Lord's cup until he should see him risen again from among them that sleep)', and again after a little, 'Bring ye, saith the Lord, a table and bread', and immediately it is added, 'He took bread and blessed and

Some scholars have theorized, based on quite credible sources, that James is actually the disciple *James* of *Peter, James, and John* fame. They suggest that his name was actually expunged and the identifier *son of Zebedee* was inserted because of Roman Catholic dogma.

Dr. Robert M. Price, reviewing Dr. Robert Eisenman's exhaustive work *James the Brother of Jesus,* summarizes:

> The Gospels give prominence to an inner circle of three: Peter, John son of Zebedee and John's brother James. And Galatians has the Three Pillars in Jerusalem: Peter, John son of Zebedee, and Jesus' brother James. What happened here? Surely the gospels' inner group of three is intended as preparatory for the Pillars, to provide a life-of-Jesus pedigree for the Pillars. But then why are there two different Jameses? Mustn't they originally have been the same? Eisenman says they were, but certain factions wanted to play up the authority of the shadowy college of the Twelve against the earlier authority of the Heirs and found it politic to drive a wedge between James the brother of Jesus and the Twelve, so James becomes James the Just on the one hand and James the brother of John on the other.

If we are willing to look beyond the carefully groomed and canonized sources, we will find that there is some very interesting history between Saul-turned-Paul and *James the*

---

brake and gave it unto James the Just and said unto him: My brother, eat thy bread, for the Son of Man is risen from among them that sleep'.

Just, before *Saul* ever changes his name to *Paul*. The *Recognitions of Clement* tells about someone named Saul:

> "...one of our enemies"—who upon "entering the temple with a few men" where James the Just was speaking "began to cry out... While he was thus speaking, and adding more to the same effect, and while James the bishop was refuting him, he began to excite the people and to raise a tumult, so that the people might not be able to hear what was said.
>
> "Therefore he began to drive all into confusion with shouting, and to undo what had been arranged with much labour, and at the same time to reproach the priests, and to enrage them with revilings and abuse, and, like a madman, to excite every one to murder, saying, 'What do ye? Why do ye hesitate? Oh sluggish and inert, why do we not lay hands upon them, and pull all these fellows to pieces?'
>
> "When he had said this, he first, seizing a strong brand from the altar, set the example of smiting. Then others also, seeing him, were carried away with like readiness. Then ensued a tumult on either side, of the beating and the beaten. Much blood is shed; there is a confused flight, in the midst of which that enemy attacked James, and threw him headlong from the top of the steps; and supposing him to be dead, he cared not to inflict further violence upon him."

Though James didn't die, both of his legs were broken, so his friends lifted him up. "When the evening came the priests shut up the temple, and we returned to the house of James, and spent the night there in prayer. Then before daylight we went down to Jericho, to the *number of 5,000 men."*[257] Then, Saul *"had received a commission from Caiaphas, the chief priest, that he should arrest all who believed in Yeshua, and should go to Damascus with his letters, and that there also, employing the help of the unbelievers, he should make havoc among the faithful; and that he was hastening to Damascus chiefly on this account, because he believed that Peter had fled thither."*[258]

Luke takes up the story in the book of Acts:

But Saul began to destroy the church. Going from house to house, he dragged off men and women and put them in prison.... Meanwhile, Saul was still breathing out murderous threats against the Lord's disciples. He went to the high priest and asked him for letters to the synagogues in Damascus, so that if he found any there who belonged to the Way, whether men or women, he might take them as prisoners to Jerusalem.[259]

Talk about a hidden piece of history! James the brother of Yeshua, who is extremely well respected and admired by many believers, survives a murder attempt by Paul in his *Saul the Persecutor* days. Eventually, Paul has a *mystic vision* of James' own brother Yeshua, and subsequently believes that based on his *vision*, he knows *more* about Yeshua and his significance than those who grew up with him and walked with him!

---

[257] See also Acts 4:4
[258] Recognitions of Clement Book 1:70-71.
[259] Acts 8:2; 9:1-2

This is a covert part of the story that we in Christianity or Messianic Judaism are never allowed to see. Instead of seeing a man who was of so great sanctity and reputation among the people that the siege and downfall of Jerusalem was believed to take place on account of his death,[260] we perceive *James the Just* as a shadow figure who "ended up ignored, an ephemeral figure on the margins of Christianity, known only to scholars and religious aficionados."[261]

We certainly never realize that,

> In the Jerusalem of his day in the 40s to 60s CE, he (James) was the most important and central figure of all—'the Bishop' or 'Overseer' of the Jerusalem Church... To have been 'Head' or 'Bishop' of "the Jerusalem Church' (Ecclesia) or 'Community' was to have been the head of the whole of Christianity, whatever this might be considered to have been in this period. Not only was the centre at Jerusalem the principal one before the destruction of the Temple and the reputed flight of the Jamesian community to a city beyond the Jordan called Pella, but there were hardly any others of any importance.[262]

This extremely provocative background information helps illustrate that there was not a glowing solidarity of brotherhood between *James the Just* and Paul, as is often preached to

---

[260] Attributed to Josephus, remarked on by both Eusebius and Origen. Additional information regarding sources at http://www.sullivan-county.com/id2/james.htm 7/27/10.
[261] EISENMAN, Robert, James The Brother of Jesus: The Key to Unlocking The Dead Sea Scrolls, Introduction.
[262] EISENMAN, Introduction

the laity. These two powerful men did not appear to get along, and their doctrinal positions were not in agreement either!

In the *Clementine Homilies*, Peter states that Yeshua gave a warning that the wicked one (Satan) *"promised that he would send apostles from amongst his subjects, to deceive. Wherefore, above all, remember to shun apostle or teacher or prophet who does not first accurately compare his preaching with that of James, who was called the brother of my Lord."* He then goes on to state that Satan would *"send a preacher to your injury, as now he has sent Simon*[263] *upon us, preaching, under pretence of the truth, in the name of the Lord, and sowing error."* The passage ends with two familiar passages. *"Wherefore He who hath sent us, said, 'Many shall come to me in sheep's clothing, but inwardly they are ravening wolves. By their fruits shall ye know them.'"*[264]

THE MARGINALIZATION OF JAMES THROUGH HISTORY

The contradictions between James and Paul have not been lost on Bible scholars through the ages. The Reformers themselves wrestled with this issue. Most of them simply chose to concentrate on the more popular Paul (he has more canonized epistles).

What is generally unknown in mainstream Christian circles is that while Luther was rejecting and excising the so-called *apocryphal* books from the Roman Catholic Bible, he also wanted to remove the book of *James* because the book of James specifically contradicts Paul's NuGospel. In Marcion-

---

[263] "Simon" or "Simon Magus" is thought by many scholars to be a well-known cipher for Paul. This will be discussed in greater detail in a later chapter.
[264] Clementine Homilies 11:35 and Matthew 7:15, 20

like fashion, it again was Paul's letters that essentially became Luther's core *canon*, his core standard by which he would measure and then judge other books of the Bible. As such, Luther removed not just some *Old Testament* books, but also attempted to remove a number of *New Testament* books as well: Hebrews, Jude, Revelation—and most especially the book of James.

However, Luther found substantially less support from his fellow Reformers for his *New Testament* deletions. Because of this lack of support, he settled for moving these books from their normal period order and placing them at the end of the Bible canon, stating that they were *less than canonical*.

The book of James was not Luther's favorite because of the book's glaring contradictions to Galatians and other Pauline epistles. Luther wrote:

> I think highly of the epistle of James, and regard it as valuable although it was rejected in early days. It does not expound human doctrines, but lays much emphasis on God's law… I do not hold it to be of apostolic authorship.

William Barclay notes Luther's reasons for rejecting James:

> First, in direct opposition to Paul and the rest of the Bible, it ascribes justification to works, quoting Abraham wrongly as one who was justified by his works.

This in itself proves that the epistle cannot be of apostolic origin.[265]

For the record, the book of James *does not* stand in direct opposition to the rest of the Bible! Unless one's notion of the *rest of the Bible* begins with Romans and ends with Hebrews, James actually stands in full harmony with Torah, the Prophets and the words of the Messiah via Matthew. The reality is that James only stands in direct opposition to Paul's antinomian (anti-Law of God) theology. Also, we have already noted that it was Paul who quoted Abraham in error from Galatians 3.

We can see in Deuteronomy where this theme of faithfulness, faith *plus* action, is driven home as the assurance of righteousness before God:

> AHYH commanded us to obey all these decrees and to fear AHYH our God, so that we might always prosper and be kept alive, as is the case today. And if we are careful to obey all this law before AHYH our God, as he has commanded us, that will be our righteousness.[266]

Here again within Scripture the theme of *obey, prosper and live* is clearly presented; and it is a recurring theme from all of the Bible's inspired authors—all except Paul, who says,

---

[265] BARCLAY, William, *The Daily Study Bible Series, The Letters of James and Peter*, Revised Edition, Westminster John Knox Press, Louisville, KY, 1976, p. 7

[266] Deuteronomy 6:24-25

> Clearly no one is justified before God by observing the law...[267]

We can clearly see from what we have read that every man who puts his faith in the Eternal One and obeys God's TRUE Law is justified by his faith and obedience working hand-in-hand. Yeshua says belief requires *deeds* (i.e. action) to be saved and that if "we want to enter [eternal] life we must obey the commandments."[268]

So who is really right here? The witnesses of Yeshua, his Disciples and the Prophets which all reflect the Character of God, and who command and affirm obedience to God's TRUE Law—or the singular witness of Paul?

---

[267] Galatians 2:16, 3:11
[268] Matthew 19:17 NIV 1984

CHAPTER 29

❖

ROBBING PETER TO PAY PAUL

If you play a simple word association game with a traditional Protestant about the first thing they think of when they think of the Apostle Peter, the top three answers often include the following:

1) Peter denied Yeshua, not only once but three times!
2) Peter was full of himself when walking on the water and started to sink because he was too proud in front of his friends.
3) Peter got on the wrong side of Paul in Galatians, and Paul sure set him straight!

Basically, we've all grown up thinking that Peter was a bullheaded, uncultured *doofus* who wasn't presentable enough to be let out in polite company. We generally ignore the fact that Yeshua seemed to value him enough to leave him *large and in charge* of the rest of the Apostles and by extension, the work of spreading the *Gospel of good news*.

Rather than looking for advice from Simon *the Rock* Peter, numerous Christian leaders and believers instead consider the writings of the Apostle Paul to be the bedrock upon which we build our churches. Paul is the one we go to for advice on how to deal with problems in our congregations. Paul is also the one we seek to be the final word when we have trouble understanding a problematic Scriptural concept. If we consider Peter to be relevant at all, it is only in that we believe he can offer us affirmation about the legitimacy of Paul.

Those who are willing to search outside of traditional canonized Scripture will find an abundance of first and second century documentation which details how the Apostle Peter bravely and consistently stood up for the TRUE Gospel that he learned at the feet of Yeshua HaMaschiach. Far from being a cartoonish buffoon, he was instead a pillar of spiritual strength in a time of instability and conflict. However, these *non-canonical* historical documents also relate in great detail the deep controversy and disagreements Peter had with Paul of Tarsus. In them, we truly see how Peter and Paul were really bitter rivals who stood for two completely different and divergent *gospels*.

Not uncharacteristically, the deep controversy between Peter and Paul has been all but expunged from Christian tradition or, where it does emerge, it is thoroughly downplayed and presented as nothing more than a *minor disagreement* between two *brothers in Christ*.

In Galatians 2, Paul very colorfully relates that Peter is the one in the wrong because it *appears* that he is attempting to *Judaize* the Christian faith. If we choose to believe this one-sided rendition of the story, Peter is the one who is actually *robbed* of the respect that we then pay to Paul, who is telling the story. It never really occurs to us that it is indeed

Peter, and *not* Paul, who is in *true apostolic authority* during this period of leadership of the *Jerusalem Church*.

The general consensus among most mainstream Christian scholars is that in this *minor* controversy between Peter and Paul, Peter, the illiterate and clumsy fisherman, had to be categorically wrong in his disagreement with the highly educated and self-actualized Paul. From the historical record however, this controversy was not a mild disagreement at all—and Paul was not the one *in the right*.

Dr. Bart Ehrman, one of the more renowned scholars of Christian history of our time, sums up the situation with a perspective that seems to be more in keeping with the historical record regarding *what really happened* between Peter and Paul. Ehrman states,

> The controversy between Peter and Paul presupposed in [the Homilies and Recognitions] is premised on a real, historical conflict between the two, evidenced in Paul's own writings. In particular, in his letter to the Galatians, Paul speaks of a public encounter with Peter in the city of Antioch over the issue of whether Gentiles who have become Christian need to observe the Jewish Law (Gal. 2: I 1-14). Paul reports the encounter and states in the strongest terms that Gentiles are under no circumstances to be required to keep the Law. As scholars have long noted, however, Paul does not indicate the outcome of the public altercation—leading to the widely held suspicion that this was one debate that Paul lost, at least in the eyes of those who observed it.
>
> The Pseudo-Clementines [ancient historical Christian documents] take up the debate to show Peter

supporting the ongoing validity of the Law against Paul, thinly disguised as Simon Magus.[269] The books are prefaced by a letter allegedly from Peter to James, the brother of Jesus and head of the church in Jerusalem (one of a number of letters we have that are forged [i.e. pseudepigrapha] in Peter's name). In it Peter speaks of his "enemy" who teaches the Gentiles not to obey the Law, and he sets out his own authoritative position in contrast:

"For some from among the Gentiles have rejected my lawful preaching and have preferred a lawless and absurd doctrine of the man who is my enemy. And indeed some have attempted, while I am still alive, to distort my words by interpretations of many sorts, as if I taught the dissolution of the Law. But that may God forbid! For to do such a thing means to act contrary to the Law of God which was made to Moses and was confirmed by our Lord in its everlasting continuance. For he said, "The heaven and the earth will pass away, but not one jot or one tittle shall pass away from the Law." (Letter of Peter to James. 2.3-5)

The Law of Moses, therefore, is always to be kept by Jew and Gentile. It does not take much to recognize who Peter's "enemy" is here, the one who opposes this

---

[269] Multiple scholars through the centuries have come to the unmistakable conclusion that *Simon Magus* is a cipher for Paul. In several historical documents such as those mentioned, Peter is constantly coming against *Simon the magician* because Simon preaches against all that Peter stood for—most especially, the law of God, not eating food sacrificed to idols, and the fact that God did not need sacrifice in order to forgive. This will be addressed in more detail later in the chapter.

view "among the Gentiles." The apostle Paul consistently portrayed himself as the apostle to the Gentiles and insisted that they not keep the Law (e.g., Galatians 2:15, 5:2-5). As to who may have been responsible for teaching that Peter himself urged "the dissolution of the law," one again does not need to look far: The New Testament book of Acts, allegedly written by Paul's own traveling companion Luke, portrays Peter as taking just that position (Acts 10-11, 15). Even though Paul and Acts eventually became part of the proto-orthodox canon, for this author they are both heretical. This Pseudo-Clementine writing, then, appears to embody an Ebionite polemic against the view adopted by proto-orthodox Christianity. The attacks on Paul and on what he stood for become yet clearer in portions of the Homilies. In one section in particular, Peter is said to have developed the notion that in the plan of God for humans, the lesser always precedes the greater. And so, Adam had two sons, the murderer Cain and the righteous Abel; two also sprang from Abraham, the outcast Ishmael and the chosen one Isaac; and from Isaac came the godless Esau and the godly Jacob. Bringing matters down to more recent times, there were two who appeared on the Gentile mission field, Simon (Paul) and Peter, who was, of course, the greater of the two, "who appeared later than he did and came in upon him as light upon darkness, as knowledge upon ignorance, as healing upon sickness." (Homilies 2.17)

A final example of this polemic comes in an imaginary scene in which Peter attacks a thinly disguised Paul for thinking that his brief visionary encounter with Christ could authorize him to propound a gospel message at variance with those who had spent considerable time with Jesus while he was still alive and well among them.

"And if our Jesus appeared to you also and became known in a vision and met you as angry with an enemy [recall: Paul had his vision while still persecuting the Christians; Acts 9], yet he has spoken only through visions and dreams or through external revelations. But can anyone be made competent to teach through a vision? And if your opinion is that that is possible, why then did our teacher spend a whole year with us who were awake? How can we believe you even if he has appeared to you? ... But if you were visited by him for the space of an hour and were instructed by him and thereby have become an apostle, then proclaim his words, expound what he has taught, be a friend to his apostles and do not contend with me, who am his confidant; for you have in hostility withstood me, who am a firm rock, the foundation stone of the Church." (Homilies 17.19)

Peter, not Paul, is the true authority for understanding the message of Jesus. Paul has corrupted the true faith based on a brief vision, which he has doubtless misconstrued. Paul is thus the enemy of the apostles, not the chief of them. He is outside the true faith, a heretic to be banned, not an apostle to be followed. The Pseudo-Clementines, then, especially in their older form, which came to be modified over time, appear to present a kind of Ebionite polemic against Pauline Christianity and against the proto-orthodox of the second and third centuries who continue to follow Paul in rejecting the Law of Moses. For these Ebionite Christians the Law was given by God, and, contrary to the claims of Paul and his proto-orthodox successors, it continues to be necessary for salvation in Christ.[270]

What we are never allowed to hear from the pulpit is that Peter *did* defend himself against Paul's accusation in Galatians 2. We see that in reality, it was not Peter who was in error regarding the Law of God, but rather Paul himself who stood against the true teachings of Christ which came directly from a *Messianic Jew,* the *firm rock, the foundation stone of the Church,* that *Judaizing* and *Super Apostle*—Peter!

The *Encyclopedia Biblica*, which was published in the late 1800s by the editors of Encyclopedia Britannica, discusses at length how *Simon Magus* was a well-known cipher for Paul. The section on Simon Magus tells how Peter had to follow behind *Simon* wherever he went to correct his erroneous teaching.

> That this is Peter's task is everywhere taken for granted as a thing of course. Take for example, Homilies 14:12, where we find Peter saying that Simon is in Antioch (with Annubion); 'when, then, we get there and come upon them, the disputation can take place'; out of a large number of other passages we may point also to 2:17 where Peter speaks of himself as having come in upon Simon 'as light upon darkness, as

---

[270] EHRMAN, Bart D., Lost Christianities: The Battles for Scripture and the Faiths We Never Knew, 2005, p. 184

knowledge upon ignorance, as healing upon disease'. According to 4:6 none but Peter can cope with Simon, and his companions complain that he has sent them on this occasion before him. In Recog. 3:65 Peter says: 'Since Simon has gone forth to preoccupy the ears of the Gentiles who are called to salvation, it is necessary that I also follow upon his track so that whatever disputation he raises may be corrected by us', and in 3:68 we read that 'Simon has set out, wishing to anticipate our journey; him we should have followed step by step, that wheresoever he tries to subvert any there he might forthwith be confuted by us'... [271]

Not only does Peter *not* support the teachings of Paul, he is also actively coming along behind him trying to do damage control! This is a very different story than the one we are used to reading from our carefully groomed and edited Bible.

---

[271] *Encyclopaedia Biblica*, pp. 4553-4. The Encyclopaedia Biblica was published between 1899 and 1903. It was a prodigious enterprise that represented the best in Biblical research of the late 19th century, featuring articles written by William Robertson Smith, Julius Wellhausen, and many, many other scholars from both the English-speaking world and Germany.
http://www.archive.org/details/ encyclopaediabib03cheyuoft

CHAPTER 30

❖

PETER AND THE WOLF

Most Christian and Messianic believers feel uncomfortable and even offended when someone dares to question Paul's apostolic credentials. The traditional line of defense is to shut the conversation down by quoting the books of Peter, specifically 2 Peter 3:16. Within this book and passage Peter is quoted as saying about Paul that,

> ...[Paul's] letters contain some things that are hard to understand, which ignorant and unstable people distort, as they do the other Scriptures, to their own destruction.

Aside from the fact that *Peter* has just belittled and bullied other Christians by calling them *ignorant and unstable*, the underlying theme here is that Peter is ostensibly issuing a warning to anyone who disagrees with Paul's words:

"If you don't believe what Paul writes, you're an unstable ignoramus and you're going to hell."

Before we start quoting the books of Peter as a defense for Paul, we need to realize that there was a deep historical controversy surrounding the adoption of these books into the Bible canon. In fact, they were considered to be *disputed books* by some influential churches and leaders of the late fourth century.

Do we not think that if the books of Peter were well known in the first or second century to be actually authoritative; that is, written by Peter, that the proto-orthodox church fathers would have *immediately* regarded them as canon from the very beginning? They would have added the books to the canon along with the Gospels and Paul's epistles, and there would be no controversy at all!

There is a huge enigma here, with deep and foundational reasons why these books were not widely quoted from nor used in the earlier centuries of Christianity. Either they were simply not around, which means Peter didn't actually write them, or they were spurious—and everyone within these periods of the early Church knew they were spurious—which again means that Peter didn't write them!

WHO REALLY WROTE THE BOOKS OF PETER?

The reason why many scholars state that the book of I Peter is not the work of the Apostle Peter is not only because of the deeply Pauline doctrines the book espouses, but also because the written Greek of 1 Peter is quite exceptional. It is, in fact, some of the best Greek in all of the *New Testament*. Its sheer eloquence surpasses even the well-educated prose of Paul, and is simply not the work of a simple Galilean fisherman. F.W. Beare observes:

> The epistle is quite obviously the work of a man of letters, skilled in all the devices of rhetoric, and able to draw on an extensive, and very learned, vocabulary. He is a stylist of no ordinary capacity, and he writes some of the best Greek in the whole New Testament, far smoother and more literary than that of the highly-trained Paul.[272]

The observant Christian will point to the fact that the book itself offers that Peter didn't write it, but rather dictated it to *Silvanus*.[273] This easily explains why the Greek can be so well notated. But who is this *Silvanus*? *Silvanus* is simply the proper name for *Silas;* the same Silas found traveling with Paul in Luke's *Acts of the Apostles*.[274]

While the casual reader will assume that Peter solicited the services of Silas to write his letter, such a concept stirs rebuttals of deep dissent within scholastic circles. When considering the deep conflicts over the keeping of the Law between the Apostles and Paul's group (which included Silas), the heavily contradictory Pauline theology being espoused by the books of 1 & 2 Peter, and the admission that Silvanus was not just the stenographer but the literary architect of the Greek of 1 Peter, educated scholars find it difficult to see how this book is anything other than a complete work of outright

---

[272] BARCLAY, William, The Daily Bible Study Series, The Letters of James and Peter, Introduction to Peter (1), p. 142
[273] 1 Peter 5:12
[274] 2 Corinthians; 1-2 Thessalonians

fraud. In other words, Peter did not write it nor did he dictate its contents.

The *Jerusalem Church* was large and well known. Peter had at his disposal any number of well-educated people there in Jerusalem to whom he could dictate his letters in Hebrew, Greek, Aramaic, or Latin. He did not need Paul's sidekick Silas—and in fact would have likely regarded him as part of Paul's rogue group. Other Bible scholars are of this same understanding:

> One cannot save Petrine authorship by arguing that Peter employed a secretary. If one argues that this secretary was Silvanus, the traveling companion of Paul (eg. Selwyn 1958) or an anonymous amanuensis of the Roman church (Michaels 1988) the letter then becomes the product not of Peter, but of the secretary, since it is the latter's language that the epistle exhibits (see Beare 1970).[275]

Other evidence contained within the book itself testifies against I Peter being a book that was actually written or even dictated by Peter. W.G. Kümmel observes:

> I Peter presupposes the Pauline theology. This is true not only in the general sense that the Jewish-Christian readers, the 'people of God' (2:10), are no longer concerned about the problem of the fulfillment of the Law, but also in the special sense that, as in Paul, the death of Jesus has atoned for the sins of Christians and has accomplished justification (1:18 f;

---

[275] EVE, Eric, The Oxford Bible Commentary, p. 1263

2:24). Christians are to suffer with Christ (4:13; 5:1), obedience to the civil authorities is demanded (2:14 f), and the Pauline formula *en xristw* is encountered (3:16; 5:10, 14). The frequently advanced proposal that I Peter is literarily dependent on Romans (and Ephesians) is improbable because the linguistic contacts can be explained on the basis of a common catechetical tradition. But there can be no doubt that the author of I Peter stands in the line of succession of Pauline theology, and that is scarcely conceivable for Peter, who at the time of Gal 2:11 was able in only a very unsure way to follow the Pauline basic principle of freedom from the Law for Gentile Christians.[276]

The book of 2 Peter exhibits even deeper problems. From the Reformation era, not even John Calvin believed that Peter wrote the book of 2 Peter! In the modern era, William Barclay notes within his *Daily Bible Study Series* that it is difficult to believe that 2 Peter was actually written by Peter the Apostle:

> It is the well-nigh universal judgment of scholars, both ancient and modern, that Peter is not the author of Second Peter. Even John Calvin regarded it as impossible that Peter could have spoken of Paul as Second Peter speak of him (3:15-16), although he [Calvin] was willing to believe that someone else wrote the letter at Peter's request.[277]

---

[276] KÜMMEL, WG, Introduction to the New Testament, p. 424
[277] BARCLAY, The Daily Bible Study Series, The Letters of James and Peter, p. 285

It is clear that these books have been in deep dispute since the Roman Catholic Church added them to the Bible! Even our own modern Christian scholars concur that the people whose names they bear did not actually write them. However, mainstream Christianity continues to insist that these very Pauline books are valid books written by the Apostle Peter. Today's evangelists and preachers continue to ignore the very deep historical disputes over such books as completely immaterial, while continuing to insist that such issues have been *settled* and are therefore no longer issues for our modern laity to review and study.

Who Really Holds Apostolic Authority?

The overshadowing reason why the books of Peter needed to be written (forged) in the first place is that Paul must be seen to have some valid tie to the authority of the *Jerusalem Church*; otherwise, Paul's ministry and apostolic credentials rest only on himself.

As the hand-selected Disciple of Yeshua and a distinguished founding member of the *Jerusalem Church*, Peter is the one in an authority position. Peter doesn't need Paul to be authoritative, but Paul definitely needs Peter and the rest of the Apostolic leadership of the *Jerusalem Church* to lend credence and authority to his other NuGospel, his NuYeshua and his NuSpirit.

Paul is, in effect, the *ravenous wolf* who is nipping at the proverbial heels of Peter's flock, not the other way around! Yet somehow Christianity has turned Peter into the *villain* and Paul into the *victim*.

The existence of letters ostensibly written by the Apostle Peter extolling Paul and his Law-less NuGospel really amount to nothing more than what Luke attempted to do with his *Acts of the Apostles;* that is, to somehow lend a modicum of Jewish and Hebraic legitimacy to Paul's Hellenistic and Mithraic version of his Yeshua.

CHAPTER 30

❖

THE REST OF THE STORY

We noted earlier in the chapter entitled *Abandoned and Alone* that most of Asia Minor, Paul's home territory, had all but abandoned his NuGospel toward the end of the first century. While a handful of Paul's followers[278] remained loyal to him and his divergent teachings, it would not be until a few decades later that Paul's NuGospel of antinomianism (Lawlessness) against the TRUE Law of God would be revived. Paul's blood-focused gospel, with its mishmash of Mithraic pagan dogma, would rise again—and soon its full impact would be felt as it reverberated throughout the known world and indeed history itself.

In the middle of the next century, Paul's NuGospel found its greatest ally in the wayward leadership of the up-and-coming, anti-Semitic, proto-orthodox and ostensibly catholic

---

[278] Such as: Luke and Mark, Tychicus, Priscilla and Aquila

(universal) Christian churches in Rome, Antioch, Carthage and Alexandria.

Take note of where this issue of two differing, two opposing *gospels* gets undeniably damning for Paul. The Apostles of Yeshua continued to keep the holy festivals of AHYH—at least to some degree. Acts 2 tells us how the Apostles had gathered for Pentecost. Pentecost is the Greek name for *Shavuot*, the *Jewish Feast of Weeks*.

However, Paul condemns and even belittles those who have been keeping God's holy days. In Paul's letter to the churches in the region of Galatia, he admonishes the churches for keeping God's Holy Festivals when he says,

> But now that you know God—or rather are known by God—how is it that you are turning back to those weak and miserable principles? Do you wish to be enslaved by them all over again? You are observing special days and months and seasons and years! I fear for you, that somehow I have wasted my efforts on you.[279]

Attempted guilt trip aside; we can see that Paul has indeed been teaching the churches in Galatia not to observe these Festivals because here Paul admonishes the churches for doing just that.

Contemporary Sabbath-keeping and/or Festival-keeping Christian denominations should have already recognized and taken steps to correct this issue of Paul's divergent gospel. These denominations rely on Torah, the Tanakh, the Messiah

---

[279] Galatians 4:9-11 NIV 1984; Paul is specifically denouncing the Holy Festivals of God as outlined within the Law of God. See also: William Barclay, *The Daily Bible Study Series, "The Letters to the Galatians and Ephesians"*, Revised Edition, ©1976, Galatians 4:8-11, pp. 37-37

and His Apostles' own examples within the Gospels for the understanding that the observance of these Sabbaths is paramount to the Character of God. Yet here Paul is unilaterally and specifically allowed to toss the Sabbath out the window as being a *weak and miserable principle!*

Paul's revisionism of the Scriptures and his tendency to use Torah passages way out of their intended context has not gone unnoticed by authentic Jewish scholars. Take serious note that this is not some personal *interpretation* issue between rival religions, Judaism and Christianity; rather it goes to the heart of who Paul says he is and what his words and actions actually reveal about himself.

Rabbi Tovia Singer[280] offers this review of Paul's scripture quotes:

> A classic example of [Paul's] biblical revisionism can be found in Romans 10:8 where Paul announces to his readers that he is quoting directly from scripture as he records the words of Deuteronomy 30:14. Yet as he approaches the last portion of this verse, he carefully stops short of the Torah's vital conclusion and expunges the remaining segment of this crucial verse. In Romans 10:8 Paul writes, But what does it say? "The word is near you, in your mouth and in your heart" (that is, the word of faith which we preach).

---

[280] Tovia Singer is a well-known speaker and Israeli talk-show host, lecturing hundreds of times each year around the globe in North America, South America, Europe and Israel. Singer harbors a vast knowledge of topics ranging from anti-Semitism, holocaust revisionism, Jewish and Christian History. He sponsors and publishes materials for Judaism aimed at countering the misinformation of Christian Missionaries.

Predictably, the last words of Deuteronomy 30:14, "that you may do it," were meticulously deleted by Paul. Bear in mind that he had good reason for removing this clause—the powerful message contained in these closing words rendered all that Paul was preaching as heresy.

This stunning misquote in Romans stands out as a remarkable illustration of Paul's ability to shape scriptures in order to create the illusion that his theological message conformed to the principles of the Torah. By removing the final segment of this verse, Paul succeeded in convincing his largely Gentile readers that his Christian teachings were supported by the principles of the Hebrew Bible.[281]

Deuteronomy 30:14
But the word is very near to you, in your mouth and in your heart, that you may do it.

Romans 10:8
But what does it say? "The word is near you, in your mouth and in your heart" (that is, the word of faith which we preach).

---

[281] To give this example a modern application, let us consider that this is very much like a well-known reporter who stated that a political candidate had said regarding a certain war, "There is a plan and it is God's plan." The meaning was found to be utterly different when the political candidate's entire statement was considered. "Pray for our military men and women who are striving to do what is right. Also for this country, that our leaders, our national leaders are sending them out on a task that is from God. That's what we have to make sure that we're praying for, that there is a plan and that that plan is God's plan." *(Example taken from an interview of Sarah Palin by ABC reporter Charles Gibson, shown on 9/11/08.)*

The question that immediately comes to mind is: How can Paul deliberately remove a vital clause from Moses' message and still expect to gain a following among the Jewish people? While considering this question, we can begin to understand why Paul attained great success among his Gentile audiences and utterly failed among the Jews who were unimpressed with his contrived message.

It is for this reason that although both Paul and Matthew quoted extensively from the Jewish scriptures, they achieved a very different result. Paul was largely a minister to Gentile audiences who were ignorant of the Jewish Bible (the only Bible in existence at the time). As a result, they did not possess the skills necessary to discern between genuine Judaism and Bible tampering. These illiterate masses were, as a result, vulnerable, and eagerly consumed everything that Paul taught them. In fact, throughout the New Testament it was exclusively the Jewish apostates to Christianity who challenged Paul's authority, never the Gentile community.[282]

Singer offers a striking historical revelation that is consistent with many other scholars of Judaic and Christian history. It is yet another nail in the coffin of the presumed infallibility of Paul's writings.

To Paul's credit, there is one issue in which he really hits the nail on the head. Paul was fundamentally and foundationally correct when he vehemently preached against the ancient pagan practice of circumcision that had been adopted

---

[282] Tovia Singer, OutreachJudaism.org/original.htm, on 08/16/2008

by Judaism as a *sign* of their covenant with God. Indeed, *circumcision of the heart*[283] is what God really desires, and this understanding is clearly expressed in the Torah and Tanakh as well.[284] Keeping in mind the extreme significance that circumcision held to traditional Judaism, speaking out against this practice in front of a crowd who considered their trimmed penises to be the greatest indicators of their covenant with God was downright revolutionary and even reformational.

In light of his spot on diatribes against circumcision, it is difficult to understand why Paul felt compelled to have Timothy circumcised, other than to somehow impress some of the Jews back home.[285] It makes him appear to be hypocritical or, in today's vernacular, *a flip-flopper*.

The lack of backbone shown by this action should make one wonder: was Paul simply an opportunist, preaching any message that would make him popular to whatever crowd he was currently with? After all, circumcision was frowned on in many parts of the Gentile world, and preaching against it would make him more popular with the Greeks and Romans. Did he really believe what he was saying about circumcision, or was *being all things to all people*[286] more important than taking an unequivocal stand?

Faced with this kind of divided and conflicting advice, the discerning Christian or Messianic believer needs to consider: If we carefully consider the context and background of *all* of Paul's referenced Scripture, can we truthfully continue to call him infallibly inspired?

---

[283] Romans 2:29
[284] Deuteronomy 10:16, 30:6 and Jeremiah 4:4
[285] Acts 16:3
[286] 1 Corinthians 9:22

CHAPTER 32

❖

SHEEPLE NO MORE

Most Christian and Messianic believers have been taught from a very early age to deeply revere the entire Bible as the inerrant and infallibly inspired Word of God. This is not what the Bible itself teaches,[287] but is the tradition that has been given to us by Protestant Christianity.

When Protestantism broke away from the assumed authority of the Roman Catholic Church during the Reformation, Rome's so-called *rebellious daughter* decided that *the Church* would no longer be her assumed authority on spiritual matters. The Bible, which Protestantism adopted from the Roman Catholic Church, would now become her lone authority. Henceforth, the doctrine of *Sola Scriptura* or *Scripture Alone* was born. The irony in this belief is that Protestants must assume that while the Roman Catholic Church erred

---

[287] Jeremiah 8:8

egregiously in almost everything it did, it somehow managed not to err when assembling the Bible that we inherited and now call our own.

As support for the doctrine of *Sola Scriptura*, believers have been taught to cite Paul as their basis for the dogma of Scriptural inerrancy. They quote,

> All Scripture is God-breathed and is useful for teaching, rebuking, correcting and training in righteousness...[288]

These faithful *Sola Scriptura* believers automatically assume that this passage in 2 Timothy includes the entire current modern Bible. The problem with that viewpoint is that when these words were written, Paul didn't have our current modern Bible! All Paul had at the time was the *Tanakh*, the *Jewish Scriptures;* our *Old Testament*. Paul didn't have the Gospels or many of the other *New Testament* books because they had not been written yet. Furthermore, it is highly unlikely that Paul would have been referring to his own letters as *Scripture*. Paul was admittedly boastful, but he wasn't that boastful!

This assurance that *all Scripture is God-breathed* (i.e. inerrant, infallible, inspired) also directly contradicts God, who, speaking via the prophet Jeremiah, in no uncertain terms stated that *"Torah* [had been] handled falsely by the lying pen of the scribes [elders]."[289]

---

[288] 2 Timothy 3:16
[289] Jeremiah 8:8

When such contradictions or historical discrepancies[290] surface within the pages of the Bible, believers feel compelled to resolve these problems in a way that ultimately preserves the Protestant belief that the Bible as a whole is inerrantly and infallibly inspired. We never really stop to consider that it is our own tradition of Scriptural infallibility itself that might be in error. It is like we're trying to prove the manmade tradition that *the Earth is flat* by explaining away all of the scientific satellite data telling us the Earth is a sphere!

God has not given us perfect Scriptures, nor do we have a perfectly assembled canon (standard of belief and understanding) that illustrates the TRUE Word of God. The dogma that declares the Bible to be *inerrantly inspired* makes us feel all warm and fuzzy, but it is not reality.

Conflicting Testimony

There came a point in my spiritual journey when the multitude of discrepancies that were facing me could no longer be explained away. After completing an intense study on the writings of Paul, I was distressed to discover that with nearly every peaceful, reasoned, and logical Character trait I discovered about Almighty God within the *Tanakh*, Paul seemed to be offering conflicting testimony. Sure, I could close my eyes to one or two problems or assumed contradictions here or

---

[290] Such as: Historical discrepancies between witnesses (did Jesus ride into Jerusalem on one donkey or two?), editorial revisions between manuscripts (scholars noting that the most reliable manuscripts do not have certain verses); current tradition versus Apostolic tradition (the Apostles kept a seventh-day Sabbath and most Christians worship on the first day of the week).

there; but at some juncture I could no longer ignore or sweep aside the veritable mountain of evidence.

Many Adventist theologians and other conservative Christian scholars that I had discussed these issues with acknowledged that Paul indeed appeared to be offering contradictory information. But because of his inclusion in the *authoritative Word of God*, the underlying advice was to just accept what he was saying, and attempt to reconcile or ignore the problem passages as best I could.

I am not good at ignoring problems, so the counsel I received from these discussions ended up being an exercise in confusion. It didn't help the situation to know that many thousands of scholars before me had recognized the problems with Paul, but had chosen to do nothing about it. It seemed to me that Paul really needed to be thoroughly and critically scrutinized—but no one that I knew within Christianity's leadership seemed willing to do so.

Eventually I realized that what I was doing was not questioning God, but rather questioning Paul's canonization into Scripture by the Roman Catholic Church—an *authority* that I as a Protestant didn't recognize anyway! Why were these early Roman Catholic Fathers trying to build upon a foundation that was errantly laid by a wayward and rogue apostle? And should I really feel compelled to follow their example?

DOES PAUL BELONG IN THE BIBLE?

The majority of Christian or Messianic believers have been completely raised and educated—even indoctrinated—within a culture and perspective where Paul is the central figure for our understandings of the Gospel. It is this education and indoctrination that becomes the basis of our perspective, a decidedly *Pauline* hermeneutic, which shapes our cultural understanding of how we see facts and history. It then helps us develop our version of what we believe to be *the truth*.[291]

I have heard the argument ad nauseum—"Well, you are totally looking at Paul from a very Jewish (i.e. *Judaizing*) perspective; of course you are going to see him as an apostate from the Law!" In reality, it was Paul himself who attempted to illustrate that he was a bona fide Jew!

God allows wicked men their evil desires—even if those desires will mean misleading other well-intentioned people for centuries. This is exactly what happened to the ancient Priesthood of Israel—the priesthood deliberately misled the whole nation into idolatry and sacrifices. Paradoxically, many Protestants have accused the Roman Catholic Church of doing the exact same thing—installing paganism and idolatry into Christendom!

Perhaps it could be argued that God indeed put Paul into the Bible—not as an apostle to be followed, but rather as a test—a test to see whom we would choose to follow. Would we chase after the sacrificial paganism of Israel and subsequent idolatry of Rome, or pursue the simple faith of Yeshua HaMaschiach, who indeed taught,

> Go and learn what this means, '[AHEYEH] desire[s] *mercy* and not sacrifice.'[292]

---

[291] In scholastic circles a biased perspective is called a *hermeneutic,* which when broken down to its most basic definition is, "how do we choose to interpret history, ancient writings, etc., and with what methods."

[292] Matthew 9:3; 12:7 quoting Hosea 6:6 which reads: "For I delight in mercy / loyalty / loving kindness / grace rather than sacrifice, And in the knowledge of God rather than burnt offerings." NIV, NASB, *Hebrew and Chaldee Lexicon to the Old Testament Scriptures* by Wilhelm Gesenius

We earlier discussed in detail how there are multiple period witnesses such as Ezekiel, James, Peter, and the author of Revelation, whom Paul has absolutely contradicted. In the final analysis, we need to look at Paul impartially, and match his words and counsel with those of other authoritative witnesses within the Bible's Scriptures. In light of these glaring contradictions, it is ironic that Paul himself wrote,

> Do not entertain an accusation against an elder unless it is brought by two or three witnesses. Those who sin are to be rebuked publicly, so that the others may take warning. I charge you, in the sight of God and Yeshua HaMaschiach and the elect angels, to keep these instructions without partiality, and to do nothing out of favoritism.[293]

In 2 Thessalonians 2:9-12, Paul predicted:

> The coming of the *lawless one* will be in accordance with how Satan works. He will use all sorts of displays of power through signs and wonders that serve the lie, and all the ways that wickedness deceives those who are perishing. They perish because they refused to love the truth and so be saved. For this reason God sends them a powerful delusion so that they will believe the lie and so that all will be condemned who have not believed the truth but have delighted in wickedness.

---

[293] 1 Timothy 5:19-21

Note the *italicized* phrase, *lawless one*. This phrase is a carryover subject from verses 7 and 8 of this chapter, where Paul is describing the *lawless one*. The terms in Paul's Greek, which he is using to describe the lawless one, are *anomia* [ἀνομία] (from verse 7), which is an adjective that describes people having:

> *iniquity, wickedness; to be in a condition of without law because one is ignorant of it or simply violating it; or having contempt for and thus in violation of law.*[294]

...and the term *anomos* [ἄνομος] (from verse 8) which is another adjective that means:

> *destitute of (the Mosaic) law; to be of the Gentiles; departing from the law, a violator of the law, lawless, wicked*[295]

So, the person Paul is warning us to avoid here is one who is:

a) In flagrant violation and contempt of the TRUE Law of God; and
b) Adversely affecting those people he is speaking to at that time, as he is speaking to a *present day* audience.

---

[294] Thayer's Greek Lexicon, Strong's G459 offers "Lawless, Lawlessness: "without law," also denotes "lawless," and is so rendered in the RV of Act 2:23, "lawless (men)," marg., "(men) without the law," AV, "wicked (hands);" 2Th 2:8, "the lawless one" (AV, "that wicked"), of the man of sin (2Th 2:4); in 2Pe 2:8, of deeds (AV, "unlawful"), where the thought is not simply that of doing what is unlawful, but of flagrant defiance of the known will of God. See LAW, C, No. 3."

[295] Thayer's Greek Lexicon, Strong's G458

This dire warning of Paul's corresponds directly with what Yeshua said about those who would not enter the Kingdom of Heaven. Yeshua warned,

> Beware of the false prophets [apostles], who come to you in sheep's clothing, but inwardly are ravenous wolves. [a reference to evil Benjamites] You will know them by their fruits. [what they preach and teach and do] ...
>
> Not everyone who says to Me, 'Lord, Lord,' will enter the kingdom of heaven, but he who does the will of My Father who is in heaven will enter. Many will say to Me on that day, 'Lord, Lord, did we not prophesy in Your name, and in Your name cast out demons, and in Your name perform many miracles?' And then I will declare to them, 'I never knew you; depart from Me, you who *practice lawlessness*.'[296]

Yeshua (via Matthew) uses the Greek word *anomia* to describe those *who practice lawlessness*. These are the people who will not enter the Kingdom of Heaven because of their "flagrant defiance of the known will of God."[297] Paul himself later uses this exact same term, which essentially describes Paul's very own antinomian and lawless ministry!

Paul is said to have prophesied. Paul performed miracles in Yeshua's name. Paul is said to have cast out demons in Yeshua's name. Yet Paul's ministry is one of almost utter hypocrisy when it comes to following the TRUE Law of God, which Yeshua said would be necessary to enter the Kingdom of Heaven. Did God really need a human sacrifice, something

---

[296] Matthew 7:15-21 NASB, [amplification supplied]
[297] Strong's G459

that is in direct violation of the Law? But that is exactly what Paul preached: Yeshua as a crucified pagan (Gentile) human sacrifice so that God could forgive humanity their sins (c.f. Mithraism).

When you really look at Paul's words and ministry without the rose-colored glasses of Christian tradition, it is *Paul* who appears to be this *great delusion* that he himself predicted. *He* is the *lawless one* that Yeshua warned us about! In stunning irony, what better way could there be to steer the unknowing away from the source of the deception than by having the deceiver himself state that there is a deception coming?

The organized Christian Church has made some terribly bad decisions in the past; and the canonization of Paul within the Bible is perhaps one of the most egregious ones. If present-day Christianity decides to purge any books from the Bible that have been found to stand at odds with the witnesses of God, she will be following an already well-established path, because the removal of books from the Bible is not the stuff of ancient history. Martin Luther's own removal of several books from the Bible may have been 500 years ago, but it wasn't until 1885 that the Protestant Church itself ultimately agreed with Luther's decision and *officially* removed these books from the Bible.[298]

We are not talking about the Stone Age here: George Patton was born in 1885 and Daimler's internal combustion engine was patented in 1885. Christians living only a century

---

[298] Well after Luther's decision to remove the Apocrypha, Bibles continued to be printed with the Apocryphal books included within them because of the demands of the marketplace. It was not until 1885, when the Archbishop of Canterbury made an official decree, that this decision would ultimately mark the official removal of the Apocrypha from the Protestant Bible canon.

ago decided that God had given them the authority to make changes to the Bible, and to once again correct the errors of the Roman Catholic Church.

THE ROAD LESS TRAVELED

After learning all of these troubling facts about Paul, I was faced with an intersection of belief. I could take the easy path and go down the wide road into *New Covenantville,* where quite a few of my friends were already headed or even residing. Paul's words would supersede those of Yeshua and the rest of the Bible, and in Marcion-like fashion I would throw out the Law of God as being required or even necessary. I would then head to the nearest church of the Northland / Willow Creek / Saddleback variety and once again become involved in praise and worship, Christian songwriting, and full participation with the Body of Christ. On this road, I could enjoy the company of some two billion other Christian believers worldwide.

The one problem with this *easy path* was that if I chose this route, I would also need to try to *close Pandora's box of knowledge* and forget everything I had ever learned about Paul's *stigmata,* his demonic *thorn* and his false and bloody NuGospel.

The other alternative was to take the other, much less populated road. I could choose to reject the antinomianism prescribed by Paul and look at the TRUE Law of God as a blessing, just like Yeshua himself did and the TRUE Prophets before him.

The thought of giving up Paul and by extension Christianity as I knew it, was very upsetting. Who can describe the anguish, grief, remorse, and anger of a Christian who realizes that the foundation of Christianity that they have built their doctrine on does not just have some minor cracks in it—but instead has some severe foundational flaws?

After learning all of this new information about my beliefs, my church's history, and my God, I finally couldn't sit in silence anymore. Instead of just *accepting* what I had been taught, I needed to start *protesting* the status quo that I had been given. I needed to stop being a *sheeple*[299] and start being a *PROTESTant!*

Like the Protestants living a century ago and the ancient Church members in Ephesus twenty centuries ago, the message was beginning to sink in that as a Christian, I had not only the God-given *authority*, but also the inherent *responsibility* that comes with that authority, to learn and to judge with impartiality *those who claim to be apostles but are not*.[300]

God entreats each one of us personally to come before Him and *reason* with His counsel.[301] I was ready to start reasoning and stop following. It was time to take action!

---

[299] *Sheeple* is a word that is often used to denote those people who accept the status quo and never question authority or the traditions they have been taught. It is a combination of the words *sheep* and *people*.
[300] "I know your deeds, your hard work and your perseverance. I know that you cannot tolerate wicked men, that you have tested those who claim to be apostles but are not, and have found them false." -Revelation 2:2
[301] Isaiah 1:18

CHAPTER 33

❖

LEAVING HOME

The weekend I really faced these facts and contradictions, I was so shocked and dismayed that I skipped church. I lay woodenly in my bed, sobbing brokenly. It felt like someone near and dear to me had died; in fact, this situation seemed even worse, because my own now-shaky faith no longer had a *Thus saith the Lord* to depend on. What was I to do now? Where was I to go? How could I live without the support and comfort of my spiritual home, and the familiar traditions I had depended on my whole life?

I did not realize it at the time, but many other Adventists have had questions about Adventism as well; in fact, it takes more than the fingers on my two hands to count how many close and devout friends have exited the Adventist Church because they can no longer reconcile what they have been taught with what they read in the Bible.

This exodus of members of my home church is not an isolated trend. In 2005, the SDA Church reported astounding membership losses. In spite of the fact that five million new believers joined the church during the 5-year period of 2000-2004, over 1.4 million members left the church during that same period.[302]

If you ask the great majority of those who have left Adventism what their reasons for leaving are, the answers will be nearly unanimous: earnest Christian people are leaving Adventism because of Adventism's obvious contradictions with Paul.[303] Paul alone creates more contradiction with the rest of the Bible than any other Biblical figure or writer. Paul *contradicts* the words of Yeshua HaMaschiach and Paul *contradicts* the prophets as well. We previously looked at such a contradiction between Mathew 5:17 versus Ephesians 2:15. These contradictions are not unknown within Christianity, but they are generally spun and smoothly marketed as *the mystery of God* or *two sides of the same coin* or whatever excuse sounds good and plausible at the time.

What usually happens in a church that correctly attempts to honor God's Law in general and the Sabbath in particular is that intelligent Christian people end up recognizing Paul's contradictions and are then forced to choose sides, so to speak. It then becomes a contest of the Apostles' *'Yeshua'* versus Paul's *'Yeshua'*, with Luke's books and the forged books of Peter running interference somewhere in the middle. Add to the mix the unknown Pauline author of *Hebrews* with its pseudo-Hebraic slant that makes everyday Gentiles think

---

[302] Vance Ferrell, More WAYMARKS - from PILGRIMS REST, "The 2005 St. Louis Session: Items of Interest General Conference Sessions: WM1305, "2005 ST. LOUIS SESSION: ITEMS OF INTEREST Nov 05 Index: General Conference Sessions / St. Louis".

[303] Anger over Ellen White's writings and the "plagiarism issue" is also frequently cited; however, even this anger comes back to noticing a difference between what Adventism believes and what is reflected in Paul's writings.

they suddenly know what it's really like to be a Jew, and you have a very potent—but altogether misguided—case for deep confusion.

It is unfortunate that Paul usually wins, because his message is the much more Gentile-centric and anti-Semitic (less culturally Jewish) option that fits within the neo-Marcionism of today's pop-Christianity—just as it did in the second century Roman Empire.

In other words, Paul is more like us!

Many God-fearing people end up leaving the Adventist Church because of Paul's anti-law counsel. Because they think that Paul is *infallibly inspired of God,* they then logically deduce and conclude that Adventist leaders are being inconsistent hypocrites with regard to Paul's *New Covenant* message within the Bible. On the one hand, these leaders claim Paul is a bona fide apostle; but on the other hand, they quietly disregard and ignore his deeply antinomianist (anti-Law-of-God) message, such as the passages contained in Galatians (the whole book), Romans 14, and Colossians 2—especially with regard to the keeping of the Sabbath.

Ask almost any Christian who is not an Adventist whether or not Christians need to be keeping the Sabbath proper (i.e. on the seventh day of the week), and you'll be met with someone quoting Romans 14 where Paul says,

> One man considers one day more sacred than another; another man considers every day alike. Each one should be fully convinced in his own mind.

Yet, if anyone within Adventist circles dares to say anything about this conflict between Paul and our Adventist tradition, it is generally resolved by reinterpreting Paul's words to make

Paul sound more logical and less confusing. The typical expression is, "What Paul really meant was ..."[304]

The American journalist, Upton Sinclair, once wrote,

> It is difficult to get a man to understand something when his job depends upon his not understanding it.

Our own Adventist leadership is deeply rooted in such a position—their very jobs and livelihood are secure only when they do not agitate and only when they conform to the mainstream of orthodox Adventist theology—even if that theology is dead wrong. When you have Adventist leadership earning their living only because they maintain an orthodox Adventist (traditional) perspective, you will not have an easy time convincing our best and brightest people to challenge any doctrine that could jeopardize their livelihoods.

Despite such criticism, it remains obvious that the SDA Church has not been without the Holy Spirit of God! What makes modern Christianity admirable is not our *beliefs*, but our actions; what we *do* in our walk with Almighty God. Christians, and Adventists especially, remain Torah-observant people at heart; Messianic believers especially so. We try to keep God's Commandments, and we also try to reach out and help others as best we can. But we still may find ourselves wondering—do these actions save us? "Are we saved by works or by grace?"

---

[304] Entire books have been written to try to help the confused Christian or Messianic believer decipher Paul's writings. There is even an Evangelical book by Catholic author Garry Wills entitled *"What Paul Meant."* This same author has also written books reinterpreting and framing *"What Jesus Meant"*, and *"What The Gospels Meant"*.

Adventists and indeed all Christians should recognize that this question itself is flawed, and designed to promote an errant either/or response. The correct answer to such a question is to first correct the question to allow for the full answer to be imparted. When asked, "Are we saved by works or by grace?" The correct answer is, *"Both!* It is not either/or! The true mechanism of God's salvation is that *Man is saved through repentance."*[305]

Repentance—the simple turning from one's sin and doing what God requests of His people—embodies both grace and works. These are not mutually exclusive components. To be forgiven requires God's forbearance, grace, and mercy. However, we cannot expect God's mercy and grace to fall upon us if we continue to be stuck in our sin. We must consistently repent, turn from our sinful ways, and stop doing those things that grieve the heart of God.

This, then, is the very heart and core of God's grace. The grace and forgiveness of God is never bestowed upon the unrepentant heart that refuses to let go of sin. While we may sin again and again, God indeed looks for a contrite heart that longs to be released from and forgiven of sin. When a contrite spirit and an eagerness to do what is right are present within the man, a beautiful thing happens within the heart and a change begins to occur. The Eternal One tells us, "In repentance and rest is your salvation, in quietness and trust is your strength". This is God's TRUE Biblical mechanism of salvation, not atonement through the blood of a sacrifice.

---

[305] Ezekiel 18

PART V
THE CALL TO "GO FORTH!"

CHAPTER 34

❖

THE GREAT CON

Several years ago I read a very exciting book entitled *This Present Darkness*, a work of Christian fiction / fantasy by the prolific author Frank Peretti. One reviewer describes the book in the following way.

> The residents of the sleepy college town of Ashton, comfortable in their middle American lifestyle, had no idea that their community was about to play a significant role in the ages-old battle between the forces of good versus evil. A malevolent storm was brewing in the nether regions, a storm that would challenge the mightiest of God's angels in their task to preserve the earth from satanic conquest. And the people of Ashton were to play the major role in equipping His angels with the power they would need to meet that challenge.

Author Frank E. Peretti weaves a tale of suspense tempered with humor in his book, This Present Darkness, which, just of late, seems to have surged into popularity since its original release in 1986. Already in its eighth printing since its debut, This Present Darkness is causing Christians to buzz with excitement at the prospect that they may have learned something new and of great importance to help them in their own struggles against the spiritual darkness that pervades the earth.

The premise of Peretti's book is the power of prayer to influence the forces in the spiritual world. When the novel's chief protagonist, a godly pastor by the name of Hank Busche, discovers a sinister plot to turn Ashton's college into a bulwark of New Age philosophy, he finds that human effort alone will not stop the advance of this evil. A novice at prayer, Hank and his wife Mary learn quickly that, unless God intervenes, their very lives are at stake.

Facing discouragement at every turn, set up for a sexual scandal intended to discredit Hank, threatened with death or worse, the Busches find that they are not alone in the fight. God has other prayer warriors they know nothing about until the chips are down and the eleventh hour has passed in the plot to turn Whitmore College over to a political machine steeped in witchcraft.

Behind the political machine is one Alexander Kaseph, holder of interests in multi-billion dollar corporations working to establish a new world order. Kaseph allows himself to be possessed by "the Strongman," chief of all demons.

Employed in Kaseph's service is professor of psychology Juleen Langstrat, known to dabble in witchcraft, and a channeler for one of the Strongman's princes, Ba'al Rafar. Through her wiles, she controls the local sheriff, Alf Brummel, and other lesser characters embroiled in their sinister plot.

But Kaseph, Langstrat, et al., do not reckon on the power of God to move the hearts of men toward good. Besides the Busches, Marshall Hogan, editor of the Ashton Clarion, discovers through some top-notch investigative work that all is not kosher in his quiet little town. With the help of an assistant, Bernice Krueger, he gathers enough evidence to indict the conspirators, provided he can overcome the superior game-playing that he is up against. And provided he doesn't get murdered as have others before him who got too nosy.

Peretti's tale braids the story of Ashton's human struggle with the "real" struggle behind the scenes: the spiritual warfare that controls the destinies of men. Demon spirits, dark, sinister, fierce in their antagonism against God and man, gather in a brooding cloud of evil, discernible only to other spirits in their realm: God's angels strategically planted to offset this attack here, that countermove there.

Flailing with swords against forces vastly superior in number, God's angels take their share of blows. A broken wing, a deep gash in the body, pain from countless injuries incurred during moments of lull in the humans' prayer lives. But with every prayer comes a new surge of strength, equipping the angels with the ability to stand against the strongest demons.

On the other side, lesser demons are terrorized by their superiors, kicked into submission, ridiculed, and abased by every means available to spirit entities. Tiny demons disappear into puffs of smoke, if not at the hands of God's angels, then at the behest of their superiors displeased with their lack of performance. And it seems that, no matter how powerful a demon, there is always one more powerful than he to keep him in place. Jealousy results in a treasonous act by one demon of high status who is rankled over the impending victory by his hated and abusive superior.

In the end, the Christians of Ashton—The "Remnant"—win the day along with a lot of souls, and keep Whitmore College free of control by the Strongman.[306]

This Present Darkness was so very pivotal to my spiritual life at the time I read it. My friends and I felt very inspired to pray after reading the story, because it really made it seem like the victory won by God was utterly dependent on the prayers of His people. *I* could help make a difference in whether God or Satan triumphed! What a heady and amazing thought!

The other thing I found intriguing was that the book shined a spotlight on the supernatural. It made me feel like I could really see what was going on behind the scenes in this epic *Great Controversy between God and Satan*. I found it easier

---

[306] This material has been adapted and/or excerpted from a 6/88 Media Spotlight Special Report – "This Present Darkness: Spiritual Warfare -- Fact or Fantasy?" by Albert James Dager. The article goes on to discuss at length many of the problems found in this book; not in the least that its pure fantasy and conjecture have shaped many erroneous opinions of how things *really* are in the spirit world. The article was found on 8/15/10 at http://www.rapidnet.com/~jbeard/bdm/exposes/peretti/ dark.htm

to visualize what was going on because the book had made it all seem so real.

What I did not realize at the time was that there are some significant problems with this particular theological point of view—one of which is that it portrays God and Satan in a very dualistic manner.[307] In some ways, the concept is similar to American politics. There is always a continuous struggle between Democrats and Republicans, and the votes (in the case of dualism, the prayers) of the people actually determine the outcome. Victory or defeat is in the hands of the people!

Adventism takes a lot of direction regarding this great dualistic struggle from Ellen White's epic book *The Great Controversy,* which was based on one of her most famous mystic visions. This *war in heaven* perspective deeply shapes Adventist doctrine, so the SDA Church is always looking for new ways to make this *Great Controversy* viewpoint fresh and relevant for the times.

One example of this attempt at relevancy was a particularly disturbing *Signs Of The Times* cover from September 2004 which showed *Yeshua,* in requisite white robe and sandals, with a light saber in his hand, duking it out with Satan in a very *Luke Skywalker battles Darth Vader* kind of manner. Relevant to the times? Yes. In good taste? Doubtful. But it did illustrate in an eye-catching manner the dualistic *struggle between God and Satan* dogma that was being promoted.

After years of study, I came to realize that a created being who is a mere speck compared to its Creator, and who draws its actual life from that same Creator cannot in any way be a

---

[307] Dualism in its purest religious sense is the belief that there is a great struggle going on at this time between two great powers – the powers of Good and the powers of Evil.

major player in any so-called controversy. The concept does not even compute! You might as well compare the Earth to Sol, our sun. Besides being much smaller, the Earth has no light or power of its own; any life and power it sustains is dependent on the light and heat of the sun.

It is unfortunate that so much of today's Christianity, as illustrated earlier by Peretti's fictitious novel based on fantasy, focuses on *The Enemy* and his assumed attributes—his great power, influence, authority, and so on. We are bombarded with stories about this "struggle between the powers of good and darkness."

Unfortunately, Almighty God's vast authority and power is lost in the wreckage of this dualistic nonsense. Instead of standing in awe of a mighty Creator and Ruler who bows to no one and is in no way threatened by us or by anything, we have created a god who has been dumbed-down to the point of lunacy; stripped and emasculated of all power, held hostage by a pitchfork-wielding, horned *Enemy* who is the *god of this world* or even the *god of this age*.[308] We remove any responsibility for obedience from our message, and we state vehemently that if any bad thing happens, it is because *The Enemy* is out to get us.[309]

The Biblical story of Job is often quoted to support this *Great Controversy*. (Yes, I have quoted it myself in the past.) Yet when considering this story, we never really focus on the fact that for every action Satan made, he had to obtain God's express consent. As we have earlier discussed, there are records in Scripture of God sending evil spirits on people, to

---

[308] Thank you, Paul. 2 Corinthians 4:4.
[309] Ironically, we also figure that if things are going well and bad things are not happening to us, that *The Enemy* is not out to get us because we are doing something spiritually wrong and are *no longer a threat!*

lie to people and persecute them. *God Almighty* sent these evil spirits; God did not just *allow* them to attack! Yet Christianity has to support such a sanitized version of a namby-pamby God that we cannot wrap our heads around the fact that our *God* will sometimes send evil spirits to do His bidding, to work His purposes—and furthermore, these evil beings, who draw their life from God just as you and I do, obey!

In addition, we insist that the God of the Universe has something to *prove* to us in this whole *Great Controversy*. We never stop to consider that the Creator of all does not have to prove a single thing to those He created. He does not have to explain Himself or His actions. If He does, then there is a natural or universal law at work that is even higher than our God is.

We are not, in our limited finite understandings, able to comprehend why God is doing what He is doing because His understandings are so far above ours. This is the essential message of the book of Job:

> Listen buddy, I tossed together a handful of molecules to make you. Yes, I did that. I don't need to explain to you why I do what I do; I gave you life, I can take it away. You exist at my pleasure. When you can create yourself out of nothing, then we might have something to talk about. Until then, I don't need to explain myself to you. Grow up and get over it.

In our efforts to understand a God who is too far above us to even comprehend, all that we have managed to do is *remake* God into something that is easier for us to grasp and fathom. First, we've recast God into the image of *someone*, like an all-powerful human being or spiritual superman who lives in this place called Heaven. We see this God as not one, but three gods; two sitting on thrones with a third god that floats around in some ghost-like manner. Second, we've stripped God of His TRUE awe and power and dumbed Him down to something we can more easily get our minds around; something *we* are more comfortable with. We've invented something that makes us *feel* better when we see God's *evil* at work in the world. No, it's not a comforting thought to hear God say,

> I form the light and create darkness, I bring prosperity and create disaster; I, AHYH, do all these things. [310]

Subsequently, we massage this understanding by saying, "Oh, God just *allows* evil to happen, He doesn't actually bring it." Poppycock! If God actively *allows* evil to happen, then God is complicit in it. This is an example of believers attempting to revise the reality of who and what God is in order to make themselves somehow feel better about a God who is not just warm and fuzzy, but truly *dangerous*. In the process, we have turned God into this spiritual Santa Clause of sorts while attempting to ignore the fact that God is at times quite *unsafe*.

Modern Christians appear to have lost sight of something that Christians just a century ago seemed to know very well. C. S. Lewis in his *Chronicles of Narnia* series paints a very interesting portrayal within the story of his god-like character, Aslan. Within the first book, *The Lion, the Witch and the Wardrobe*, Narnia has been suffering for a century under the

---

[310] Isaiah 45:7 NIV 1984; Note that the term translated as "disaster" within the NIV is רע (ra`) in the Hebrew which means, literally: evil, distress, misery, injury, calamity.

rule of an evil witch. Aslan could easily destroy the witch—but for some unknown reason, he doesn't. In the course of the story, a very revealing exchange takes place between the children, or *Sons and Daughters of Adam and Eve,* and the Beavers, who act as the wise historians. This conversation illustrates how Christian believers a century ago perceived God, as opposed to the understanding that is generally taught today:

> "Ooh!" said Susan, "I'd thought [Aslan] was a man. Is he—quite safe? I shall feel rather nervous about meeting a lion."
> "That you will, dearie and no mistake," said Mrs. Beaver; "if there's anyone who can appear before Aslan without their knees knocking, they're either braver than most or else just silly."
> "Then he isn't safe?" said Lucy.
> "Safe?" said Mr. Beaver; "don't you hear what Mrs. Beaver tells you? Who said anything about safe? 'Course he isn't safe. But he's good."[311]

As believers, we want a *tame* and predictable God who makes us feel all warm and safe and secure. This is what *sells* in today's churches, because no one wants to feel powerless! However, it is *not* the truth or an accurate reflection of the One TRUE God and Eternal One.

A Facebook friend recently posted,

> It is hard to understand why Satan does cruel things and then points at God as the culprit. Cripple and

---

[311] LEWIS, C.S., *The Lion, The Witch and the Wardrobe,* from the Chronicles of Narnia series, p. 146

maim—then blame God. Cause a divorce—tell them that God should have stopped it. If you really want to see what God desires for you, read Jeremiah 29:11. Have a blessed day.[312]

There was a chorus of agreement for my friend's post. No one seemed to want to look at the fact that God sometimes does things that are—shall we say, unpopular and even seemingly unfair—to His people. Unwilling to let things stand as they were in this Utopian Happyville where God was essentially wrapped up with a pretty "God only brings good things" bow, I posted,

> If someone asks you if they can hurt someone; you can approve or disapprove and you give them permission, are you responsible? See the book of Job for an example.
>
> IMO, man's ultimate struggle is not with Satan but with God, as Satan cannot do anything without God's approval.

Herein lies the crux of the difference between Christianity's God and Judaism's God. Because of this *Great Controversy* dualism, Christianity's God has no shades of gray. Christianity's God would never bring calamity, is incapable of deception (i.e. lying), would *never* actually *send* an evil spirit to do anything, and does not truly know the end from the beginning. Christianity's God is limited in many ways and must learn from his actions and His mistakes. So badly does

---

[312] This is actually one of my favorite texts, as long as we do not look at it in a vacuum. "For I know the plans I have for you," declares AHYH, "plans to prosper you and not harm you, plans to give you hope and a future."

Christianity's god mess up that he also changes his mind (and his covenant) if he figures out that what he has done is just not working. He is so fickle that he changes his *chosen people* at the drop of a hat, blessing his second *chosen people* for doing the very thing that he rejected his first *chosen people* for doing![313]

Judaism's God, on the other hand, is harder to stereotype. There seem to be a lot more shades of gray, more things that cannot be understood, and above all, less certainty that you actually *know* or can predict this Being. Despite the fact that He doesn't need or want sacrifice to forgive, Judaism's God seems more dangerous somehow, mainly because He is unpredictable and will do some rather drastic things in an effort to get His point across to an un-listening generation.

Ancient Jews realized that God was the only one that mattered. They did not worry about an *Enemy* that was the *god of this world* that was out to get them; their epic struggle was not with this *Satan (Adversary)*, but with God Himself, as the entire book of Job and Jacob's nighttime struggle both aptly illustrate. At the end of the day, they accepted that they might never know the answers to why bad things happened to them. They were content in the knowledge that God was in control. This was God's world, and they needed to trust that God had their best interests at heart.

Despite Christianity's watered down *no-responsibility* message, there are still people out there of all religious persuasions who seem to really *get* the fact that God is a

---

[313] Christianity's *New Covenant* is all about God rejecting the Jews for not being able to obey enough to *keep his covenant,* but then realizing that this covenant is not working and changing it for the Gentiles. Henceforth, they do not have to *keep* God's law because they have *a better covenant* that does not require obedience. (Hebrews 7)

mystery that is far beyond what our feeble minds can comprehend. One Episcopalian believer rather eloquently described God by explaining,

> The most profound verse written in the Bible (is) Exodus 3:14. "I am that I am." Why do you think God describes himself that way to Moses? God spoke these words because he understands we haven't the capacity to comprehend him in our infinitely limited, three-dimensional world with our linear thinking.
>
> One of the many profound quotes from Albert Einstein, with which I whole-heartedly agree: 'My religion consists of a humble admiration of the illimitable superior spirit who reveals Himself in the slight details we are able to perceive with our frail and feeble mind.'
>
> Trying to comprehend God is like trying to explain the view from an airplane by looking out of a window that is only open by a millimeter. That's all our windows are allowed to open. I dare not compartmentalize God or pretend to understand Him when my capacity to do so is so unbelievably limited. I pray and do what God asks me to do ... I am endlessly and tirelessly hammering home the Golden Rule—which so many of us have forsaken.[314]

This is an amazing description of God. This God is wild, untamed and unpredictable. This type of viewpoint of the Divine helps explain the Old Testament's frequent use of the Hebrew word *yirah*, which is used to describe *fear of God*,

---

[314] K. Rowland posted this on a message board on 2/17/10: www.topix.com/forum/city/keene-tx/TT8T357910R4AFHB5/p6

reverence, piety. *Yirah* is used in this capacity more than 40 times in the Hebrew Scriptures. This usage has pretty much been removed in our current more popular paraphrases, because the concept of *fearing God* doesn't bring in believers in today's *seeker-sensitive* world. Rather, *being buddies* with God is what sells in today's mega-churches. For example, "Come my children, listen to me, I will teach you the fear of AHYH" has been changed to "Come children, listen closely, I'll give you a lesson in God worship."[315]

Since rediscovering this truly loving but dangerous God, I have had a startling shift in thinking. In my *This Present Darkness* days when I would feel an *attack of the enemy* occurring, I would rebuke the devil, as is the Christian custom. Now, realizing that nothing happens that is not approved by God, I go straight to the Source. "Father, what is the problem here? What are you trying to tell me?" I plead.

Interestingly, I can't tell you the last time I had one of these *attacks by the enemy*—they have all but disappeared since I have begun a direct relationship with the One Source that is God.

It turns out that *The Great Controversy* is in fact just *The Great Con*. Man's struggle is not in fact with some nameless, faceless *enemy* but with the God who created him.[316] *God* is the one in power, and *God* is the one with whom we should worry about being right with. We have utterly lost sight of the Authoritative Creator that Job actually discovered; the Ruler who challenged,

---

[315] Psalm 34:11 NIV vs. *The Message* paraphrase.
[316] Consider the story of Jacob, struggling all night with God. *The Enemy* was in no way involved – Jacob's struggle–as is ours–was with Almighty God!

> Will the one who contends with the Almighty correct him? Let him who accuses God answer him![317]

There is no sacrilege whatsoever in challenging God with your questions. God is big enough to take your toughest questions and challenges; big enough for the struggle. And God can handle your emotions as well; your anger, your frustration, your pain, and your anguish. He made you, gave you life, and knows the innermost desires of your heart.

When you search for God with all your heart, you *will* find Him.[318] He may just look quite a bit different than you have expected all your life!

---

[317] Job 40:2
[318] Jeremiah 29:13

CHAPTER 35

❖

GOD IS

There is another significant difference between the God of non-Talmudic Judaism and that of Christianity, which relates in a very personal way to God's beloved daughters. Women throughout Christian history have been put down, marginalized and disenfranchised by a religion that insists that its principal God consists of three men. It is rather ironic that in light of the fact that we tell our children how important a mother/father family unit is, the Christian version of our own heavenly Parent is a family of males.

We support this very patriarchal viewpoint by quoting a plethora of texts that seem to uplift the male and downplay the female, as far as we can tell by reading our English translation, starting with Genesis 1:27, which we read as saying,

God created man in His own image, in the image of God He created him; male and female He created them.

We then read multiple stories of deceptive or promiscuous females throughout the Bible, and condemn God's *Bride* for being a whoring woman. This women-hate begins to really accelerate by the time we start talking about that other whoring woman, Babylon, which we all need to come out of. (From what I have been told by my more frank male friends, this is an especially masculine and very literal characterization that a woman cannot hope to understand in the same way a man can.)

The marginalization of women reaches full force by the time we reach Paul's writings. How many godly women have been shushed and shamed by a reading of 1 Timothy 2:12 which states,

> A woman should learn in silence and full submission. I do not permit a woman to teach or assume authority over a man, she must be quiet.

1 Corinthians 14:34 then seals the deal with,

> Woman should remain silent in the churches. They are not allowed to speak, but must be in submission, as the Law says.

Because we have been raised with this not-so-hidden chauvinistic viewpoint, there exists a deep and aching wound in the heart of God-fearing females. First of all, we internalize that we were an afterthought in Creation and we remain so now, a necessary evil to be tolerated in order to perpetuate the species. Secondly, we feel like we don't even have the right to speak up and be heard in some circles because, well, we are obviously not worthy in the minds of many because *Saint Paul* said so and he's in the Bible. Thirdly, and this is the hardest one of all to even express and is one that many people have not even considered—we feel deep in our feminine hearts that our Creator could not possibly understand us and in some ways may even be biased against us because of the fact that we are women and He isn't.

It is good to remember that things are not always as they appear. Hebrew is a very basic and simple language. There are far fewer words in the Hebrew because it does not incorporate pronouns and many of the connecting words that we use in English. Imagine how different our language would be without pronouns? As well, imagine how different Scripture would look without pronouns, especially when referring to God?

To illustrate this concept, let's look at Genesis 1:27 in the Hebrew.

Elohim (a plural form of God) *bara'* (created) *adam* (adam in this instance denotes all mankind and not specifically someone's name) *tselem* (in the image of, favoring, likeness); *tselem Elohim* (plural form of God) *bara'* (created) *zakar* (male) *neqebah* (female) *bara'* (created).

> "God created mankind in the image of God; in the image of God created male and female, created."

Contrast this with the traditional English translation that states,

> "God created man in *His* own image, in the image of God *He* created him; male and female *He* created them."

The difference between the two translations is important. In the traditional English offering, the female's creation is an afterthought; the man is discussed first and is obviously the most significant. Furthermore, the number of pronouns included in the English translation that refer to God as *He* leaves no doubt in the reader's mind that *God* is distinctly male, with all that that involves. In the Hebrew version, we simply have God creating male and female in God's own image. Period.

Rather than getting into a huge discourse on gender issues, I just want to simply put in plain words that in Judaism, God is not even looked at as having a gender, as the main purpose of gender is for the physical act of procreation. *Genderizing* or assigning a gender to God is a holdover from the ancient peoples who were trying to relate to God in a very patriarchal society. In reality, the Eternal One is spirit and indescribable in composition.

In Judaism, all of the traits of male and female are found in *Elohim*. The Spirit of God—*Ruach*—is a feminine word in the Hebrew. *Wisdom*, which brought about Creation in the book of Proverbs, is feminine, and the *Shekinah* is held by many within Judaism to be the feminine attributes of God. There are many extra-canonical writings which refer to the Holy Spirit as our Mother, such as the writing in which Yeshua is quoted as stating,

> Even so did my mother the Holy Spirit
> one of my hairs and carry me away t
> mountain Tabor (in Galilee).[319]

Reform Judaism has recently introduced a new prayer book that incorporates more *gender neutral* or *gender-free* language for God in an effort to better reflect the totality that is God, as well as to honor the matriarchs of the Jewish faith. Instead of using words such as Father, Lord, and other male-specific terms, the book uses terms such as *Sovereign Ruler, Living God* and *Eternal One*.[320] Reform Judaism has also introduced a Scripture translation that is closer to the thought of that reflected in the simple Hebrew and which actually ends up being more gender-neutral. For example, instead of adding in those thousands of masculine pronouns (*He*) to refer to God, when the original writings only state *AHYH*, they have brought it back to a more gender inclusive reflection of the Almighty as being, well, genderless.

How does this make any difference, you wonder? I'll tell you how! Realizing that we are not children of a single heavenly Dad (or trio of dads, in Christianity's case) but that

---

[319] Gospel of the Hebrews

[320] *The Quixote Center and Priests For Equality* (PFF) have also published an Inclusive Bible, with inclusive language and more Hebraic language. They have also portrayed the Tetragrammaton as YHWH where it appears in the original text instead of substituting the title "The LORD". One can tell that the translators have tried very hard to make this translation welcoming to both genders; even going so far as to say "The Great Idolater" instead of "The Whore" of Babylon, as they feel that the idolatry portrayed in the example is more accurately relayed in the updated language.

Here is another example of how they have translated a familiar psalm: "The LORD is my shepherd, I shall not want" turns into "YHWH, you are my shepherd – I want nothing more." In my opinion, this is a step where a Catholic organization is heading in a very positive direction!

...ay claim the entire reflection of emotions brought on by having both a mother and a father is significant. It really is the best we can ever imagine; we have a strong, protective heavenly Father but we also are also sheltered under the wings of a protective Mother, as is reflected in the Psalms.[321]

God is—simply—God. Everything. AHEYEH Is. And because AHEYEH Is, I can be, and am significant, no matter which set of reproductive organs I have been provided with or what color my skin is or how my eyes or nose are shaped. God does not see me or judge me by the composition of my body, but by the spirit that makes up who I am. My Creator judges me by the choices I make, the kindness I offer, and the love that I share when I reach out to others. I am significant because God sees my heart.

Those qualities that make me female are also reflected in the great Heart of the Divine, because Almighty God made *me* after God's own image. No longer do I need to feel like a lonely child who longs for the tender, sheltering arms of a Heavenly Mother and is slightly frightened by the grandness and power of my Heavenly Father. Almighty God is not only my Creator but my Father, my Mother, my Comfort, my Strength, my Shelter, my Protector, my Sword, my Shield, my Inspiration and my Song. God, simply, Is.[322]

---

[321] Consider Psalm 57:1, 61:4, 63:7, and Psalm 91. Realizing that all of the male pronouns that have been added are not in the original Hebrew causes one see this passage in a completely different way. After all, the very concept of *hiding under the wings* brings to mind a mother hen protecting her chicks.
[322] Because we are so used to hearing the title *Heavenly Father* and referring to God with a male pronoun, I have continued to do so in this book in order to not distract the reader from the points being made. - Author

CHAPTER 36

❖

GOD ACTS

*God creates out of nothing. Therefore, until a man is nothing,
God can make nothing out of him.*
~Martin Luther

We in Christianity have been so broken down and convinced that we are complete rubbish when looked at and judged on our own merit, that we can't even conceive of being able to communicate directly with God without the presence of an *Intercessor*. We just feel *spiritually invisible*; way too unworthy to even be acknowledged by our own Holy God.

We promote this mindset by narrowly quoting half-verses such as,

> All of us have become like one who is unclean, and all our righteous acts are like filthy rags.[323]

We postulate,

> Behold, I was shapen in iniquity and in sin did my mother conceive me.[324]

Seems like a slam-dunk, doesn't it? We're hopeless and unrighteous wretches! We're so sinfully ugly and repugnantly repulsive that our Almighty God cannot even look upon what He created!

But as we have seen multiple times, the Scriptures that we were taught to view through a decidedly Christian lens do not always look the same when viewed from a Hebraic perspective or from within the full context in which they were written. Let's examine for a moment the Isaiah text in context.

> You come to the help of those who gladly do right, who remember your ways. *But when we continued to sin against them, you were angry.* How then can we be saved? All of us have become like one who is unclean, and all our righteous acts are like filthy rags; we all shrivel up like a leaf, and like the wind our sins sweep us away.[325]

In context, this text is not directed at all of humanity in general, but is specifically directed at a precise group of

---

[323] Isaiah 64:6
[324] Psalm 51:5
[325] Isaiah 64:5-6, emphasis supplied

people who have admitted to deliberately sinning against God's righteous people. This bunch of *filthy rags* folks reflects some truly evil individuals who are effectively being cursed by God for their abominable and hateful actions toward those who are trying to obey God's Law and live righteously. The passage is a lament, not an actual fact. It is an isolated situation for a certain group of people at a particular time, not a general directive about every person who has every lived in the whole world. Yet Christendom paints all of humanity with the broad brush of this select group of sinners!

Some will want to take issue with this more precise reading and say, "Well, you're not looking at the fact that the verse has a *double meaning*. It means what you are saying, but it also applies to all of humanity!"

In reality, the verse does not specifically have a so-called *double meaning* other than to illustrate that people who do really bad things are really bad people! Not every text in the Bible applies to every person. In fact, most, if not all, of the so-called *double meaning* passages are designed to do nothing more than push a Scriptural passage out of its original context, in order to support a flawed tradition instituted by inaccurate scholars a long time ago.

Let's look at the next quote:

> Behold, I was shapen in iniquity and in sin did my mother conceive me.

King David rather forlornly penned this psalm after Nathan the prophet confronted him for David's own sinful behavior with Bathsheba. Obviously, David was feeling guilty about his actions, as he had very spectacularly broken God's Law and been "taken out back behind the woodshed", so to speak, for it. Feeling contrite and useless, David rather dramatically elucidated his feelings of worthlessness before God. Exploring the context of his situation helps explain his pessimistic "woe is me I am so guilty" rant.

You and I both know that David did not feel that hopeless and pessimistic all the time! Compare and contrast the "in sin my mother conceived me" text with the hope-filled optimism of the following passage,

> For you created my inmost being; you knit me together in my mother's womb.[326]

And,

> From birth I was cast upon you; from my mother's womb you have been my God.[327]

In order to maintain our guilt-inducing rhetoric, we first must ignore the context of these very dismal and depressing texts. Then, in order to keep our "I'm a horrible, worthless, pessimistic sinner" vibe going, we ignore the multitude of verses that talk about the fact that there are many *righteous* men and women whose righteousness is *not filthy rags*, and indeed, God will exalt and bless them![328]

---

[326] Psalm 139:13
[327] Psalm 22:10
[328] For example; Genesis 6:9, Job 17:9, Psalm 5:12, Isaiah 33:15, Isaiah 42:6, Malachi 3:18, Matthew 25:37, Luke 5:32

The Doctrine of Original Sin is Not of God

The dogma of *Original Sin* is not original to Christianity, but came straight out of primitive Judaism. This ancient doctrine initially began in a theme that was repeated throughout Torah and can first be found beginning in Genesis, with the sin of Adam and Eve damning the whole human race for *their* personal sin. Then we see this dark misnomer theme repeated again within the Ten Commandments, in Exodus 20:4-6, when we are told that God says,

> You shall not make for yourself an idol, or any likeness of what is in heaven above or on the earth beneath or in the water under the earth. You shall not worship them or serve them; for I, the Lord your God, am a jealous God, visiting the iniquity of the fathers on the children, on the third and the fourth generations of those who hate Me, but showing loving kindness to thousands, to those who love Me and keep My commandments.[329]

'Wow,' we think, 'God is *really serious* about this idolatry thing, even damning our kids for our sin!' This theme (of God "visiting the iniquity [sin and punishment] upon the children" of the original sinners as deep as the third and fourth generation) gave rise to a saying within ancient Israel. The saying declared that "the fathers had eaten sour grapes (i.e. sinned) and their children's teeth were set on edge (i.e. punished) for it!"[330]

---

[329] Exodus 20:4-6, NASB
[330] Genesis 15:16; Exodus 20:5; Exodus 34:7; Numbers 14:18; Deuteronomy 5:9; Jeremiah 18:1-4; Jeremiah 31:29-30

While this sounds all well and good from the traditional Christian perspective, the doctrine of *Original Sin* is actually a man-made dogma and a deep misunderstanding that is *not* of AHEYEH God. To the contrary, the Eternal One Himself firmly took action to correct the ancient Israelites for even establishing such a notion!

Jeremiah 31:31 is regularly quoted to support Paul's *New Covenant* doctrine. However, no one ever really notices a somewhat random passage a couple of verses above it that reads,

In those days people will no longer say,

> *The fathers have eaten sour grapes,*
> *and the children's teeth are set on edge.*

Instead, everyone will die for his own sin; whoever eats sour grapes—his own teeth will be set on edge.[331]

This isolated passage just sits out there like a kind of enigma leaving most of us just scratching our heads and mumbling, "Huh?" And then we move quickly on to the more familiar *New Covenant* passage; skipping over a colossal and important issue that fundamentally illustrates and clarifies the Character and Word of God.

Fortunately, this concept is also found in the writings of another major prophet, Ezekiel, where we get a much more

---

[331] Jeremiah 31:29-30. In Jeremiah 31 we see only a snippet of God's correction, but it is enough to provide one witness. Perhaps the fuller understanding and context was edited out of the original writing of Jeremiah by later scribes.

specific understanding of what God is really trying to tell us through this little snippet of Scripture in Jeremiah.

CHAPTER 37

❖

GOD SPEAKS

Imagine for a moment that you are in a conversation with God. You have just thanked God for saving all of Humanity from the *original sin* of Adam and Eve; and you are now mentioning how unfortunate it is that the sin of your human ancestors has followed everyone throughout time. "The children's teeth were definitely set on edge from their parent's 'eating sour grapes!'" you lament. Naturally, you're expecting God to maybe discuss in a little more detail why Yeshua had to die in order to *pay* for the misdeeds and sin of everyone, but there is only an odd silence from God. You open your mouth to continue, but close it when you hear God speak.

Believer, what do you people mean
by quoting this proverb about Christianity:

> 'The fathers eat sour grapes,
>> and the children's teeth are set on edge?'"[332]

Opening your mouth to answer, you realize that God has not yet finished speaking, so your jaws snap closed again. AHEYEH sounds very solemn as He issues a bit of a reprimand.

> As surely as I live, you will no longer quote this proverb in Christianity! For every living soul belongs to me, the father as well as the son—both alike belong to me. *The soul who sins is the one who will die.*[333]

'What?' you think to yourself in alarm, 'This makes no sense at all! Did God just say what I think He said? Did God just destroy Christianity's entire doctrine of *Original Sin*?'

Yes, that is exactly what the Almighty has just done.

You mentally replay God's statement in your mind and realize that God is not only correcting much of Torah—but He is correcting much of the *New Testament* as well! God has just done away with what has been a deep misunderstanding that Christianity has harbored for a very long time. Indeed, it isn't the sin of the fathers that is being pronounced upon—and the punishment inherited by—their children. What has actually been happening is that the sinful *traditions* and *tendencies* of the fathers are being handed down, passed on, and taught to their children, who then continue to keep and perpetuate the same sinful behavior and pagan beliefs as their parents![334]

---

[332] Ezekiel 18:1-4; amplification to "Christianity" and *emphasis* supplied
[333] Ibid.
[334] One example of a harmful tendency that can be passed down from parent to child is a propensity (both genetic and cultural) toward alcoholism.

You listen carefully as God now goes into a generous explanation of what He means when He says, "the soul who sins is the one who will die." God starts by reciting a laundry list of character traits that define a righteous man:

> Suppose there is a righteous man
>> who does what is just and right.
>
> He does not eat at the mountain shrines
>> or look to the idols
>> [or pagan practices] of Christianity.
>
> He does not defile his neighbor's wife
>> or lie with a woman during her period.
>
> He does not oppress anyone,
>> but returns what he took in pledge for a loan.
>
> He does not commit robbery
>> but gives his food to the hungry
>> and provides clothing for the naked.
>
> He does not lend at usury
> or take excessive interest.
>
> He withholds his hand from doing wrong
>> and judges fairly between man and man.
>
> He follows my decrees
>> and faithfully keeps my laws.
>
> That man is *righteous*;
>> he will surely live![335]

'What? Righteous? Just by his works? How?' you ponder to yourself. But you remember that this is GOD speaking to you. You mentally set aside your "righteousness is as filthy rags"

However, it is up to each individual to determine whether or not that harmful tendency will rule over him or her.

[335] Ezekiel 18:5-9; amplification to "Christianity" and *emphasis* supplied

doctrine that Christianity has taught you, and continue listening intently as God goes on to describe the contrasting actions of the righteous man's evil son:

> Suppose he has a violent son, who sheds blood or does any of these other things (though the father has done none of them):
>
> > He eats at the mountain shrines.
> > He defiles his neighbor's wife.
> > He oppresses the poor and needy.
> > He commits robbery.
> > He does not return what he took in pledge.
> > He looks to the idols [or pagan practices]
> > He does detestable things.
> > He lends at usury and takes excessive interest.
>
> Will such a man live? He will not! *Because* he has done all these detestable things, he will surely be put to death and his blood will be on his own head.[336]

It could not be made more clear. God is adamant that the righteous father will bear *none* of the guilt of his unrighteous son! All of Humanity is *not* inheriting the sin of one man! But then God, seeing the awestruck look on your face, takes His explanation a generation further.

> But suppose this son has a son who sees all the sins his father commits, and though he sees them, he does not do such things:

---

[336] Ezekiel 18:10-13; amplification to "Christianity" and *emphasis* supplied

> He does not eat at the mountain shrines
>> or look to the idols [or pagan practices]
>> of Christianity.
> He does not defile his neighbor's wife.
> He does not oppress anyone
>> or require a pledge for a loan.
> He does not commit robbery
>> but gives his food to the hungry
>> and provides clothing for the naked.
> He withholds his hand from sin
> and takes no usury or excessive interest.
> He keeps my laws and follows my decrees.
>
> He will not die for his father's sin; he will surely live![337]

God's great Voice then softens to a solemn whisper,

> But his father will die for his *own* sin, because he practiced extortion, robbed his brother and did what was wrong among his people.[338]

You can see that your Creator has now gone into more detail than should be necessary to illustrate His own Word and Character; which is, that He will not visit the iniquity of the wicked father on the righteous son who does what is just and righteous.

'But that makes no sense!' you think to yourself. 'I have been taught my whole life that the sin of one man will be inherited by the whole human race; and that we all have to

---

[337] Ezekiel 18:15-17; amplification to "Christianity" and *emphasis* supplied
[338] Ezekiel 18:18

live totally perfect lives in order to be righteous! How can this be? This is a huge contradiction!'

But the Eternal One is not finished yet. His next words continue to drive home His point. You flinch a little as He looks straight at you and answers your unspoken question.

> Yet you ask, 'Why does the son not share the guilt of his father?' Since the son has done what is just and right and has been careful to keep all my decrees, he will surely live.[339]

Reiterating, God clarifies once again,

> The soul who sins is the one who will die! The son will *not* share the guilt of the father, nor will the father share the guilt of the son. The righteousness of the righteous man will be credited to him, and the wickedness of the wicked will be charged against him.[340]

At this point, it is crystal clear to you that Christendom has all but totally ignored this foundational aspect of God's eternal and unchanging Character. In Christianity's rush to embrace the completely condemning doctrine of *Original Sin*, Christendom has completely swept the fact that God does not allow the sin or punishment of one man to be borne by another under the proverbial rug!

It is a foregone conclusion that if one man cannot inherit nor pay the price for the sin of another, then the entire foundation of the (Pauline) Christian message—that Yeshua

---

[339] Ezekiel 18:19
[340] Ezekiel 18:20; *emphasis* supplied

has somehow paid the price for everyone's sin—has just been unilaterally *voided* by God Almighty.

"But, but," you stammer, "if Yeshua cannot pay the price for my sin, then *how* will you forgive me—forgive all of us, for our sins?"

Your Creator, responding to your internal confusion and conflict, answers firmly and without ambiguity,

> But if a wicked man turns away from all the sins he has committed and keeps all my decrees and does what is just and right, he will surely live; he will not die. *None* of the offenses he has committed will be remembered against him. *Because of the righteous things he has done, he will live.*
>
> Do I take any pleasure in the death of the wicked? Rather, am I not pleased when they *turn from their ways* and live?[341]

God is being perfectly clear. He has given you and everyone else the ability and the power to turn away from your sin—and live! But now the Eternal One also issues a warning that somehow catches you by surprise. God continues,

> But if a righteous man turns from his righteousness and commits sin and does the same detestable things the wicked man does, will he live? None of the righteous things he has done will be remembered. Because of the unfaithfulness he is guilty of and because of the sins he has committed, he will die.[342]

---

[341] Ezekiel 18:21-23; *emphasis* supplied
[342] Ezekiel 18:24

You stand there silently. Stunned.

You can quote entire chapters and even whole books written by Paul, but this is the first time you have ever really thought about what *these* verses illustrating God's TRUE Word, His TRUE Character are really saying. After all, it is not standard sermon material—what responsible Christian pastor wants to point out these admonishments and clarifications by our own God to all of us, thus causing us to have all manner of disputes and uncertainty about Yeshua's final *atoning sacrifice* on the cross? Furthermore, your church's beloved *once saved, always-saved* doctrine is now in utter shambles!

At this point, you abruptly get mad. Furious, even. Despite your better judgment, you cannot help the words that come pouring out of your mouth in defense of your beloved tradition and doctrine. Your horror overcomes your fear, and you address the Almighty One Himself.

"Hey, now wait just a minute here, God! All of my life I have been following and even preaching to thousands, maybe millions of people, about this doctrine of Yeshua paying the price for my sin and being my atoning sacrifice and my salvation! And now you're suddenly telling me that all of it is bunk? That is just not fair! How could you have let me believe it if it wasn't the truth?" you demand.

The silence is deafening.

You could hear the proverbial pin drop as the thought hits you: "Haven't I sincerely been seeking God's Truth? Could this conversation with the Almighty be my answer— the answer I have been waiting for God to give me?"

So you stop ... You wait ... And finally, you really *listen* as the clear voice of the Eternal One gently answers the deepest cry of your heart:

> Yet you say, 'The way of AHEYEH is not just.' Hear, O believer: Is *my* way unjust? Is it not *your* ways that are unjust?
>
> If a righteous man turns from his righteousness and commits sin, he will die for it; because of the sin he has committed he will die. But if a wicked man turns away from the wickedness he has committed and does what is just and right, he will save his life. Because he considers all the offenses he has committed and turns away from them, he will surely live; he will not die.

His Voice softens in astonishment as He says,

> Yet the house of Christianity says, 'The *way of the Lord* is not just?'[343]

His Great Voice finally drops to a silent whisper that you somehow hear with every fiber of your being,

> Are *my ways* unjust, O believer? Is it not *your ways* that are unjust?[344]

Logic.
Reason.
Fairness.
Mercy.
Your Father exemplifies all of these characteristics and so many more!

---

[343] Ezekiel 18:25-29a; amplification to "Christianity" supplied
[344] Ezekiel 18:29b

Your Creator's Voice now rises in a solemn conclusion of the matter:

> Therefore, O believer, I will judge you, each one according to his ways. Repent!

His words resonate through every cell of your body,

> Turn away from all your offenses; then sin will not be your downfall. Rid yourselves of all the offenses you have committed, and get a new heart and a new spirit.

The Almighty's words are transforming and so encouraging. You marvel to yourself, 'I can get a *new heart* and a *new spirit* without Yeshua's sacrifice? God gives me this ability all on my own?'

You continue to listen as His Voice, great and solemn, reaches out across the ages,

> Why will you die, O believer? For I take no pleasure in the death of anyone. Repent and live![345]

The words of Almighty God now ring over and over again throughout your being.

"Repent and live! Repent and live! Repent and live! ..."

You begin to realize that *nowhere* within this conversation has God ever mentioned that blood or sacrifices of any kind are necessary for righteousness, salvation or forgiveness. His

---

[345] Ezekiel 18:30-32; amplification to "Christianity" and *emphasis* supplied

whole conversation has been all about personal *repentance*, about personal *responsibility,* about turning away from your sinful actions and *doing*—not just *believing*—the right thing.

No one else can pay the price for your sin. This pagan doctrine has been completely and absolutely corrected and abolished by Almighty God!

Forgiveness That Is Truly "Free"

What believer has not heard from the pulpit that salvation and God's forgiveness are freely given? That is what we have been taught and that is what we repeat to our children. But is the blood-based version of God's forgiveness really *free?* No, it is not! Only because Yeshua *paid* the blood price for our sin, is forgiveness and salvation said to be free. But the fact of the matter is, according to Christian soteriology and Christology, God *needed to be paid* for the gift of His forgiveness. Something *perfect* had to *die* to somehow pay for our imperfections—imperfections that God created us with, I might add.

This dichotomy or non sequitur logic has never made much sense to me. God created imperfect beings so that He could rescue them from their inherent imperfection by supposedly demanding the death of *Himself* to appease His own anger/wrath/holiness about some beings He Himself created as fallible in the first place? It makes no rational sense to the God-given mind!

Christianity deliberately and artificially elevates righteousness to some mythological and utterly unattainable state of perfection (i.e. never having sinned) so that people must rely on its Mithraic version of *Yeshua* to be made right(eous) with God. "Without Yeshua's perfection," Christianity opines, "you cannot come before God." However, God speaking through the prophet Ezekiel unilaterally destroys these Pauline/Mithraic constructs and returns true righteousness to the logical and reasoned simplicity that God originally designed. There is no sacrifice, human or otherwise, required.

The Ezekiel understanding of God's forgiveness is one that is not only logical, but is also truly free! No payment is required; all that is necessary is just a repentant heart and mind before God. The salvation of God can be easily summed up in these Words of God,

> ... if a wicked man turns away from all the sins he has committed and keeps all my decrees and does what is just and right, he will surely live; he will not die. None of the offenses he has committed will be remembered against him. Because of the righteous things he has done, *he will live.*

CHAPTER 38

❖

GOD SEES ME!

In order to cope with the inclusive and innate guilt that is an inherent part of Christianity, the Christian believer learns to utilize a type of religious *shields down* technology, to use Star Trek vernacular. From childhood you are consistently taught that no matter what you do, God only sees Yeshua instead of you. If you sin, God still sees Yeshua. No matter what horrid thing you have done, if you are *saved* (each denomination has different definitions of what being *saved* actually means), God magically sees Yeshua instead of you. In a nutshell, God only perceives you as righteous because the sacrificial death of his Son *cleansed you* from your horrible and otherwise unforgivable sins and pathetic *filthy rags* attempts at righteousness.

Once you fully embrace the foundational message of Ezekiel 18 and let go of the pagan doctrine of *Substitutionary Atonement*, things start to look a lot different in your relationship with God. Rather than disappearing into Yeshua, as it were, you begin to get the distinct feeling that God wants you to be accountable for your *own* behavior. You are now suddenly responsible for your own relationship with God, you no longer have or need an *Intermediary,* and you will receive your own consequences. It's a bit like growing up. And at first, admittedly, it's a little scary.

I cannot tell you how long it took for me to get accustomed to this new paradigm of understanding. I felt grief and anger, because I missed being able to just punt the responsibility over to someone else. I felt fear, because all of a sudden I was in the direct line of sight of God Almighty. And somewhat oddly, I also felt a deep longing for God to see me! As a Christian, I *knew* that I was significant but only because Yeshua was significant. But now? Now I was being judged on my own merit, as God's own daughter. How on earth could I measure up? I wanted to jump up and down to get my Father's attention, yet hide at the same time.

God was willing to forgive me without blood and without sacrifice; God wanted to have a direct and deeply personal relationship with me, with no one in between. But that also meant I had to take responsibility for my own actions.

The fact is, God knows what He made. We do not have to achieve some unattainable level of perfection; that is, being sinless or never having sinned, to be perfectly forgiven of God. God will forgive us as many times as we truly repent of our sins. We fall, and fall often. Repentance, and forgiveness, is just a decision and an action away.

One day, I was feeling particularly lonely in a spiritual sense. I felt so insignificant. Invisible. Colorless. Spiritually drab. If God was looking at me to be some rock star believer, then I knew for sure He'd be disappointed because I just had nothin' on this particular day.

I took myself out for a solitary walk and inwardly raged, at my circumstances, at my loneliness, and even at God. How I longed to get some *message from God* that I mattered! How I wanted to know that even though Yeshua was not *standing in the gap* between us, I was still valuable!

Just a couple of days before on this same walk, I had been talking to God when some sand hill cranes trumpeted in reply, almost like they were a direct voice of God saying, "Hey, you! You're not alone!" Well, this time, lost in my own thoughts, I didn't even notice these lovely birds until they called out to me again. Immediately, I remembered the last time I had heard them—when they had trumpeted after I cried out to God. Now that they had gotten my attention on God's behalf, I waited.

You know, God is the great Innovator! God will use whatever means is necessary to get a message across. With Moses, it was an oddly burning bush. With Balaam, it was a talking donkey. With me, it was trumpeting sand hill cranes and a song that immediately followed on the radio playing directly into in my ears. As the song started, the words seemed to be coming directly at me from my God above.

You with the sad eyes; don't be discouraged,
Oh, I realize it's hard to take courage
In a world full of people you can lose sight of it all
And darkness still inside you makes you feel so small

But I see your true colors shinin' through
I see your true colors and that's why I love you
So don't be afraid to let them show
Your true colors, true colors, are beautiful,
like a rainbow.

> *Show me a smile then, don't be unhappy,*
> *Can't remember when I last saw you laughing*
> *If this world makes you crazy*
> *and you've taken all you can bear*
> *You call me up because you know I'll be there*
>
> *And I see your true colors shinin' through*
> *I see your true colors and that's why I love you*
> *So don't be afraid to let them show*
> *Your true colors, true colors, are beautiful,*
> *like a rainbow.*[346]

I bet you didn't know that God sounds an awful lot like Phil Collins... but on this day, God did. It was so amazing because it was just what I needed to hear right then! With tears flowing from my eyes and a giant smile on my face, I just basked in the glory that was my Father's Presence. With nothing, and no one, between us—I knew that far from disapproving of me—God saw me! My Father indeed saw my heart; saw my "true colors, so beautiful, like a rainbow." And now that He had gotten my attention, I was finally able to see myself through God's eyes—and what I saw was, for just one moment, beautiful. Yet because of my insecurities and timidity, it was a lesson that I would have to learn over and over again.

---

[346] *True Colors*, written by Tom Kelly & Billy Steinberg. ©Sony/ATV.

CHAPTER 39

❖

BECOMING AN ANCESTOR

A day or two after my *True Colors* experience, I was once again hurting. The SDA *General Conference* Session, attended by seventy-thousand members of the world church, was taking place in Atlanta, GA, and I was experiencing the loss of my *religious homeland* very deeply. Watching my friends and family members excitedly attend the *GC* Session brought on excruciating feelings of pain and longing. I cannot tell you how much I grieved at the loss of my church, my SDA culture, and my utter significance itself, since embarking on this journey of question and discovery.

My entire identity as a sixth-generation Adventist had always been wrapped up in *being a good Adventist*. Because of this religious birthright, my ongoing journey *away* from Adventism was unspeakably difficult. What made it even more heartbreaking was the knowledge that I had so utterly devastated my parents with my deliberate choice to leave the spiritual *land of my fathers*. How could I expect them to understand my choice? They had dedicated their entire lives in service to the Adventist church, and had always been good and faithful servants for her cause!

In my *Serena the Adventist musician* past, my godly parents had always been so proud and supportive when I was writing and performing music for church. They would travel long distances to hear my programs in person, and listened with love and anticipation every time I would call them up to tell them, "I've written another song!" So you can only imagine their utter consternation, anguish, and heartfelt grief to realize that their very faithful, very visible, yet very inquisitive daughter had been questioning the faith of her fathers.

I will never forget the knockdown, drag-out argument that occurred one evening when Luc and I were visiting my parents in another state. My mother flat out challenged me very strongly and vocally about the fact that I was questioning Paul's inspiration and inclusion in the Bible. I was in tears, sobbing, as I stated my case. I wanted only to please my beloved mother, and it was killing me to cause her this kind of distress! Yet I could not recant what I believed to be the truth. And while the *little child* part of me could not understand why my Mama was attacking me in this manner, the wiser, more mature part of me realized that she was passionately and desperately trying her best to reach me out of the depths of a mother's loving heart, as one who truly must have believed that her daughter was on the path to hell!

After that, we just really didn't speak of our differences in belief. Mom and Dad invited us to church on rare occasions and we would generally decline, because we just felt that to attend would be an utter lie. After all, we understood and believed so very differently now! Furthermore, our children did not subscribe to some of the most precious fundamental beliefs of Christianity: the need for blood sacrifice, Communion, and the Trinity. How could we expect them to attend *Sabbath School* with other children and keep their conflicting opinions to themselves? That wouldn't be fair to them or to the other children! So we refrained from family church attendance and tried to keep quiet about our beliefs during family gatherings, just to keep the peace.

Yet it still hurt during the time of the *General Conference* Session, knowing that my loved ones were rejoicing in this big worldwide SDA event, and I wasn't there. The grief of my self-imposed exclusion just wouldn't go away.

What made it even worse was that while I truly believed in my heart that my beliefs were now a lot more in line with those that Yeshua followed, I still had Adventist programming inside my brain that said, "God only sees you if you are Adventist. You are only chosen of God if you are SDA. After all, Adventists are *The Remnant People*. There can be only *One Remnant!*" I knew in my mind that this was not true—but my heart still felt like it had been taught to feel all its life. This is what made the week when everyone was at *General Conference* so difficult.

I cannot tell you how much my heart longed to be there, visiting old friends, meeting new ones, and feeling like a part of a larger, greater entity. I literally felt like crying all week—and did so frequently. The loss of my religious homeland—my spiritual inheritance, as it were—was never more profoundly felt.

The last day of *General Conference*, those feelings came to a head. I was looking at pictures that family members had posted on Facebook of the *GC* session, and reading their comments of how it was simply *Heaven on* Earth to be there with so many other friends and family members. I felt so alone, left out, and invisible. Utterly despondent, I once again cried out to my heavenly Father in my grief. I so longed to know, in what was becoming a regular refrain, that God saw me, that He loved me, and that He still had meaning for me, even though I was no longer an Adventist. I wanted to matter to my Creator!

In tears, I started searching online and ran across a passage in a book on Amazon that struck me like a bolt of lightning from above. Somehow, God knew the exact words I needed to read to realize that I still had extreme significance, meaning, and favor in His eyes.

The passage I read talked about how Abraham, the father of the Jews, start out living his life by following the path that his ancestors had walked before him, honoring God as he had been taught. But when AHEYEH God called him to go on a journey to parts unknown, Abraham said, *I will.*

> The Bible portrays the origin of Judaism in God's call to Abraham. Abraham is told to leave his childhood home, told to go "to the land that I will show you" (Gen. 12:1). The life he has known is overthrown in that instant. Abraham has been fated to follow something grander and deeper.
>
> God does not tell Abraham his destination, because the goal cannot make sense to someone who has not yet experienced the journey. Arrival is not the essence. The lesson that Abraham will pass on to his descendants is that the key to the journey is the journey.
>
> The command to Abraham "Lech L'chah" (Go forth) is literally "Go, you." The Hebrew can also be read as "Go to you," that is, journey inside yourself. Moving through this world is always an expedition

into the "you"—into one's own soul. Abraham must be willing to leave the community that will not accept his changed spirit. But even more important, he must be willing to break with what has been inside of him until this moment.

In Abraham's time as in our own, most are content to skate along the surface of their lives. God's call in Judaism is a challenge to go deeper, which means a challenge to wrestle with difficulty. Abraham must stop looking back on the life that has been provided for him; he must change his focus and look forward to the life he is fashioning for those who will come after. He is no longer just an inheritor but a creator, not only a descendant but an ancestor, no longer a passive recipient of the ideals of others but an idol smasher. The moment that Abraham responded to God's call by saying, "I am here," his soul burst out of the cage of convention and began its journey.

This is the model and the challenge for one who undertakes a truly Jewish journey. Quiet and complacency tempt one all along the way. But the call to depth is always there. "Go forth" has no ending—not in the world and not in the terrain of the individual soul.

Jews are called the children of Sarah and Abraham. That is not a statement of biology; it is a statement of destiny. But none can claim a destiny who will not journey.[347]

---

[347] WOLPE, David J., *Why Be Jewish?*, pp. 4-6. Emphasis supplied.

Eureka! My tears of sadness turned to tears of joy. I sat quietly in reverent submission, head bowed and heart fully exposed in the brilliant spotlight of Heaven's stage. Finally, it had sunk in. I *knew* in the deepest part of my soul that my Father was looking at me and Actually Seeing Me. ME! Non-Adventist, sort-of Jewish Me! Once again, the Eternal One had heard His beloved child's cry and cared enough to answer. I was still beloved of God!

Finally, my Father got through to my quiet, hesitant, tentative heart. I realized that I *do* have a mandate from above as to why I am still here. I am *not* to be defined by where I have been, but by where I am going. I am "no longer a passive recipient of the ideals of others but an idol smasher". I have a purpose! The journey, which I have always had difficulty appreciating in my grand rush to get to the destination, IS the purpose. And in traveling the long, solitary road, with no one but my precious husband and my God to cling to, I finally found not only my voice, but also the courage to use it.

Most exciting of all, I now had a God-given mandate: from now on, I would not just be a passive descendant—but an ancestor!

CHAPTER 40

❖

TAKING BACK GROUND

As I gradually began to figure out what it meant to live a godly life free from an overwhelming dependence on bloody doctrine and pagan practices, I started feeling melancholy about some of the inspirational Christian songs I had written in the past. One of them entitled *It Was Me* provoked a special sadness. This anthem, which was one of my best known and most loved songs, held incredible personal significance. The problem was that the lyrics were based entirely on imputed guilt and *Substitutionary Atonement*, and these religious constructs held no place in my life anymore.

It Was Me was originally inspired by an emotional conversation with a dear friend. This devout Christian woman confided that during a particularly dark time in her life, she found herself very angry with Yeshua, or "Jesus" as she thought of him. Because she believed that he was responsible for not rescuing her from her personal pain, her therapist advised her to physically mimic the action of nailing Yehsua to the cross. Finally she could show him just how angry she was at him!

Having worked for many years as a psychiatric nurse, my heart was touched and saddened by the depths of her pain. As I reflected on the event and viewed it through the Christian lens of *Substitutionary Atonement*, the thought struck me like the proverbial ton of bricks: "Hey! I did kill Yeshua, for all intents and purposes. It was my own personal sin that killed him!" and thus the following lyrics were born.

It Was Me

*When I'd hear about the age-old story
of how Jesus died for me
I always wished that I had been there by His side
I would have stayed right there beside the Master
as His closest, dearest friend
I would have comforted His mother while she cried*

*I believed, that I was very different; that I'd never run away
If it were me, I'd fight for Him, I'd stand my ground
But then, the Lord revealed to me a vision
of that day on Calvary
and to my horror and my astonishment, I found*

*That it was me that nailed him to the tree
I'm the one who shouted "Crucify the Son of God!"
It was my sin that pierced his holy side...
When I saw who killed the Savior, it was me!*

I was overcome with pain and sorrow;
I cried bitter tears of grief
I couldn't understand the price he had to pay
For I knew I simply was not worthy of the sacrifice he made
What was my worth to him, that he would die that way?

It was for me, He laid there on the tree
The price of sin was paid, by the life He gave for free
For my eternal soul He died and rose again
I'm the child He gave His life for: it was me.

Now look, the cold, hard truth laid bare for all to see
Those gentle nail-scarred hands were pierced
and bruised for me
The Father's precious, perfect Son
was in this world the only One
who could pay that fatal price to set me free.

It was for me, He laid there on the tree
The price of sin was paid, by the life He gave for free
For my eternal soul He died and rose again
I am the child He gave His life for: it was me.

It Was Me was a heartfelt and touching song that encapsulated and illustrated in a nutshell the traditional Christian message. But I could no longer buy into those doctrines anymore. Rather than agonizing about my utter worthlessness that was supposedly responsible for nailing Yeshua to the cross, I had found a loving Father who actually *saw* me—ME!—and loved me for the precious child that I am; with all my faults, quirks and foibles, idiosyncrasies and emotions.

Because God truly saw *me*, He had no need for Yeshua to *stand between us* in order to tolerate the sight of me.

It Was Me was a kind of skeleton from the *land of my fathers* that would not remain buried. In all honesty, I did not want to leave it in the past! I longed to be able to bring this heart-felt tune into the *Promised Land* with me. But in order to do so, I needed to make some substantial changes to the lyrics so that they would now reflect the TRUE God and not the pagan one I had inherited from the land of my fathers.

Even though I was the author, the thought of rewriting such an epic inspirational song was daring, and a not little bit intimidating. Because of the emotional significance the song held for so many precious friends and family members, I ran the risk of upsetting them greatly when they found out that I had changed the lyrics. But how could I remain honest to myself as well as to God if I did not rewrite the lyrics? The melody would never be purged from my mind! Would I just continue to be overcome with sadness when I heard it playing on my mental soundtrack, or would I reclaim it and use it to testify about the beauty of the new spiritual homeland I had found?

The answer was obvious. The replacement lyrics came more easily than I had expected, even though the restrictions of rewriting an established song made it more challenging than if I had just started a new song from scratch. My goal was to keep the same *look and feel* of the original lyrics, using as many of the same phrases and rhyming structures as possible so it still sounded *right* to my ears. This presented a bit of a puzzle, but I knew instinctively that the result would be worth the challenge.

When the rewrite had been completed, I was excited to find that the redux version of *It Was Me* now beautifully illustrated the love and compassion and outstanding character of the God I had come to know. Now, rather than being a leftover relic of the land of my fathers, my signature anthem had become a testimony that illustrated the glorious beauty of the Promised Land.

It Was Me

From the time that I was young and fragile,
as an innocent should be
I knew my sins were like a thorn in Father's side
I was told I could not stand before Him,
for these sins were all He'd see
And for atonement, precious Jesus had to die

I was told that God had found me "guilty",
placed my shame on full display
That all my righteous deeds were filth upon the ground
But then my questing heart began a journey
to discover His true way
And to my joy and my astonishment I found

That it was me my God could clearly see!
Perfect love, undoubted, was the love He had for me!
He longed to draw me to His holy side
Precious child loved by Heaven, it was me!

I was overcome with joy and gladness;
I cried tears of sweet relief
I was so thrilled to know He would not turn away
For I was a child of my Father much adored beyond belief
Of matchless worth to Him, beloved in every way

For it was me my God could clearly see!
Perfect love, undoubted, was the love He had for me!
He longed to draw me to His holy side
Precious child loved by Heaven, it was me!

Now look, such glorious Truth revealed for all to see
God finds me worthy; from His eyes I should not flee
No need to offer up a lamb
"Appease His wrath" with blood-drenched hands
For when I repent, He'll always pardon me!

Yes, it is me my God can clearly see!
Perfect love, undoubted, is the love He has for me!
He longs to draw me to His holy side
Precious child loved by Heaven, it was me!
I am a child beloved of Heaven, it was me!

The salient points of the original version of *It Was Me* based on traditional Christian doctrine were:

1. I am, on my own, worthless.
2. I am so vile that my actions caused the death of Yeshua. I might as well have driven the nails in myself.
3. God needed to be appeased with the blood of Yeshua in order to forgive me for my sins and transgressions.

By comparison, the salient points of the redux version of *It Was Me* held a much more loving understanding:

1. God loves me so very much and looks on me with pride and joy.
2. When I repent of my sins, God is faithful to forgive me. No blood or sacrifice is required or even desired.

Tell me, which one of these song variations illustrates the most loving God? Even so, why are we so reluctant to accept this viewpoint? Is our deep-seated tradition the only thing that keeps us from accepting and embracing a more loving God? Can we not see? This is the epitome of *Good News!*

CHAPTER 41

❖

CONSIDER THE COST

As Luc and I have undertaken this long and lonely journey, we have been very curious to see if any of our friends have taken or are taking this same path. We have found a few who have come to a lot of the same conclusions, and this has given us great comfort. However, there are others who have arrived at these same conclusions but have not let these conclusions alter their behavior. They are still doing what they have always done; taking their kids to their local Protestant church service, teaching them that Yeshua died for their sins, and endorsing the belief that God needs sacrifice to forgive.

This puzzles me a great deal. I understand completely that it is very hard to leave the comfort and fellowship of one's home church or denomination. "Being an Adventist" has always been very important to me! But when it comes right down to it, I just choke up at the thought of teaching my kids that "God needs a battered and bloody human[348] sacrifice in order to forgive." Furthermore, there is no way on earth that my kids would accept being told that they should "pretend to drink Yeshua's blood and eat his body." Why do something—even symbolically—that is so heinous in real life?

The "ROI" of Reformation

I work in a field that is dominated by the analysis of "return on investment" or *ROI*. In simple terms, *ROI* is:

> A performance measure used to evaluate the efficiency of an investment or to compare the efficiency of a number of different investments. To calculate ROI, the benefit (return) of an investment is divided by the cost of the investment; the result is expressed as a percentage or a ratio. The return on investment formula:
>
> $$ROI = \frac{(\text{Gain from Investment} - \text{Cost of Investment})}{\text{Cost of Investment}}$$
>
> Return on investment is a very popular metric because of its versatility and simplicity. That is, if an investment does not have a <u>positive</u> ROI, or if there are other opportunities with a higher ROI, then the investment should be not be undertaken.[349]

---

[348] Or even "part human, part divine" as is commonly believed in Christianity.
[349] http://www.investopedia.com/terms/r/returnoninvestment.asp#ixzz1xMnkmsOx, 06/10/2012

In plain terms, this simple formula boils down to this: are the benefits I have gained greater than the price I have paid? Is the result worth the cost?

In current Christian vernacular, the saying we have from Yeshua is "consider the cost."[350]

Cost of Investment

Every searching Christian or Messianic believer who is considering following a different spiritual path than the one on which they are currently traveling will need to undertake a serious evaluation of their own *spiritual ROI;* perform their own religious cost-benefit analysis, as it were. I will give you an example of how mine looks. On the *Cost of Investment* side, I have:

A. Losing my home church, my community, my sense of belonging.
B. No longer being able to participate in very important family functions that revolve around church.
C. Not having an outlet for my music; in fact, pretty much having to put aside a whole library of music I have loved because I no longer believe the doctrinal beliefs contained in it.
D. Losing the significance of my heritage as a sixth-generation SDA.
E. Losing friends who no longer feel they can relate to me, and who cannot understand my choices.

---

[350] Luke 14:28

F. Watching my children feel left out of major holidays such as "the religious significance of Christmas".
G. Being made to feel like a nutcase over and over because people do not want to understand the choices I have made and why I have made them.

It is easy to see the common thread of loss in all of these items; loss of identity, loss of pride, and even loss of culture. It is finding that where I am, my beloved family members and friends are not. It is an utter sense of loneliness. With all of these liabilities—*costs* as it were—it is easy to see that a huge benefit—*return*—is going to be required in order to see a positive return on my investment in the process of Reformation. Sometimes the return on this investment will not be realized immediately, but rather will take some time to come to fruition and full realization.

God Speaks in Many Ways

King Nebuchadnezzar of Babylon once fretted, "I have had a dream that troubles me and I want to know what it means."[351] I personally had that same feeling some time ago when I awoke from a disturbing dream with the distinct impression that perhaps God was trying to tell me something. In the dream, I had been in a regular suburban house, with friends and family all around me. Everyone was laughing and having a good time. The house was fairly nondescript, except for the fact that the entire floor was covered with this sticky, gloopy black stuff, much like an oily tar. I tried to wipe

---
[351] Daniel 2:3

it off my shoes as I left the house. One little bit was left on the sole of my shoe.

As I exited the building, I wiped the remaining little patch onto the front step. I watched in horrified disgust and amazement as this black goop began to multiply to the point where it covered the whole front lawn and started running down the street! My one prevailing thought was, "Think of how much of this horrible stuff is still in the house with all of my loved ones!"

The meaning of the dream weighed heavily on my mind and my heart. After realizing how much pagan practice, ritual, and belief still permeated my beloved Christianity, it was not a stretch to understand that the goopy black stuff represented these pagan beliefs. Furthermore, far from being removed to the distant past, these heinous beliefs still permeate every aspect of our Christian doctrine and practices! Consider the whole "blood of Yeshua" issue; being "washed in the blood of the lamb", "eating and drinking" Christ's blood and body, "one man must die for the sins of another", and the absolute worst, "God requires the death of one animal or person to forgive the sin of another person. Mere repentance is not enough."

This, then, was the bulk of the gloopy substance—the paganism that we in Christianity still hold dear.

In the dream, I was so very relieved to be out of that house containing all the icky black stuff—but I felt so bad that my loved ones were still in there!

I saw a very memorable children's story at a large Adventist church several years ago. The extremely popular pastor had spent a lot of time preparing for the presentation, even building and assembling some sort of mock-up of the early Hebrew tabernacle. Right in the middle of his story, surrounded by tots to teens, he went through the motions of stabbing a lamb; animatedly informing the children that this is what God wanted! "This," he emphasized, "illustrates God's *plan of salvation.*"

As a parent and a Christian, I found the pastor's actions utterly appalling. I left the church utterly grateful that my children were not present, because this *children's story* would have permanently damaged their tender psyches by teaching them that this violent deed is what God really wanted. I wonder if any other parent that day wondered for even a moment if this is really the image we want our children to have of God—that God is a demander of death and blood?

A Positive Return On Investment

This brings us to the *Benefit* portion of my personal cost/benefit analysis, the *Return on my Investment* that comes down to one thing: All of the gloopy black substance has been washed off of my view and understanding of God! No longer do I have to try to convince myself that bloody sacrifice was and is somehow beneficial. No longer do I have to rationalize that "it's just too mysterious to understand—but surely, God incorporated sacrifice into a *requirement* for salvation so that I could understand how *heinous* sin is." (In effect, negating a heinous activity by doing something even more heinous.) No longer do I have to try to sell this monstrous and detestable pagan doctrine to my compassionate children; and no longer do I have to secretly shudder at the thought of trying to make the entire book of Numbers, with all of its bloody paganism, somehow *relevant* to my Christianity.

In a word—with the ugly and confining cocoon of paganism stripped away, a fresh new Christianity has emerged. I now have the privilege of seeing my Creator God as a beautiful, compassionate, merciful, and kind butterfly. And that, my friend, is priceless.

A few weeks ago, I was feeling sorry for myself. I was sorry that I had come on this journey; sorry that I was all alone in my beliefs, and most of all, sorry that my friends and family members thought I was nuts. I had a really nice pity party going until the Eternal One put an end to it by dropping eight simple words into my head.

"Would you rather still be in the house?"

Instantly, I was transported back to the sense of horror and repulsion I had felt being surrounded by all of that black gloopiness; symbolizing my previously pagan beliefs and views of God. Just as quickly, my pity party was over, because I had nothing but thankfulness to express for the fact that my beloved heavenly Father had honored my request for truth, and had brought me out of my house of paganism into His glorious light!

WHAT DOES THE FUTURE HOLD FOR YOU AND FOR CHRISTIANITY?

AHEYEH'S advice given to and through Ezekiel offers a firm mandate to His children regarding our responsibility to correct the error Christianity has been preaching about His Character. Consider this a personal message from Father to you:

> AHEYEH then said to me: "Son or daughter of man, go now to Christendom and speak my words to them. You are not being sent to a people of obscure speech and difficult language, but to Christians—not to many peoples of obscure speech and difficult language, whose words you cannot understand. Surely if I had sent you to them, they would have listened to you. But Christendom is not willing to listen to you because they are not willing to listen to me, for all of Christendom is hardened and obstinate. *But I will make you as unyielding and hardened as they are. I will make your forehead like the hardest stone, harder than flint. Do not be afraid of them or terrified by them, though they are a rebellious house.*[352]

The task at hand is daunting, but AHEYEH has promised to give those who are willing to stand up for His Character clarity, focus, and strength for the mission ahead. By working together to share the message about the TRUE Gospel, we can rescue Christianity from the erroneous doctrines it has inherited and adopted over the centuries.

There will very likely always be Roman Catholics and Protestants, those who will continue to be thought of as *traditional Christianity*. But future generations centuries hence will thank the modern Reformers of today—you and I—for taking a stand and investing themselves in returning Christianity to the roots and faith of the God Yeshua knew.

The full measure of the positive return on the investment in a Second Reformation of the Christian Church may not be felt today, this week, this month or this year or this decade.

---

[352] Ezekiel 3:4-9, amplified and made specific to Christianity

But it is coming; slowly, steadily, believer-by-believer, it is coming! There is nothing we can do to stop it, because like the last Reformation, this Second Reformation is also being directed by the Hand of God; and whatever the Hand of God touches will bring forth fruit in abundance. We may not see the full measure of this new Reformation in our lifetimes, but the foundation of reform has already been laid by the many who have come before us.

You and I are adding on to what others have already built; and many more reformers will come after us to continue the building process. If we work together, the future return on the spiritual investments we are making will yield a return far beyond what any of us can imagine today!

CHAPTER 42

❖

DISCOVERING THE TRUE GOSPEL

There are a thousand answers
    all claiming to be true
    To solve the age-old question
    "What must I do?
To enter life eternal and pay salvation's cost
If I've got faulty doctrine will I be lost?
What dispensation must I claim to qualify for Heaven's gain?"

    What does our Father require of you?
    What has He shown to be good?
    Act justly, love mercy; walk humbly with your God
    Act justly, love mercy; and walk humbly with your God.

    It's not so complicated; it's rudimentary
    If you confess your sins His pardon you'll see
    If you show true repentance and step into His light
    Our God will hold you close for you're His delight!
    Don't let your sorrow weigh you down;

One day He'll offer you a crown!

What does our Father require of you?
What has He shown to be good?
Act justly, love mercy; walk humbly with your God
Act justly, love mercy; and walk humbly with your God.[353]

Questions will always remain about which of our cherished doctrines truly reveal the Character of God. In our family, with our children, we have found that perhaps the simplest way to look at who God is and what He is truly like with regard to His Word and His Character are these words from the prophet Micah (6:8):

> He has showed you, O man, what is good. And what does AHYH require of you? To act justly and to love mercy and to walk humbly with your God.

More powerful words have perhaps never been said. Solomon summed it up this way,

> Now all has been heard; here is the conclusion of the matter: Fear God and keep his commandments; for this is the whole duty of man.[354]

Throughout this book you have frequently seen God's "TRUE Laws" referenced, as if to emphasize that there are some laws that have been written into Torah that are in essence, not true—that is, there are indeed laws have been man-made

---

[353] BEAUCHAMP, Serena, What Does Our Father Require of You (Micah 6:8) 2010
[354] Ecclesiastes 12:13 NIV 1984

additions to the original TRUE Laws of God. So the question naturally arises, if you cannot wholly trust what is written or translated in the Bible, how does one recognize a true Law from a false or man-made one?

What are God's TRUE Laws and Commandments?

The tests are very simple, actually: Anything that attempts to change our unchanging God is likely not of God. Anything that requires the *temporary* is likely also not of God. And finally, such a Law should have the *witness* of two or three.

For instance: Paul's so-called *New Testament* (or *New Covenant*) unilaterally changes God's plan of salvation. It fails the first test. Second, Paul is really the only witness of such a massive change in the Character (i.e. the Word) of our Creator. Paul contradicts the previous witness of several canonical and historical sources. Finally, the sacrificial system implemented *things* that were obviously temporary; the Temple, the Ark, the Priesthood, etc. These things have all passed away and are no longer with us. To tie forgiveness via sacrifice to the ephemeral Temple and priesthood is to foundationally illustrate that these things were not and could not be of an unchanging God to begin with!

Many scholars, both Christian and Jewish understand that a lot of the so-called *Law of God* was highly cultural and written for an ancient period people in a specific geographical situation. Do today's ladies really need to sit outside the city at "that time of the month" in order to keep from sinning? Should the responsible parent *kill* his or her child if he or she becomes an alcoholic?

At the heart of it, the TRUE Law of God is about how we honor our Creator, treat others, and conduct ourselves. It is about being responsible for those created beings, both human and animal, that AHYH has given us to care for. It requires no blood price for forgiveness and no previous, current, or future sacrifice of the innocent.

> "Hear the word of AHYH, you rulers of Sodom; listen to the law of our God, you people of Gomorrah! The multitude of your sacrifices—what are they to me?" says AHYH. "I have more than enough of burnt offerings, of rams and the fat of fattened animals; I have no pleasure in the blood of bulls and lambs and goats. ...
>
> Your hands are full of [sacrificial] blood; wash and make yourselves clean. Take your evil deeds out of my sight! Stop doing wrong, learn to do right! Seek justice, encourage the oppressed [rebuke the oppressor]. Defend the cause of the fatherless, plead the case of the widow."
>
> "Come now, let us reason together," says AHYH. "Though your sins are like scarlet, they shall be as white as snow; though they are red as crimson, they shall be like wool. If you are willing and obedient, you will eat the best from the land; but if you resist and rebel, you will be devoured by the sword. For the mouth of AHEYEH has spoken."[355]

My friend Shaynie who grew up in Satanism—having to participate in both animal and human sacrifices—has fiercely embraced the concept that "GOD can forgive without blood." That really is the best kind of news—the best *Gospel* that can

---

[355] Isaiah 1:10-20

be preached to someone who has grown up in a culture of actual blood and death!

Shaynie still has many flashbacks to rituals that trouble her a great deal. A very kind Christian friend whom I'll call Lauren[356] sometimes helps Shaynie out on days when she is having trouble with her past memories. The other day Shaynie was having a *call back date* to the cult, and Lauren was helping make sure that Shaynie couldn't actually respond and return to the cult. In situations like this, you sometimes have to hold Shaynie down because she is having multiple flashbacks to some very horrible abuse, much of which is blood-related. She can easily hurt herself if she is not gently restrained.

Being a devout Christian, Lauren had been quite upset that Shaynie had embraced the "God does not desire sacrifice" message. So she told her, while holding her tightly to keep her safe, "You are covered with the blood of Jesus." She repeated this over and over, and started singing Christian "blood" songs to Shaynie.

When you actually *say* something like this to someone very suggestible and who has been through years of satanic blood-related abuse, to him or her it is practically the same as doing it because of his or her incredible susceptibility to guided imagery. All of a sudden, Shaynie was again, in her mind, literally covered in blood. She panicked and started screaming until she had no voice left. Although well-intentioned, the mental scars from that experience remained for a long time.

This incident really helps illustrate from a practical standpoint that instead of preaching that "I'm gonna be the

---

[356] Not her real name.

ultimate blood sacrifice, so drown yourself in my blood," Yeshua's much more compassionate and less ritualistic *good news* was, "My Father is not like that! He is not like the pagans! He doesn't need blood to forgive!"

A TRULY BEAUTIFUL STORY

The TRUE Gospel is not the tale of a harsh Father who has condemned you on sight and considers you flawed from birth. It is not the fable of a bloodthirsty tyrant who can only forgive if he is *appeased* with the blood of an innocent man. The TRUE Gospel is not the cruel account of an unforgiving judge who can only stand to look at you if he sees someone else—Yeshua—instead of you. It is not the legend of a brutal despot who plans to make you "burn in hell" forever if you do not *believe* the right doctrine or have enough *faith*.

Neither complicated nor a mystery, the TRUE Gospel is the beautiful story of how the Creator of the Universe made you in the image of God and has nurtured and cared for you ever since. It is a narrative of a loving Parent who smiles when seeing your true colors; who laughs when you do something funny; who encourages you when you are feeling down; and who truly understands the pain of your darkest hour and will help you get through it. Your Creator longs to pick you up when you fall, smile at you when you reach up out of the depths of your heart, and comfort you when you are hurting.

Most importantly of all—your Creator is a God who longs to have you see Him for who He really is—merciful, compassionate, kind, and long-suffering. He wants you to see Him *without* the bloody glasses of paganism and realize that He forgives you *without* sacrifice! Nothing had to die in order to purchase His forgiveness, for His forgiveness is freely given.

All you have to do is repent! That is the TRUE definition of God's amazing grace and His unfailing love for *you!*

It is very likely that you are taking all this in and thinking to yourself, "Sure, there may be some—or a lot of—truth in what I have been reading. I love the view of God I am seeing and am pretty sure that this may even be the TRUE Gospel! But I can't turn away from my church and the gospel Paul preaches! My whole family and community will ostracize me if I choose to no longer believe as they do! Besides, why does it even matter? If what you say is true, God is going to love me no matter what!"

Indeed, our loving Father is merciful and gracious. But if you are truly intent on following in the footsteps of Yeshua, the one who inspired the name *Christian* which you wear so proudly, you need to responsibly do your best to honor the God that Yeshua himself knew. Yeshua stated,

> ...any of you who does not give up everything he has cannot be my disciple.[357]

What do you think Yeshua would say if he were sitting right beside you? Would it be so scary to follow in his footsteps, even if it made you feel like a pioneer on a brave new path? Of course not! And would it be worth the cost to embrace the TRUE Gospel he spoke of, even if it took you out of the comfort zone of your chosen denomination and belief system? Undoubtedly, yes!

Brave friend, are you ready to step out and begin your own journey of discovery? By traversing down this *road less traveled,* you too will find that even though your belief system

---

[357] Luke 14:33

will experience necessary changes, your faith in and love for God will grow stronger. Rather than depending on the Bible alone to be the purveyor of truth, you will learn how to reach out directly to the God of Abraham, Isaac, and Jacob. Your journey will be hard, but satisfying beyond measure.

A sincere seeker's earnest journey of faith will bear its own reward. Like countless others, my own spiritual quest has shown that once the facts and history of my faith are openly on the table in full view and I am able to fully consider this history, knowledge and data with the sound God-given logic and reason He has provided, my change in perspective has been quite astonishing. Because He has helped me overcome my fear of challenging the hypocrisy and illogic and untruths that are prevalent within the orthodox Christian (and even orthodox Judaic) faith, the Biblical contradictions have melted away and *my loving Heavenly Father has became much more real and personal in my life.*

By discovering the really Good News of the TRUE Gospel that Yeshua talked about, I have finally started to see a clear picture emerging of AHEYEH, the amazing, astonishing, and above all, *loving* God that Yeshua knew. And I have never seen anything more beautiful ...

Afterword: Notes from Israel

Israel. The Promised Land that Moses longed to enter, and the place that Yeshua called home. This is the place where most of the Bible was written, and even now remains a location of indescribable significance for three major world religions. A trip to the Holy Land is at the top of nearly every Christian or Messianic believer's bucket list, and I recently had the joy and privilege of making my own pilgrimage. Looking forward to the trip, I didn't know what to expect. Hoping for the best, yet uncertain and hesitant, I penned the following.

On the Way to Israel

I live in one of the top tourists destination in the world; Orlando, Florida. Orlando is a huge tourist destination for many reasons including numerous fantastic theme parks, historic Kennedy Space Center and beautiful beaches a short distance away, and even many random nature opportunities such as the chance to ride an airboat, or see alligators up close.

Because Orlando caters to the world traveler, we residents regularly see all sorts of people from destinations across the globe. On any given day there is likely to be a young man in Japan who is carefully planning his family's itinerary for when they visit Disney World in November. A young lady in Austria will be combing through her list of wardrobe choices over and over again, as she tries to figure out which outfits will be most appropriate for both Sea World and Kennedy Space Center. A child in England is excitedly jumping up and down at the thought of seeing Mickey and Cinderella in just a few short days. And a soon-to-be bride in Georgia is delighted she will be able to send her thank-you cards with a postmark from Kissimmee, Florida.

The young man, the young lady, the small child, and the bride-to-be – they are all thoughtfully considering how they are going to fit into and interact with and gain incomparable memories from MY town. They know nothing of who I am, but they know that this spot on the rock is exceptional. They will arrive with wide-eyed wonder; ready for the vacation of a lifetime.

I have become accustomed to the fact that the weather is gorgeous in winter, and there are palm trees in my front and back yards. I can wear flip-flops and shorts nearly all year. But none of that really matters that much to me because when I wake up each morning, I don't spend one moment worrying about what I am going to wear, how I will fit in with my environment, and how my environment will relate to me that day. I just work, play, raise my children, and love my husband. No matter what the tourists think or what they do or what they wear, I am just – home.

This week the flip-flop is going to be on the other foot. You see, I am going to go from *jaded Floridian* to *wide-eyed tourist* myself! I am going to visit a place that is arguably the Number One religiously significant destination in the world; a piece of ground incredibly meaningful to the "Big Three" religions of Judaism, Christianity, and Islam. I'm going to walk where Yeshua, his brother James the Just, and Abraham and Moses walked. I'm going to see where brave nationalist warriors killed themselves at Masada rather than be tortured and killed by the brutal Roman army. I'm going to rest my forehead on what remains of the wall surrounding the last standing Israelite temple; the same temple Yeshua learned at and taught others in. I will see where the Dead Sea Scrolls were buried, and I will sail on the Sea of Galilee. History – the history that I have been taught reflects holy events – will come alive.

For the last year I have been working on a historical fiction book about a young man who interacted with Yeshua and whose life became inextricably intertwined with Yeshua's family during the time of Yeshua and for decades afterward. I have researched the area, read multiple books, watched videos, and immersed myself in first century historical accounts. But what I lack is the experience of walking where Yeshi walked; looking at Jerusalem from the vantage point he would have seen it from, and traversing the streets of old Jerusalem by foot, just like Yeshi would have done it. Yeshi's experience is in my brain, but it is not yet powered by my heart. That is one of the main reasons I am making the trip – so my experience with the land of my religious forefathers and Yeshi's religious forefathers will intersect and overlap and infuse the story with a reality of color and sensation.

It's all a little much to take in, on a profound level, so instead I focus on the things I can control. What will I wear? Will I fit in or stand out like a sore thumb? If I bring just the right outfit, will the country like me? I have been anticipating this trip for a year; can it even hope to live up to the anticipation that has been increasing by the day? How let down will I feel when the trip is over and I do not have this *trip of a lifetime* experience to look forward to?

Those who know me realize that I have been on a very foundational religious quest and resultant transformation over the past few years. I have questioned practically every belief I have ever had, but the one thing that I have not ever done is doubt that God loves me and has a plan for my life. Will being in the country of so many previous spiritual giants bring me closer to realizing what that plan is? Is God truly closer in Israel, as billions of people secretly and not-so-secretly hypothesize, or is latitude and longitude of the ground I stand on ultimately meaningless when it comes to drawing close to my heavenly Father?

This trip will provide a multitude of experiences, and I have no doubt I will come back changed. Ultimately, will that change affect my life, my writing, and my relationships? Or will the trip simply be eventually classified as a *fabulous memory* with its pictures filed away to be looked at on select occasions? When Israel is in my rear-view mirror, what will I see straight ahead?

Lessons From Israel

I came for answers, but what I got was assurance.
I came for information, but what I found was an invitation.
I sought to find the God of Israel,
but instead reconnected with the God of my heart.

I listened to story after story about how
God interacted with others
But was most touched with how God
interacted with me.

People have sought God on this very soil for thousands of years. They have fought battles for Him, taken their own lives rather than be controlled by those who wish to enslave them, offered multitudes of sacrifices in an attempt to appease or entice Him, and looked for deliverance in the religion of their fathers. They have gazed at the same moon, shining softly in the sky. They have lain on this same ground offering praises or wrestling with His will for their lives. Their circumstances and backgrounds were different than mine, but the longing in their hearts was the same.

Is our Creator really closer in the *Holy Land* of Israel? Or is He willing to draw near to you and me whenever we put down our electronics and TVs and music and busyness and seek Him in His most unmatchable cathedral of holiness; this amazing world that He has created?

As I lay here on the ground beneath a big spreading tree under a beautiful moonlit sky, I look up at a landscape that has come straight from the pages of the Bible. Do I feel somehow connected with the past by virtue of the latitude and longitude I am currently occupying? In some ways, yes.

But the real take-home message for me is how I can feel God's arms of love wrapped firmly around me. That is what I have longed for; to know that He still sees me and knows me and loves me! But this assurance is not based on some mystical belief that He has drawn closer to me because I am in Israel. Instead, I am firmly convinced that His comforting Presence has less to do with location and more to do with the eventual silence, longing, searching, and submission of my own heart.

∽

MUSIC FOR THE SECOND REFORMATION

As a songwriter, music has always been my favorite method of communicating my feelings and beliefs to others. I've always felt the closest to God when reaching out in song, and in this era when I've finally found the compassionate God that Yeshua knew, I want to praise Him even more joyfully!

There are so many Christian, Gospel, and Messianic songs that have been written over the past few hundred years, that the music-loving Christian needs look no further than his or her local church or even the Internet in order to find rousing worship music. This wealth of music does not help the Christian who is on the path of personal and religious reformation much! In fact, sometimes it feels like trying to find inspirational music that doesn't offend our "non-blood" sensibilities is like trying to find crystal clear water in the Sahara Desert. That is why one of the things I have missed the most over the past few years has been music that accurately reflects the reformed beliefs I have come to cherish. I have also dearly missed having like-minded believers to play and sing this music with! So through the years I have started writing music that can comfortably be sung by those on the path of religious reformation.

In order to aid, comfort, and inspire you on your own quest to find the God that Yeshua knew, I have included some of my original song lyrics throughout this book, and have added some favorite additional song lyrics on the following pages. Even though we are not worshiping together in person, we can at least praise AHEYEH together through the lyrics of these songs![358]

You will find that many of these songs have been inspired by the psalms, because the psalmist seemed to have such an amazing spiritual and emotional connection with our Creator.

---

[358] *All songs ©Serena Beauchamp / 2NRITER MUSIC*

God

All my life I was told You needed blood to forgive
If I sinned something had to die just so I could live
I didn't really know You; and Lord, I could not see
That in Your great compassion, Your forgiveness was for free

All my life, I was told it took the death of a man
To take my place, purchase grace
that this was part of Your plan
I didn't really know You; and Lord, I'd not been shown
That a repentant heart would for my wrongs and sins atone

Mercy and honor and faithful compassion
That's just the God that You are!
Gracious, abounding in love without ration
Possessing a tender and gentle heart

You were clear; sacrifice never was part of Your plan
You sought obedience, that's all You needed from man
You told us very clearly Your TRUE *law was where to start*
You said that we'd be happy if we wrote it on our hearts

Mercy and honor and faithful compassion
That's just the God that You are!
Gracious, abounding in love without ration;
Possessing a tender and gentle heart

I Worship You

You are life to me; You are breath to me
and I worship You, I worship You, Lord
You're my destiny; my soul's reality
and I worship You, I worship You
Lord, let me seek You in everything I do
Let every road lead back to You

Every hour, every minute, I am sheltered in Your care
On the mountain, in the valley, I can find You anywhere
When I kneel in holy worship
when I'm seeking You in prayer
I feel Your Presence Lord, and I know
that You are there

I am so amazed at Your transforming ways
and I worship You; I worship You, Lord
I will sing Your praise for my remaining days
and I worship You, I worship You
Lord, I am willing to obey Your perfect plan
I give You everything I am

Every hour, every minute, I am sheltered in Your care
On the mountain, in the valley, I can find You anywhere
When I kneel in holy worship,
when I'm seeking You in prayer
I feel Your Presence Lord, and I know
that You are there

Prayer for Blessing (Jabez' Prayer)
Based on 1 Chronicles 4:9

Lord, that You would bless me, indeed
Enlarge my territory
Lord, that Your loving Hand would be with me
and keep me from all evil

Let me not cause pain; take away my shame
Cleansed with holy flame, transformed by mercy
All the love You've shown leads me to Your throne
I am not alone, for You are with me

Lord, that You would bless me, indeed
Enlarge my territory
Lord, that Your loving Hand would be with me
and keep me from all evil

I can only stand sheltered in Your hand
From Your holy Presence I cannot flee
Let Your kingdom come, and Your will be done
Make your perfect law reside within me

Lord, that You would bless me, indeed
Enlarge my territory
Lord, that Your loving Hand would be with me
and keep me from all evil

Aheyeh

Praise the Name, the sacred Name, Aheyeh
Praise His Name and honor Him alone
The earth has one foundation and He's the cornerstone
To make His glory known; praise His Name

Praise the Name, the sacred Name, Aheyeh
Praise the Name ten thousand angels sing
Our fortress and salvation, the Rock to which we cling
In honor of our King, praise His Name

Aheyeh; He reigns, let the nations fear
Aheyeh; He reigns, He will be revered
Aheyeh; He reigns, all the earth's His throne
Aheyeh; He reigns, we are His alone

Praise the Name, the sacred Name, Aheyeh
Praise His Name and honor Him alone
The earth has one foundation and He's the cornerstone
To make His glory known; praise His Name

Elohim
(Inspired by Psalm 61, Psalm 42:2)

Elohim, Elohim, I will hide in the shelter of Your Wing
Elohim, Elohim, I will hide in the shelter of Your Wing

From the ends of the earth I will call to You
I will call as my heart grows faint
You have been my strength, and a strong tower
I will ever fear Your Name

Elohim, Elohim, I will hide in the shelter of Your Wing
Elohim, Elohim, I will hide in the shelter of Your Wing

How I long to dwell in Your tent forever
Will You lead me to Your Rock?
You have cleared my path, and made sure my steps
as a Shepherd guides His flock

Elohim, Elohim, I will hide in the shelter of Your Wing
Elohim, Elohim, I will hide in the shelter of Your Wing

You have heard my prayer, You have heard my cry
You have heard my song of praise
With a thirsting soul and a steadfast heart
I will serve You all my days

Elohim, Elohim, I will hide in the shelter of Your Wing
Elohim, Elohim, I will hide in the shelter of Your Wing

Everywhere I Go, You Are There
(Based on Psalm 139)

Where shall I hide from Your Spirit,
or flee from Your Presence?
Everywhere I go, You are there
If I ascend to the heavens
or lie in death's peaceful slumber
Everywhere I go, You are there…

If I could just ride away on the gossamer wings of dawn
Or dwell in the depths of the sea
Even there Your mighty Hand will hold me close and guide me
Apart from you, AHEYEH, I could not be

Lord, I lift my voice in thanks and offer You my praise
With exquisite care You fashioned me
All the days I have to live were written in Your record
Before one of them had come to be

How precious to me are Your thoughts, how vast the sum of them
Outnumbering the sands of the sea
Before a word is on my tongue, You know it, Lord, completely
Such knowledge is too wonderful for me!

Search me, Lord, look in my heart, and know my secret fears
Please test the anxious thoughts to which I cling
Filter out offensive traits that fester deep within me
And lead me in Your way eternally

God of the Morning Sun

God of the morning sun
Like a day begun make me fresh and new
God of the wind and rain
To Your holy Name make me ever true

Touched by Your Spirit when I seek Your face
I am transported to a heavenly place
God of the stars above, fill my heart with love
Let it beat for You

God of the morning sun
Like a day begun make me fresh and new
God of the wind and rain
To Your holy Name make me ever true

You cannot be constrained by time or space
The universe cannot contain Your grace
God of the stars above, fill my heart with love
Let it beat for You

Alleluia, alleluia, glory rises from Your throne
Alleluia, alleluia, I will worship You alone

God of the morning sun
Like a day begun make me fresh and new
God of the stars above, fill my heart with love
Let it beat for You

I Will Awaken With The Dawn!

I will awaken with the dawn
Music will fill my heart and my voice
I will exalt the Lord, my God
I will awaken and rejoice!
I will awaken and rejoice!

I will follow God my Father
He will lead the way
My heart rejoices in this truth
God is in charge of every day

And I will sing! Glory and honor to my King!
Sing! I will exalt the Lord and sing!

I will awaken with the dawn
Music will fill my heart and my voice
I will exalt the Lord, my God
I will awaken and rejoice!
I will awaken and rejoice!

In the darkness God is faithful
Never to depart
His arms of love are holding me
Keeping me safe within His heart

And I will sing! Glory and honor to my King!
Sing! I will exalt the Lord and sing!

Aheyeh Is My Shepherd
(Based on Psalm 23)

Aheyeh is my Shepherd; He takes care of me
In pastures and valleys He leads me to me

Beside the still waters he makes me feel whole
In paths of His righteousness He restoreth my soul

Though I walk through the darkness
and feel threatened by sin
I will surely fear no evil
for the Shepherd is my friend

He is with me in darkness and with me in light
He comforts my heart in the dark, lonely night

In front of my enemies He prepares me a feast
He brings me such blessings, for nothing I need

When all of my troubles and trials are past
I'll be with my Shepherd forever; forever
I'll be with my Shepherd in heaven
at last

Tabernacle

Who will come, who will tabernacle
Who will stretch forth his hand and open the gate?
Who will come, who will tabernacle
Who will walk the hills of Zion with an offering of praise?

Who will run, who will run away to dwell with the King
Who will fly, who will fly away on the breadth of His Wing
When His call rings out, who will hear?
Our Lord is waiting now to see you draw near

Will you come, will you tabernacle
Will you stretch forth your hand and open the gate?
Will you come, will you tabernacle
Will you walk the hills of Zion with an offering of praise?

Join and sing, lift your voice in praise to our Father above
Come and bow, let His peace rain down; He's the Author of love
When His call rings out, He will draw us near
We'll feel His Presence for His Spirit is here

Let us come, let us tabernacle
Let us stretch forth our hands and open the gate
Let us come, let us tabernacle
Let us walk the hills of Zion with an offering of praise

A Psalm for Jerusalem

God of Isaac and Abraham
How You have shaken our land!
We have been living in desperate times
Now save us with Your Hand

All of our enemies gather round
Rejoicing at what has been done
They have made pagan Your dwelling place
Just look what it's become...

Evil runs rampant in the city streets
Murder and violence abound
Malice and sorrow dwell in freedom here
And peace cannot be found

Pray for the peace of Jerusalem
May those who love her be blessed
Lord, in Your mercy, forgive her sins
And let her soul find rest

Peace be upon the land of Israel
Bring health and prosperity
Lord, build a temple where Your Name will dwell
And make all Your children free[359]

---

[359] Based on passages found in Psalm 38:2,3,5; Lamentations 1:10; Psalm 55:9-11; Ezekiel 7:25; Psalm 122:607; Psalm 99:8-9; Psalm 128:6; Zechariah 14

Living Water

Come you who are thirsty, come you who are hungry
   I will lead you to drink of the river of life
Be washed in the fountain; be cleansed in the water
   that flows from My mountain and never runs dry

Come you who are thirsty, come you who are hungry
   I will lead you to eat of the bread of life
Like manna from heaven, TRUE *Words I have spoken*
   your spiritual hunger to satisfy

Precious son or daughter; do not be dismayed
I AM your Living Water; do not cast Me now away

Have you trials and temptations?
Is there trouble anywhere?
In My Arms I'll take and shield you
You will find a solace there

Come you who are tired, come you who are weary
in the warmth of my Presence, find safety and rest
My yoke, it is easy; My burden's not heavy
if you walk in My precepts your heart will be blessed

Children of your Father; do not be dismayed
I AM your Living Water; do not cast Me now away[360]

---

[360] Lyrics Serena Beauchamp; "What A Friend" Joseph Scriven, 1855
Music Serena Beauchamp; "What A Friend" Charles C. Converse, 1868

He Loves You

I know He loves you, He really loves you
He gave His law so you could live
I know He really loves you
This I know, your Father loves you
Gave His law, a gift of love; abundant life to give

Heaven's own perfect law was shared,
sent to transform each heart
A beautiful blessing undeclared; a work of art

He knows your name, He sees your face
Cares when you're all alone
Someday your tears He will erase
when you get Home!

I know He really loves you
This I know, your Father loves you
He gave His law so you could live

He loves you, He loves you
You've got to know your Father loves you
Gave His law, a gift of love, abundant life to give

He'll be your Friend
Won't you trust in Him...
And live

I Will Come and Worship You, O Lord

I will come and worship You, O Lord
I will lift my voice in song
I will thank You for Your loving grace
I will praise You all day long

I will bow my knees to You, O Lord
I will fold my hands in prayer
I will raise my eyes to heaven's throne
I will seek to find You there

I sing to You, although I am unworthy
I bring to You an undeserving heart
I cling to You, for You're my only source of hope
From Your love I'll never be apart

You are faithful and eternal, Lord
You are merciful and just
You are righteous in Your judgment, Lord
You are worthy of our trust

I will come and worship You, O Lord
I will lift my voice in song
I will thank You for Your loving grace
I will praise You all day long

The Lord Has Been So Good to Me[361]

The Lord has been so good to me
Though I cannot fathom why
I will worship Him on bended knee
And I'll praise Him 'til I die

Amazing grace, how sweet the sound
That saved a wretch like me
I once was lost but now am found
Was blind but now I see

When we've been there ten thousand years
Bright shining as the sun
We've no less days to sing God's praise
Than when we've first begun

---

[361] Lyrics Serena Beauchamp; Amazing Grace lyrics by John Newton

INDEX

A

Abraham Ibn Ezra
  commentary on Isaiah 14 · 15
Abraham, binding of Isaac · *See*
  Akeda
Adventism
  Adventist Review article
    Crossing Over · 64
  Bible & EGW approved study
    sources · 7
  Biblical infallibility · 16
  conflicted about Paul · 151–52
  endorses *Lucifer* lie · 13, 16, 17
  GC President advises against
    textual criticism · 14
  growing up Adventist · 2, 8
  Adventist Talmud · 70
  membership losses · 291–92
  prophet · *See* White, Ellen
  viewpoint regarding *NCT* · 225
  Youth Prayer Conference
    Just Claim It · 66
AHEYEH *ashar* AHEYEH
  TRUE Name of God · 23
Akeda
  Abraham and Isaac · 137–41
  Christian perspective · 141
  Rashi commentary · 139–40
angels, helped give law · 154–57
  Jude's warning · 153
  Paul's slander · 154–57
Apocrypha · *See* Scripture
Asher, Dr. Shmuel
  God's TRUE Name · 22, 23
  Jesus knew TRUE Name · 30
  original Scriptures doctored · 25
  the trouble with *YHWH* · 23
  יהוה*Tetragrammaton* a scribal
    invention · 21

B

Bacchiocchi, Dr. Samuele
  Rome changed Sabbath · 143
  Sabbath research · 10
  the Bible canon/Catholic Church
    · 58
backslider, definition of · 2
Barclay, William
  history of *Hebrews* · 230
  James opposes Paul · 256–57
  who wrote 2 Peter? · 268–71
Bellinger & Farmer, Isaiah 53
  Suffering Servant · 133–36
Bentham, Jeremy
  Paul vs. Jesus · 242
Bible · *See* Scripture

C

Christianity
  competing versions · 109–10
  dualistic philosophy · 302–6, 308
  great controversy · 303–4
  illustrated in *This Present*
    Darkness · 299–302
  story of Job · 304
  early history · 102–6
  original sin · 323–25
  pagan rituals
    blood atonement · 91
    blood sacrifice · 90
    demon possession · 200–202
    power in the blood · 93
    washed in blood · 91
  seeker-sensitive · 63
circular reasoning, definition · 14
  examples · 41–42
circumcision
  frowned on in Greece · 279
  in early Egypt · 85–86
  in Judaism · 85, 86–87

of the heart · 279
Paul's viewpoint · 278
Clementine Homilies
  early records about Jesus · 69
  God abhors sacrifice · 112–14
  Jesus warns of wolves · 255
  Moses and sacrifice · 121–22
  Paul attacks *James the Just* · 251–53
Communion · *See* pagan rituals
Conflict of Adam and Eve
  Cain and Abel · 127–30
Council of Laodicea
  Bible canon development · 49
  changes to God's Law · 50
Cumont, Franz
  Mithraism similar to Christianity · 147–48

D

Damasus I
  commissions Latin Vulgate · 57
dualism · 302–6, 308

E

Ehrman, Bart
  apostolic rivals · 260–65
  Biblical contradictions · 103
  Misquoting Jesus · 53
Eisenman, Robert
  James, brother of Jesus · 254
Emmerich, Anne Catherine
  stigmatic · 163
  visions of glory · 162
Encyclopedia Biblica
  Paul and Simon Magus · 265–66

F

Fecko, A.J.
  Targums on sacrifice · 125–26
food sacrificed to idols
  Hebraic perspective · 234–37

Paul's perspective · 237–41
Freze, Michael
  stigmata · 171–73

G

God
  Christianity vs. Judaism · 308–9, 313–19
  has feminine qualities · 316–17
  sends evil spirits · 205–6, 305
  wants humility · 94–96
God is
  incomprehensible · 305
  not above questions · 311–12
  unchanging and eternal · 309
  unsafe, untame · 306–7, 309–11
God speaks
  through dreams · 358
    escaping paganism · 358–59
  through Scripture
    a message for you · 326–36
    words of encouragement · 340

H

Hebraic perspective
  food sacrificed to idols · 234–37
  Isaiah 14 · 14
  virgin birth story · 54
Hebrews
  riddle of the NT · 229–32
  who is the author? · 229–32
Howard-Browne, Rodney
  holy laughter · 201
  mystic calling · 200

I

I AM THAT I AM · *See* AHEYEH *ashar* AHEYEH
International Bible Society
  removes *Lucifer* from Bible · 10
Irenaeus
  why four Gospels? · 52

Isaiah
   Chapter 14
      Abraham Ibn Ezra's
         commentary · 15
      does it refer to *Lucifer*? · 10
      Hebraic perspective · 14
      Jerome adds *Lucifer* · 12
   Chapter 53
      Jewish viewpoint · 135
      Suffering Servant · 133–36
   Chapter 64 · 319–21
   Chapter 7
      virgin birth · 54
Israel
   lessons · 373
   personal experience · 377

J

James, brother of Jesus
   attacked by Paul · 251–53
   background · 250–51
   Head of Jerusalem Church · 254
   marginalization · 255–58
   opposition to Paul · 256–57
Jeremiah
   God never wanted sacrifice · 95, 116–17, 122
   NIV mistranslation · 117
Jerome of Antioch
   adds *Lucifer* to Bible · 12
   Latin Vulgate · 57
Jerusalem Church
   differences with Paul · 242–44
Jerusalem Church
   James the Just, Head · 254
Jesus
   born to die? · 99
   foundational teachings
      beware of false christs · 211
      false things in Scripture · 112–14
      God's TRUE Law is eternal · 116
      importance of humility · 190
      none good but God · 72
      standing against blood sacrifice · 110–11
   warning about wolves · 204, 287
   Jewish reformer · 100–101
Judaism
   doctoring the Scriptures · 25
   hiding God's TRUE Name · 21
   Messianic, personal experience · 233–35
   pagan practices
      circumcision · 85
      sacrifice · 79–82

K

King Jr., Martin Luther
   Mithraism similar to Christianity · 145–47

L

Laney, Deanna
   killed her children · 138
Lateau, Louise
   stigmata · 164–65
Lewis, C.S.
   God is unsafe, untame
Lucifer
   KJV declares Satan *Lucifer* · 10
   name transliteration issue? · 16
   NIV removes from Bible · 10
   removed from Bible · 13
   Satan before Fall? · 10–12
Luther, Martin
   Man needs to be nothing · 319
   mystic calling, aborted · 185
   removes *Apocrypha* · 58

M

Maimonides · *See* Rambam
Marcion
   brief biography · 103
   canon · 51
Marcionism
   early influence · 106

in current Christianity · 106–8
Metzger, Bruce
  Bible canon development · 59
  NT canon development · 52
Mithraism
  competitor of Christianity · 143
  pagan rituals · 145
  similar to Christianity
    Cumont, Franz · 147–48
    MLK Jr. · 145–47
Moses
  learns God's TRUE Name · 21
mystic / visionary
  initial calling · 179
    Ellen White · 182–83
    Joseph Smith · 181
    P. Yogananda · 180
    R. Howard-Browne · 200
    Saul-turned-Paul · 177–79
    Therese Neumann · 180
  stigmata
    Anne Emmerich · 163
    Louise Lateau · 164–65
    Paul · 158–60
    Therese Neumann · 165–67
  supernatural phenomena · 186–87
  visions of glory
    Anne Emmerich · 162
    Ellen White · 183
    Joseph Smith · 181
    Martin Luther · 185
    P. Yogananda · 180
    Saul-turned-Paul · 177
    Therese Neumann · 183

N

Name of God
  God's TRUE Name
    AHEYEH · 23
    AHEYEH ashar AHEYEH · 22
    hidden by God · 25
    hidden by Judaism · 21, 24
    ignored by Christianity · 27
    profaned by Israel · 26
    pronunciation variants

      Yahweh, YaHuWaH, Jehovah,
      Yahowah, Yehovah · 20
    Tetragrammaton · 19
    the LORD · 19
    told to use TRUE Name · 29
NCT · *See New Covenant Theology*
Nebuchadnezzar, king of Babylon
  death · 15
  troubling dream · 358
Neumann, Therese
  mystic calling · 180
  stigmata · 165–67
  visions of glory · 166
New Covenant Theology
  a *better* covenant? · 309
  Adventism's viewpoint · 225
  basic tenets · 224–25
  can God look upon sin? · 226–28
  comparison to Judaism · 69
  dependent on *Hebrews* · 229–32
  food sacrificed to idols · 237–41
  Galatians 3 · 215
  is obedience to the Law
    unnecessary? · 226
  Paul is the crucial authority · 223
  Romans 14 · 71
  spreads to Rome, Asia · 274–75
  Substitutionary Atonement · 224
  supported by *Hebrews* · 229
NuGospel · *See New Covenant Theology*

O

obedience to God
  expectation of believer · 66
  what God really wants · 94–96, 365–69
original sin · 323–25

P

pagan rituals
  Christianity
    blood atonement · 91
    blood sacrifices · 90
    demon possession · 200–202

power in the blood · 93
washed in blood · 91
Judaism
   blood sacrifices · 84
   circumcision · 86–87
Mithraism · 145
paganism
   circumcision · 85–86
Satanism
   blood atonement · 91
   blood sacrifices · 90
   Communion · 91
   power in the blood · 93
   washed in blood · 91
Paul
   a rabbi reviews Paul's scholarship · 276–78
   antitype of Saul · 202–4
   attacks *James the Just* · 251–53
   bitter rival of Peter
      Bart Ehrman · 260–65
   circumcises Timothy · 279
   circumcision, views on · 278
   compares self to Jesus · 207–8
   condemns Sabbath & Sabbathkeepers · 275
   differences with *Jerusalem Church* · 242–44
   foundational passages
      Galatians 1 · 153
      Galatians 3 · 215–17
      Romans 14 · 71
   his self-fulfilling prophecy · 287
   inclusion in Bible · 283–84
   James opposes Paul · 256–57
   marginalization of women · 314–15
   marks · 158–59
   misquoting Abraham · 216–17
   mystic calling · 177–79
   NuGospel · 215
      food sacrificed to idols · 237–41
      New Covenant Theology · 224–25
      Substitutionary Atonement · 224
   rejected by churches · 209–10
   Scripture is *God-breathed*? · 281
Simon Magus
   Encyclopedia Biblica · 265–66
   slandering celestial beings · 154–57
thorn
   aggelos satan · 195–202
   background · 189–94
   tormented by demon · 206
   visions of glory · 177
   vs. Super Apostles · 244–49
   warns of *great delusion* · 285–86
Peter
   books in deep dispute · 268
   Clementine Homilies
      Jesus on wolves · 255
   defends the TRUE Gospel · 260
   Paul's bitter rival
      Bart Ehrman · 260–65
   who wrote 1 Peter? · 268–71
   who wrote 2 Peter? · 271
prayer
   does prayer authorize God to act? · 302

R

Rambam's commentary on sacrifice · 120–21
Reformation, personal
   benefits · 360
   cost of investment · 357
   spiritual ROI · 356
Reformation, Protestant
   Sola Scriptura · 280–81
Reformation, Second · 361
Richards, Larry
   determining inspiration · 39–45
   Young, Edward J. · 39–41

S

Sabbath
   changed by Rome: · 143
   doctrine · 9
   kept by Jesus · 69
   made for man · 70
sacrifice

Abraham and Isaac · 137–41
　Christian perspective · 141
　Rashi commentary · 139–40
Adam and Eve · 124–27
adopted by Israel · 84
Conflict of Adam and Eve
　Cain and Abel · 127–30
Deanna Laney · 138
God hates sacrifice · 119
God never wanted sacrifice · 95, 116–17, 122
in Judaism · 79–82
personal experience · 77–78
Rambam commentary · 120–21
Suffering Servant · 133–36
Targums on sacrifice · 125–26
Satan, *angel of light* · 184
Satanism
　growing up in Satanism
　　Shaynie's story · 87–94, 367–69
　pagan rituals
　　blood atonement · 91
　　blood sacrifices · 90
　　power in the blood · 93
　　washed in blood · 91
Saul, Israel's first king
　disobedience · 204–5
　type of Paul · 202–4
Schweitzer, Albert
　Paul vs. Jesus · 241
Scripture
　additions to Bible manuscripts
　　Mark 16 verses 9-20 · 55
　　virgin birth story · 54
　Apocrypha · 51
　　extended controversy · 58
　　removal by Luther · 58
　Bible
　　Codex Claromontanus · 52
　　Codex Sinaiticus · 52
　　deep contradictions · 58
　　developing Bible canon · 51
　　historical roots · 48
　　Latin Vulgate · 57
　　multiple canon changes · 55
　　showing respect for · 47
　　virgin birth story · 53
　　why four Gospels? · 52

Bible canon exclusions
　Shepherd of Hermas · 52
cherry-picking · 32–34
gender-neutral language · 317
mistranslations
　Isaiah 53 · 133–36
　Jeremiah 7 · 117
seeker-sensitive Christianity · *See* Christianity
Simon Magus and Paul
　Encyclopedia Biblica · 265–66
Smith, Joseph
　mystic calling · 181
　visions of glory · 181
Sola Scriptura, definition · 42
　Catholic vs. Protestant · 42
　during Reformation · 280–81
　Scripture is *God-breathed*? · 281
songs
　Beauchamp, Serena
　　A Psalm for Jerusalem · 391
　　AHEYEH · 384
　　AHEYEH Is My Shepherd · 389
　　Elohim · 385
　　Every Time I Fall · 132
　　Everywhere I Go · 387
　　God · 381
　　God of the Morning Sun · 387
　　He Loves You · 393
　　His Law Is · 67
　　I Will Awaken With the Dawn · 388
　　I Will Come and Worship You, O Lord · 394
　　I Worship You · 382
　　It was Me, original · 349–50
　　It Was Me, redux · 352–53
　　Living Water · 392
　　Prayer for Blessing · 383
　　Tabernacle · 390
　　The Lord Has Been So Good to Me · 396
　　The Sacrifice · 118–19
　　What Does Our Father Require of You? · 364–65
　Jones, Lewis E.
　　Power in the Blood · 93
　Kelly, Tom & Steinberg, Billy
　　True Colors · 341

Lowry, Robert
   Nothing but the Blood · 94
Sczebel, Pat
   Jesus, Thank You · 92–93
Shabbazi, Shalom
   song with TRUE Name · 22
Thiem, James
   Sons of God · 88
stigmata, significance · 160–62
   early history · 169–71
   Louise Lateau · 164–65
   Paul · 158–60, 171–73
   Therese Neumann · 165–67
Super Apostles vs. Paul · 244–49

T

Tetragrammaton, definition · 19
   substitute, YHWH · 25
   TRUE, AHYH · 26
The Great Controversy
   usage of *Lucifer* · 11
This Present Darkness, review · 302
Toronto Blessing · 201
TRUE Gospel, TRUE God
   the God Jesus knew · 369–97
TRUE Law of God
   curse or blessing? · 218–21
   gift spoken of by Psalmist · 66
   Jesus versus Paul · 72
   moot for salvation? · 73
   promoted by Jesus · 69

U

Ulansey, David
   Origins of the Mithraic Mysteries · 144

W

White, Ellen
   Adventist prophet · 11
   mystic calling · 182–83
   Pen of Inspiration, SOP · 11
   The Great Controversy · 303–4
   usage of *Lucifer* · 10
   visions of glory · 182
Wilson, Ted
   how Adventists should interpret the Bible · 14
Wolpe, David J.
   Abraham told to 'go forth' · 346
wolves, ravenous
   Clementine Homilies · 255
   Jesus' warning · 204

Y

Yogananda, Paramhansa
   mystic calling · 180
   visions of glory · 180

Made in the USA
Lexington, KY
17 November 2015